Paulo Freire

Volumes of the *Continuum Library of Educational Thought* include:

Aristotle	Alexander Moseley
St Thomas Aquinas	Vivian Boland
Pierre Bourdieu	Michael James Grenfell
Jerome Bruner	David Olson
John Dewey	Richard Pring
Michel Foucault	Lynn Fendler
John Holt	Roland Meighan
John Locke	Alexander Moseley
Maria Montessori	Marion O'Donnell
John Henry Newman	James Arthur and Guy Nicholls
Plato	Robin Barrow
Lev Vygotsky	Rene van der Veer
Rudolf Steiner	Heiner Ullrich
Jean Piaget	Richard Kohler
Jean-Jacques Rousseau	Jürgen Oelkers
EG West	James Tooley
Mary Wollstonecraft	Susan Laird
St Augustine	Ryan Topping
Loris Malaguzzi and the	Kathy Hall, Mary Horgan, Anna Ridgway, Rosaleen
Reggio Emilia Experience	Murphy, Maura Cunneen and Denice Cunningham
Robert Owen	Robert Davis and Frank O'Hagan

See www.continuumbooks.com for further details.

Members of the Advisory Board

Robin Barrow, Dean of Philosophy of Education, and former Dean of Education, Simon Fraser University, Canada.

Peter Gronn, Professor of Education, Department of Educational Studies, University of Glasgow, UK.

Kathy Hall, Professor of Education, National University of Ireland, Ireland.

Stephen Heyneman, Professor of International Educational Policy at the College of Education and Human Development, Vanderbilt University, USA.

Yung-Shi Lin, President Emeritus and Professor, Department of Education and Institute of Graduate Studies, Taipei Municipal University of Education, Republic of China, Taiwan.

Gary McCulloch, Brian Simon Professor of the History of Education,

Institute of Education, University of London, USA.

Jürgen Oelkers, Professor of Education at the Institute of Education, University of Zürich, Switzerland.

Richard Pring, Lead Director of the Nuffield Review of 14–19 Education and Training for England and Wales; Emeritus Fellow, Green College Oxford, UK.

Harvey Siegel, Professor of Philosophy, University of Miami, USA.

Richard Smith, Professor of Education and Director of the Combined Degrees in Arts and Social Sciences, University of Durham, USA.

Zhou Zuoyu, Professor of Education, Beijing Normal University, People's Republic of China.

Paulo Freire

DANIEL SCHUGURENSKY

Continuum Library of Educational Thought
Series Editor: Richard Bailey
Volume 16

continuum

Continuum International Publishing Group

The Tower Building	80 Maiden Lane,
11 York Road	Suite 704
London SE1 7NX	New York, NY 10038

www.continuumbooks.com

© Daniel Schugurensky 2011

British Library Cataloguing-in-Publication Data
A catalogue record for this book is available from the British Library.

ISBN: 978-0-8264-8415-4 (hardcover)

Library of Congress Cataloging-in-Publication Data
Schugurensky, Daniel, 1958-
Paulo Freire / Daniel Schugurensky.
p. cm.—(Continuum library of educational thought; v.16)
ISBN 978-0-8264-8415-4—ISBN 978-1-4411-6788-0
1. Freire, Paulo, 1921–1997—Criticism and interpretation.
2. Education—Philosophy. 3. Critical pedagogy.
4. Postmodernism and education. I. Title.

LB880.F732S37 2011
370.1—dc22

2010052753

Typeset by Newgen Imaging Systems Pvt Ltd, Chennai, India
Printed and bound in Great Britain

Contents

Series Editor's Preface

The books in this series take the form of what might be called "philosophical biography" in the area of educational studies. Their shared purpose, simply put, is to understand the thoughts and practices of certain educational philosophers.

Straight away this project is confronted with some potential difficulties. As even a cursory read of the list of thinkers whose names provide the titles within the series will testify, many are not ordinarily considered to be philosophers. Some can be more sensibly located in other areas of the academy—sociology, economics, psychology, and so on. Others seem unsuited to the label because their contribution to education is primarily in terms of its practice. In the narrow, disciplinary sense, then, many of the subjects of this series are clearly not philosophers. In another sense, however, and this is the sense employed by Jean-Paul Sartre in his own attempts in the genre, a philosophical biography can be written about anyone whose thought is important and interesting. In this sense, I suggest, each of the thinkers acknowledged in this series is a philosopher.

Implicit within the *Continuum Library of Educational Thought* is an assertion that theories and the practices that follow from them (and equally, practices and the theories that lie implicitly within them) are vitally important for education. By gathering together the ideas of some of the most important and interesting educational thinkers, from the Ancient Greeks to contemporary scholars, the series has the ambitious task of providing an accessible yet authoritative resource for a generation of students and practitioners.

It will always be possible to question the list of key thinkers that are represented in this series. Some may question the inclusion of certain thinkers; some may disagree with the exclusion of others. That is inevitably going to be the case. There is no suggestion that the list of thinkers represented within the *Continuum Library of Educational Thought* is in any way definitive. What is incontestable is that these thinkers have fascinating ideas about education, and that, taken together, the *Library* can act as a powerful source of information and inspiration for those committed to the study of education.

Richard Bailey
University of Birmingham

Acknowledgments

I would like to express my deep gratitude to my wife Laurie, and to our children, Alejandro and Ana, for their understanding, love, and support at a time that our lives were complicated with an international migration.

Special thanks go to Hugh Oliver, editor, poet, friend and musician extraordinaire, for his tremendous help with editing this manuscript, to the Continuum team (especially Rosie Pattinson, Alison Baker, P. Muralidharan, and Series Editor Richard Bailey) for their assistance and encouragement.

I also want to thank Peter Mayo, Carlos A. Torres, Lutgardes Freire, Moacir Gadotti, Rosa María Torres, Gustavo Fischman, José Clovis, Ana Freitas, Budd Hall, Darlene Clover, Jack Quarter, Ed O'Sullivan, D'Arcy Martin, Anne Goodman, Paula Allman, Beth Lange, chris cavanagh, Danilo Streck, Elizabeth Pinnington, Nelly Stromquist, Linzi Manicom, Shirley Walters, John P. Myers, Monica Kronfli, and Kevin Kester for their help and friendship.

Last but not least, I want to thank the many Freirean educators from all regions of the world that I have had the fortune to meet. Your commitment, enthusiasm and efforts to build a better world inspired me throughout the writing of this book. As usual, all errors and omissions are my own.

Introduction

My encounters with Freire

I first came across the ideas of Paulo Freire in the early 1970s, when I was a teenager living in Argentina. That initial encounter was through *La educación como práctica de la libertad*, his first book published in Spanish. I still remember the orange tones and the dramatic pictures of the cover. I also remember the impression that the prologue of Uruguayan philosopher Julio Barreiro had on me. But what called my immediate attention early on, and prompted me to continue reading, was Freire's understanding of education as praxis: reflection and action upon the world in order to transform it. I suddenly discovered a different way to look at education and politics, and soon thereafter I found myself reading *Pedagogy of the Oppressed*. As a young reader with limited knowledge and experience, I missed important concepts, but I still remember taking careful notes and starting to think of education as an exciting field to be involved in. Needless to say, Freire's books were not required readings in the school curriculum, or even extracurricular assignments suggested by progressive teachers. As with other interesting texts I read at that time, they came recommended by my friends from the student movement, in which I was active since entering secondary school at age 13. In that politically, socially, and culturally effervescent period of' Latin America's history, it was not uncommon for curious and politically engaged teenagers and youth to read a variety of materials dealing with social critique and social change or to discuss them in self-organized study groups outside of school and unbeknownst to teachers. Books circulated hand to hand among students, educators, community organizers, social workers, academics, and political activists, and were read with enthusiasm by many who thought that the main task of the day was to change the world. It was just something that was in the air at that time. A few years later, both *Education as a Practice of Freedom* and *Pedagogy of the Oppressed* would be included among the list of books that were forbidden and burned by the military dictatorship that took power in Argentina in 1976.

My next association with Freire's ideas was in Mexico where I moved in January 1978 when I was 19 years old. There, I had the opportunity to encounter Freire in my work at different institutions and organizations over 10 years. I also encountered Freire as a student at the Universidad Nacional Autónoma de México (UNAM), in my relations with social movements, labor and grassroots organizations, liberation theology groups, exile communities, and especially through many inspiring popular educators in Mexico and in Central America. In the early 1980s, I had the opportunity to attend a public talk given by Freire in Mexico. It was a fascinating experience, because I had never been before at a lecture on education (let alone on adult literacy) that was so massively attended, with people sitting in the aisles and on the stairs in a crowded auditorium. By then, Freire was one of the world's most famous educators. Around the same time I made a short visit back to Argentina where I met some of my former classmates from the Universidad de Buenos Aires and asked them whether they had read any texts of Paulo Freire. I was surprised to discover that these young and curious people, who by then had spent several years studying educational theories, had never heard of Freire. By that time Brazil was in transition to democracy and Freire had returned to his home country, but Argentinean universities, still tightly controlled by the military regime, kept Freire's books away from education students. Away from the gaze of the military watch, however, popular educators continued studying, discussing, and applying Freire's ideas. Those were not easy times for them. Among the 30,000 people who were disappeared by state terrorism there were many educators and students.

My third encounter with Freire took place in the late 1980s and the 1990s in North America. It started in Canada, where I pursued graduate studies in education at the University of Alberta and learned new insights from my courses and through informal discussions over coffee with my classmates. Freire's ideas provided much input for our debates on the role of education in social reproduction and social change. This encounter was also marked by the geographical and thematic expansion of Freire's ideas, especially with the publication of the "talking book" with Ira Shor (*A Pedagogy for Liberation*) in 1987. Until then, Freire's ideas were regarded as significant for adult education in the global south, but largely irrelevant for the school system or for the context of advanced capitalism. This book played a significant role in changing that assumption. In the mid-1990s, I also encountered Freire during the 3 years I spent in Los Angeles as a visiting professor at UCLA, where I found many bright and engaged colleagues and students and witnessed the preparatory work for the establishment of the first Paulo Freire Institute of North America, founded a few years later by Carlos Torres.

My fourth encounter with Freire took place during the first decade the twenty-first century. Through my research and travels to different parts of the word, I had the opportunity to observe the creativity of educators and educational policymakers in adapting and reinventing Freire's ideas to address the challenges of their particular contexts. In Toronto, where I lived and worked at the Ontario Institute for Studies in Education for a dozen years, I met with Freire's ideas again through many colleagues, students, friends, and community organizers, who felt inspired by Freire's proposals but at the same time read him critically. In Toronto, I also had the opportunity to learn more about Theatre of the Oppressed, and to witness many public discussions on Freire's ideas, as in October 2003 when I acted as a translator in an intense debate between Moacir Gadotti, director of the Paulo Freire Institute and a close collaborator of Freire, and Chet Bowers, one of Freire's most persistent critics. In Arizona, where I now reside, I encountered Freire again in the legacy of Cesar Chávez, in the work of my colleagues at the School of Social Transformation and the School of Public Affairs, in the courses on Freire offered by the Faculty of Education, in the Paulo Freire Freedom School and in many grassroots community groups struggling for social justice. Throughout my life, I had the pleasure and privilege of learning from many great Freirean educators from around the world in a variety of settings: universities, schools, community centers, church basements, popular education programs, libraries, unions, and grassroots organizations. Today, I continue meeting Freire when people who I don't know tell me, often unprompted, about the significant influence that Freire has had in their personal biographies or in educational projects in which they have been involved.

Twenty lessons I learned from Freire

When Paulo Freire passed away, I wrote a short text about the impact of his work and predicted that it would grow over time. Taking an autobiographical license, I also mentioned how my early readings of Freire helped me to articulate many of my intuitions about education, how they inspired me to read more about education, and how they guided me in my subsequent educational practice. Had it not been for that early exposure to Freire, I probably would have not chosen the path of adult education. In that brief text, I outlined 20 things that I learned from Paulo Freire:

1. I learned that education is not neutral: it can be used to reinforce structures of domination, but it can also be used to promote social transformation.
2. I learned that oppressed people have part of the oppressor within themselves.
3. I learned that people learn faster and are happier when educational content is relevant to their lives and when the method is based on dialogue and respect.
4. I learned that ignorance is a relative concept because all humans have considerable knowledge, experience, skills, and values. At the same time, I learned that rejection of popular knowledge is as dangerous as its exaltation or mystification.
5. I learned that the authoritarianism of many schools is part and parcel of larger societal dynamics and that an emancipatory education can contribute to the development of a more democratic society.
6. I learned that implementing an educational model promoting democracy and critical thinking is sometimes frustrating and usually takes longer than traditional models. Consequently, temptation to return to the banking approach in which the teacher talks and the students listen is always present.
7. I learned that teachers can proclaim—and sometimes believe—to be implementing an emancipatory pedagogical model, yet in practice impose a traditional banking education.

8. I learned the importance of being consequent to core principles and values while being flexible enough to accept mistakes and change ideas and practices accordingly.
9. I learned that both the content and the method are important. A progressive content imposed through an authoritarian method is antithetical to a genuine learning process. An interactive method that avoids critical reflection and transformative action is antithetical to a liberating education.
10. I learned that it is possible to reconcile apparently contradictory concepts: reason and passion, teaching and learning, education and organization, technical skills and political activism, reflection and practice, leadership and humility, knowledge and love, academic rigor and compassion, structural analysis and individual anecdotes, religiosity and Marxism, intellectual freedom and social commitment, and denunciation of present conditions and annunciation of a better future.
11. I learned of the dangers of both voluntarism (a kind of idealism that attributes to the will of the individual the power to change everything) and determinism (a sort of mechanistic structuralism that downplays the role to human agency in the historical process), because each of these approaches alone is incapable of resolving the tension between consciousness and the world.
12. I learned that it is possible to reject a loan from an international financial institution when it imposes unfair conditionalities and priorities, and when it places an unnecessary burden on the next generations. Paulo suggested that something was wrong when a country like Brazil needed financial assistance to educate its own citizens.
13. I learned that educational processes can be directive without being authoritarian or manipulative: directiveness can be compatible with dialogue and respect for differences in ideas and opinions.
14. I learned that education is communion: "I cannot think authentically unless others think. I cannot think for others, or without others."

15. I learned that the curriculum is not something given, a universally accepted truth to be transmitted, but a social construction in which the word of the oppressed is seldom included.

16. I learned of the importance of recognizing both the political dimension of education and the pedagogical dimension of politics.

17. I learned that any process of social change starts with the hope that history can be modified and the belief that oppressors are not invincible, and that it progresses with the development of an "inédito viable," a sort of untested feasibility or possible dream.

18. I learned about the urgency of building "democratic radicalness," which calls for a new ethics and a new educational practice based on respect and emancipation, and aims at assisting subordinated groups to develop political determination.

19. I learned the potential of a work that is genuinely interdisciplinary and combines theory and practice.

20. I learned that if your ideas challenge domination and oppression, and you stand for those ideas in your everyday practice, you are likely to be persecuted by the powerful, and you must be prepared to face jail, exile, and censorship. At the same time, I learned that despite suffering hardship, you are going to be supported and encouraged by the oppressed and disenfranchised, and by those whose ethics value social justice and solidarity (Schugurensky 1997:104–7).

Today, 14 years and many grey hairs later, I might assemble a different list of 20 lessons, but I venture to say that it would not be substantially different from that one. I want to clarify from the outset that the fact that I gained insight and inspiration from reading Freire does not prevent me from recognizing some of his shortcomings and contradictions and from seriously considering the criticisms that other colleagues have raised about his works. I admit that I have learned many things from Freire, that I find many of his arguments appealing, and that I share his concern with injustice, suffering, and oppression as well as his desire to forge collectively a more democratic and happier society. However, this does not mean that I am willing to accept all his propositions, follow him blindly, and treat him like an infallible guru. I attempt to engage critically with his ideas, and at the same time, I do my best to situate his texts in the context in which they were written.

This book

Paulo Freire was a twentieth-century educator who made an important contribution to the deepening and expansion of the progressive education movement that preceded him. In developing his philosophical approach to education, he stood on the shoulders of several notable thinkers, some of them included in this *Library of Educational Thought*. Examining Freire's work in relation to those educators, it is possible to find some continuities and ruptures. Like many progressive educators before him, Freire managed to articulate, in a coherent framework, a stark criticism to the traditional education system with an alternative proposal that had democracy at its center. From a historical perspective, it is possible to argue that Freire extended the ideas of progressive education with three original contributions. First, his educational proposals expanded the scope of progressive education beyond the confines of school settings, including other settings such as adult education, community education, and rural extension. It is not that before Freire progressive education ignored nonschool settings, but its focus was on educational institutions. At the same time, although Freire's most famous work was on adult education, he neither ignored the role of schools nor called for the deschooling of society. On the contrary, he recognized the potential role of schools to equalize opportunities and nurture a more democratic society. Second, Freire transcended the liberalism of many progressive education predecessors (and their view of education as a relatively neutral space) by arguing that education is a political act, by locating himself explicitly on the side of the oppressed in their project for social justice, and by connecting power dynamics in the classroom with broader dynamics of domination. Third, he deepened progressive education's conceptualization of education (the reorganization of learning experiences) by incorporating the concept of praxis, understood, as mentioned before, as reflection and action upon the world in order to transform it. Education, in Freire's view, includes both social critique and social transformation, and as such it aims at examining the causes of unjust social relations and at strengthening collective efforts for democratic change. This explicit connection between education and politics, integrated to a larger project aimed at humanization, constitutes, in my view, his main contribution to the progressive education movement.

This book provides an introduction to the life, the work, and the ideas of Paulo Freire, and also discusses other people's reactions to those ideas. As with all the other volumes in this collection, this one is organized in four chapters: intellectual biography, critical exposition of the author's work, reception and influence of that work, and contemporary relevance. Chapter 1 is organized in three sections that cover the main phases of Freire's life: "early Brazil," "exile," and "late Brazil." Chapter 2 deals with the work of Paulo Freire. Since I contend that his work can be understood only in the context of his life experiences, I had no choice but to organize this chapter along biographical lines similar to those that I used in Chapter 1. Had Freire been a traditional philosopher who wrote his books in the quiet of his university office, I would have organized Chapter 2 around key themes or issues. However, insofar as Freire was not a classic academic but a public intellectual whose books consist mainly of his reflections on his own interventions, I decided to discuss Freire's works in relation to his experiences in Brazil and abroad and to the evolution of his ideas over time. I realized early on that this decision could lead to some overlap with the intellectual biography presented in Chapter 1, but I reckoned that this was a worthwhile trade-off if I was to discuss his work in the context of his life. Having said that, in an attempt to balance the two approaches, in the second part of Chapter 2 I include a discussion on key issues and themes that arise from his work. Chapter 3 deals with the reception and influence of his work. In the first part I advance six explanations for the fast and wide impact of Freire's early work, and discuss both the early praise and the early criticism that *Pedagogy of the Oppressed* received immediately after its release. Building on that discussion, I devote the rest of Chapter 3 to the main criticisms of Freire's work over the last four decades, as well as the responses to those criticisms put forward by Freire himself and by others. Chapter 4 addresses the relevance of Freire's ideas for today's world and explores his legacy for twenty-first-century education.

This book draws from Freire's own writings, but it also builds on the insights provided by many other colleagues over the last decades. As of today, there are hundreds of books about Freire in different languages, and thousands of edited volumes, theses, articles, letters, and other documents accumulated over four decades. I acknowledge that the list of references that I consulted, extensive as it is, only constitutes a portion of the existing literature on Freire. Although it would be impossible to cover everything written by and about Freire, I made an effort to cover as much material as possible, especially works published in English, Spanish, and Portuguese. I apologize in advance for any important omission I may have incurred. I want to end this introduction by saying that it is both an honor and a privilege to publish this manuscript with *Continuum*, which has made an invaluable contribution to disseminating the work of Paulo Freire to the English-speaking world, starting from the pioneering publication of *Pedagogy of the Oppressed* in 1970. I commend Continuum for developing the *Library of Educational Thought*, and I express my gratitude to Richard Bailey, the series editor, for trusting me with this volume. I hope that this book makes a valuable addition to this collection and to the literature on Freire.

Chapter 1

Intellectual Biography

Introduction: "Scratch a theory, you will find a biography"

As sociologist Troy Duster likes to say, "If you scratch a theory, you will find a biography."[1] This dictum applies particularly well to Paulo Freire, a twentieth-century educator, writer, philosopher, public intellectual, and political activist. He was born on September 19, 1921, in Recife, the capital of the state of Pernambuco, in northeast Brazil, under the official name of Paulo Regulus Neves Freire and died of heart failure on May 2, 1997, in the city of Sao Paulo. Paul Taylor (1981:1), writing when Freire had only produced a small portion of his published work, already noted that he had been called "the greatest living educator, a master and a teacher, first among a dying class of modern revolutionaries who fight for social justice and transformation." Others have called Freire "the Messiah of Geneva" (Kleinman 1978), "a myth in his own lifetime" (Furter 1985:301), "the most widely known educational theorist now living" (Weiler 1996:353), "the exemplary organic intellectual of our time" (West 1993:viii), "the Rousseau of the 20th century" (Bhattacharya 2008:101), "the John Dewey of the present era" (Kanpol 1997:13, Guilherme 2002:31), "the most important educator of the second half of the 20th century" (Elias 1994:151, Carnoy 2004:7), "one of the most heralded educators of the 20th century" (Mayo 2004), "the most original educational thinker of the last half of the 20th century" (Siddhartha 1999), and "a radical hero of adult education" (Coben 1998:148). Like wise, Roberts (2000:1) claimed that "few educational thinkers have been more widely influential than Paulo Freire," Gronholm (1999:161) argued that Freire was "the most important educationalist of the twentieth century"; and Darder (2002:149) stated that "more than any other educator of the twentieth century, Paulo Freire left an indelible mark upon the lives of progressive educators." C. A. Torres (1998a:ix) referred to Freire as a "wonderful and spiritual man who inspired a whole generation of critical educators" and as "one of the most vibrant educators and philosophers of education." Hall (1998:95) stated that by the 1970s and 1980s, Paulo Freire had already become the world's best-known intellectual voice supporting a socially transformative vision of adult education, and Gadotti (1994:141) argued that because Freire's educational proposals have been connected to so many settings and movements around the world, the universal extension of his thought "has no parallels in the history of pedagogical ideas."

If these claims seem exaggerated, it is beyond doubt that, at least in the subfields of critical pedagogy and popular education,[2] no other educator had the worldwide impact of Paulo Freire. Both the *Critical Pedagogy Reader* (Darder, Baltodano, and Torres 2003) and the *Critical Pedagogy Primer* (Kincheloe 2008) acknowledged Freire as the most influential philosopher in the development of critical pedagogy. Likewise, Giroux (1994:141 and 2010:1) recognized Freire as one of the main founders of critical pedagogy and noted that in some quarters his name has become synonymous with the very concept and the practice of critical pedagogy, and thus anyone who would like to engage with critical pedagogy has to begin with Freire, whether they like him or not. Along the same lines, McLaren (1989, 2000a) called Freire "the inaugural philosopher of critical pedagogy" because he was one of the first internationally recognized educational thinkers who fully appreciated the relationship among education, politics, imperialism, and liberation. Guilherme (2002:31) went one step further, identifying Freire as "the founder" of critical pedagogy. With regard to popular education, Freire is not only the most prominent name associated with this movement in Latin America, but is also recognized as its main guide and inspiration (Kane 2001, Nuñez 2007). For instance, the Consejo de Educación de Adultos de América Latina, the umbrella organization of popular education organizations in that region, has Freire as its first honorary president, and its website highlights prominently pictures and quotes of Freire. The stature of Paulo Freire in the popular education movement is not only limited to Latin America though. His contributions to this field have been highly influential in all continents (Gadotti 2001b, Mayo 2004, C. A. Torres 2008). Like most influential thinkers, Freire has his detractors. As we will see in Chapter 3, he has been criticized for different reasons, ranging from his particular writing style to issues related to perceived flaws in his theoretical analysis. Regardless of the different opinions on his work, his contributions can be better understood when they are situated within the specific sociopolitical and economic contexts in which they were formed. Indeed, Freire's intellectual biography was influenced in different ways by diverse political, economic, cultural, and social dynamics that took place around him throughout his life. Although Freire's life began and ended in Brazil, in between he lived and worked in many countries. For this reason, I have organized his intellectual biography into three distinct moments: "Early Brazil" (1921–64), "Exile" (1964–80), and "Late Brazil" (1980–97).

Early Brazil: From the mango tree to a prison cell

Paulo Freire was born into a middle-class family, the youngest of four children, in northeast Brazil, one of the most impoverished and unequal regions of that country. His mother, Edeltrudis Neves Freire, was a church-oriented Catholic. His father, Joaquim Temistocles Freire, was a military police official and a Spiritist, although not religiously affiliated. Freire adopted his mother's religion from childhood. His father not only respected that decision, but also attended Paulo's Communion ceremony. In examining his past, Freire said that with this and other similar gestures, his father taught him the importance of respecting the ideas of others even if he did not agree with them. He also noted that from his father he learned to distinguish between legitimate authority and authoritarianism, an issue that he would later address in his writings when analyzing power dynamics in pedagogical relations. Through conversations with his father, the young Paulo was introduced to information about social injustices and political struggles in Brazil. From his mother, he learned to embrace Catholicism, a belief that would influence his future worldview. At the same time, whereas his upbringing was deeply framed in religious values, it was not tarnished by an uncritical acceptance of reality. As he said, recalling the financial hardships faced by his family: "I never accepted our precarious situation as an expression of God's wishes" (Freire 1996:14). Through early family socialization practices, Freire also acquired a disposition toward dialogue and its attendant skills. He carried this competency into adulthood to the point where dialogue became central to his educational approach. He also learned from his parents to read and write at an early age, before attending school, in fact. Interestingly, they taught him literacy skills in a playful way: as a game, writing words on the earth with a stick under a mango tree. Freire (1983) recalled that his own literacy learning was pleasurable, largely because it started with concepts and sentences related to his own experience as a young child.

Freire noted that, seemingly unconsciously, the method used by his parents would inspire him later on to develop his famous approach to adult literacy, which starts from the vocabulary used by the learners in their daily lives and not with the words chosen by curriculum developers (Freire and Guimarães 1984). In a dialogue with Canadian adult educators Roby Kidd and Alan Thomas, Freire discussed his relationship with his parents and their influence on his attitudes toward adult education. At one point during the conversation, Freire said that he learned how to read and write under the shadow of a tree, writing in the earth with a stick: "The words that my parents used to introduce me to the literacy process were my words. It is very interesting to note that many years after that, when I started working in adult literacy, I started precisely with the words of the illiterates and not with my own words."[3]

Freire's initial educational experience at home found continuity at the local elementary school. His first teacher was a teenager named Eunice Vasconcelos. Freire remembered her with fondness, noting that she was particularly caring and constantly stimulated students' curiosity for learning. Moreover, Eunice's method of teaching writing skills was consistent with Freire's parents' approach to teaching reading skills. Eunice asked first-grade children to write in a piece of paper as many words as they knew, and then asked them to write sentences using those words. Finally, she discussed with each student the meaning and context of each sentence (Freire 1994a). This early school experience also contributed to developing Freire's approach to literacy teaching, particularly reliance on the vocabulary of the learners as the departure point for sentence making and for connecting sentence making to meaning making through dialogue and discussion.

Although Freire's family's social status could be characterized as middle class, its purchasing power declined drastically during the economic depression of the 1930s: the stock market crash of 1929 had a severe impact on the Brazilian economy, causing the price of coffee to fall dramatically, and affecting large sectors of the population. At that time, his father became very ill and his family struggled to make ends meet, and when Freire was 10 years old he endured hunger for the first time in his life. In 1932, the family had to move to nearby Jaboatão dos Guararapes, where the cost of living was lower than in Recife. Moving away from the house where he was born was a traumatic moment for Freire: "More than anything else, I felt like I was being expelled, thrown out of my sense of security. I experienced a fear that I had not felt before. It was as if I had died a little" (Freire 1996:36). In Jaboatão, Paulo spent the last part of his childhood and his adolescence. There, many of his friends lived in extreme poverty. As in many middle-class families that become suddenly impoverished, there was a disconnection in his house between cultural environment and concrete material conditions, illustrated by the juxtaposition of a German piano—a symbol of a better past and a sign of middle-class identity—and an empty fridge: "The piano in our home was like the tie around my father's neck. In spite of all difficulties, we did not get rid of the piano, nor did my father do away with his necktie" (Freire 1996:21).

The experience of living in poverty among poor rural families and laborers helped Freire to become familiar with the language and grammar of the people, something that would be important later on in his work as a popular educator. It also helped him to become more aware of the social world around him: "In Jaboatão, when I was ten, I began to think that there were a lot of things in the world that were not going well" (Freire 1978:10). He also learned to empathize with the oppressed, with whom he shared the difficulties of attending school on an empty stomach: "I didn't understand anything because of my hunger. I wasn't dumb. It wasn't lack of interest. My social condition didn't allow me to have an education. Experience showed me once again the relationship between social class and knowledge" (cited in Gadotti 1994:5). Moreover, in *Letters to Cristina*, Freire recalled how his experiences in Jaboatão marked his life with a deep sense of solidarity and human respect and helped to develop a critical and humanistic perception of the world. Toward the end of his life, he reminisced that he was a "connective child" in the sense that he was able to establish meaningful relations with people from different social, economic, and cultural backgrounds. Gadotti (2001a:29) argued that this ability to connect with others would help Freire to link different fields, disciplines, and categories ("episte- mological connectivity"). The finances of the Freire family became even more desperate in 1934 when his father passed away. The psychological impact of the death of his father, together with the consequences of the move and of financial difficulties, exacted a toll on Freire's academic performance. He received low grades, and some of his teachers diag- nosed him with a developmental disability (Facundo 1984, Elias 1994). Because he had problems being admitted to a secondary school, he had to remain out of school for 2 years.

At that time, in the midst of an economic crisis, Freire was bound to never complete secondary school. Two fortuitous events made a crucial difference to his educational future. The first was that Freire's mother was able to persuade Aluizio Pessoa de Araujo,[4] the director of the private high school Oswaldo Cruz, to accept Paulo as a student and to waive his fees. Surrounded by upper-class boys, it took some time to adapt to the new milieu, but eventually Paulo managed to find his place. The second was that his eldest brother got a job and started to make an economic contribution to the family, which helped Freire to enhance his academic performance: "the eldest in my family began to work and help our condition, and I began to eat more. To the extent I began to eat better, I began to better understand what I was reading" (Shor and Freire 1987:29). By the late 1930s, Paulo's other brothers were also working, and the economic situation of the family further improved. In these favorable circumstances, Freire made remarkable intellectual progress. Whereas up to the age of 15, he used to spell "rat" with two r's, a few years later he mastered Portuguese language so well that he became a teacher of grammar and syntax while still in high school and for several years after. As a young teacher, he asked his students to pay attention to the rules of language but, at the same time, he nurtured the role of creativity and recognized that creativity requires freedom. This early insight was key because creativity and freedom would become important principles in his educational philosophy and in his political approach: "As a young teacher, I changed my teaching and gave greater value to creativity. This was also a basis for me to understand later that creativity in teaching is linked to creativity in politics" (Freire and Shor 1987:20).

In his early twenties Freire started to study philosophy and sociology of language, and in 1943 was admitted to the law school at the University of Pernambuco. Soon thereafter he would discover that teaching was his true vocation. Paulo was invited to teach part-time at the same high school where he had studied (Oswaldo Cruz), and through his teaching he met adult workers and also Elza Maia Costa Oliveira, a primary school teacher who was preparing for an exam to qualify for the position of school principal. Freire became her tutor for the syntax part of her preparation. They fell in love, were married in 1944, and subsequently raised five children (María Madalena, María Cristina, María de Fátima, Joaquim, and Lutgardes). Throughout her life, Elza provided Paulo enormous emotional and intellectual support, and as a fellow educator she helped him to elaborate many of his innovative proposals and worked with him on several projects around the world.[5] Her experience teaching literacy to children played an important role in helping him develop and refine his adult literacy method.

During the 1940s, Elza constantly motivated Freire to continue his university studies. After passing the bar exam and becoming a lawyer, Freire defended his first client, who would also be his last: a young dentist unable to pay back a loan that he used to set up his dental office. Freire recalled that moment: "I had to collect my fee. After talking to my client, a young shy, frightened dentist, I decided not to charge him. He was happy because I was this kind of lawyer, and I was happy when I stopped being one" (Freire, cited in Gadotti 1994:8). After this experience, Freire confessed to Elza: "You know what, I'm not going to be a lawyer." She responded: "I was hoping for that. You are an educator" (Freire 1994:17). Then he returned to his high school teaching job, wearing black clothes to express his protest and sadness for the tragedy of World War II (Gadotti 1994, Garrido 2005). Partly because of his work as a high school teacher and his new role as parent, and partly because of his linguistics studies and his conversations with Elza, Freire's interest in educational theories and methods grew, and he read enthusiastically books on education, philosophy, psychology, and language in Portuguese, Spanish, French, and English, taking detailed notes (Freire 1985a:175). His transdisciplinary orientation, which would characterize most of his later work, was slowly beginning to take shape.

In terms of professional occupation, after his brief encounter with the practice of law and several years of high school teaching (1941–47), Freire started to work as a welfare official and then served for 10 years (1947–57) as director of the Department of Education and Culture of the Social Service of Industry (SESI) in the state of Pernambuco. SESI was an agency that channeled funds from a national confederation of factory owners to create programs for the betterment of the standard of living of their workers (Lownd 2001). Through his work at SESI Freire gained valuable insights that he would later develop in his educational theory. In *Letters to Cristina*, Freire (1996, 81) described his decade at SESI as the most important political-pedagogical practice of his life. SESI constituted a sharp change in Freire's professional trajectory. If he had not been invited to work at SESI, he probably could have ended up working as a high school language teacher or as a traditional university professor.

To understand how the transition from lawyer to progressive educator occurred, it is necessary to remember that during the 1940s Paulo and Elza started to participate in educational activities of the Catholic Church. There, through the Catholic Action movement, Freire became familiar with an incipient progressive movement that expressed a "preferential option for the poor" and would later be known as "liberation theology." He became acquainted with this movement through his involvement with the Christian Base Communities [Comunidades Eclesiales de Base], an initiative that sought to connect biblical study with local realities and social issues faced by the poor, and particularly through Dom Hélder Câmara (1909–99)[6], the Bishop of Recife who would be his mentor. It was precisely through his participation in this movement that Freire was invited to work at SESI. At SESI, Freire became the coordinator of an education and culture program directed to workers, where he interacted daily with various social groups. This provided Freire with a second opportunity—after his interactions with working-class children and peasants during his childhood in Jaboatão—to learn about popular culture and about class oppression. "Now as a young man, working with laborers, peasants, and fishermen, I once more became aware of the differences among social classes" (Freire 1985a:175). This position also allowed him to travel extensively throughout northeast Brazil and to be involved in a variety of projects.

For instance, he was one of the founders of the Capibaribe Institute in Recife, a school with a strong commitment to high-quality scientific inquiry, ethical education, and democratic principles and practices (Lownd 2001, Souto-Manning 2010). It was also in SESI, through his daily relationships with workers and peasants, that Freire made a transition toward a more radical understanding of education and developed his first ideas about the role of dialogue and culture in education (Shor and Freire 1987:29). At that time, however, he was not yet fully aware of the political implications of his educational practice (Freire 1985a:179).

As director of SESI, Freire implemented a democratic, open, and flexible management system and learned a good deal about school/family relations. In the educational institutions managed by SESI, Freire invited students and parents to participate in debates about education and society. He believed that social problems such as malnutrition and child labor could only be resolved with the participation of parents and the community. He also believed that this initial involvement could enable parents to participate in the design of the educational policies to be implemented in the schools and eventually take part of decision-making processes regarding the curriculum. At SESI, Freire also created "workers' clubs" in which members could examine their problems and seek collective solutions. Despite institutional constraints, Freire tried to reorient the management of SESI around the principles of dialogue, self-management, and "parlamentarization" (a combination of study groups and action groups). Due to the criticisms he received for this unprecedented administrative approach, Freire resigned from his position at SESI in 1957 (Freire 1994b, Gerhardt 1993). Around that time, he was appointed to the Board of Educations of Recife and coordinated the drafting of a paper by the state of Pernambuco to be presented at the Second National Conference on Adult Education, which took place in Rio de Janeiro in 1958. In his paper, Freire argued that adult education—and particularly adult literacy work with marginalized populations—should begin with the day-to-day situations experienced by learners. He also pointed out that for any educational project oriented toward democracy to be successful, educators should work with learners in co-creating knowledge. In the context of a traditional society characterized by elitism, authoritarianism, discrimination, paternalism, and exploitation (Brazil was the last country of the Americas to abolish slavery), these ideas were regarded as particularly innovative and progressive, and helped to establish Freire as a leading democratic adult educator (Ibid).

In 1959, Freire defended his doctoral dissertation at the University of Recife and was appointed professor of the history and philosophy of education at the University of Pernambuco. The thesis, entitled *Educação e atualidade brasileira* [Education and Present-Day Brazil] dealt with silence and resistance in postcolonial Brazilian education. In his doctoral thesis, based on his experience at SESI, Freire made references to John Dewey (1859–1952), whose pedagogical ideas were introduced to him by Anisio Teixeira (1900–71), a Brazilian intellectual and prolific writer who studied at Columbia's Teachers College in 1928–29 with Dewey and some of his disciples, such as William Kilpatrick, Harold Rugg, and George Counts. Impressed by progressive education, pragmatism, and humanism, Teixeira introduced Dewey's ideas to an entire generation of Brazilians through his translation of *Democracy and Education* in 1936, and tried to implement some of them in the public education system (Geribello 1977, Gadotti 2001a). In that period, Freire also became acquainted with the work of Soviet educator Anton Makarenko, especially with his texts on authority, obedience, and freedom (De Castro and Ghiggi 2009). By then, Freire was ready to put together the experience accumulated during the previous two decades and to make some original contributions of his own. All those years in public service and the different activities he had engaged in helped him to formulate the incipient ideas for an educational approach based on dialogue and social transformation. To put those ideas into historical perspective, it is pertinent to say a few words about Brazil during that period.

Throughout the 1950s and early 1960s, Brazilian political, social, and intellectual life was burgeoning. It was a historical moment characterized by the emergence of developmentalism, an independent model of national development that took into account the needs of the poor. Among the leading exponents of this movement were Hélio Jaguaribe, Anísio Teixeira, Roland Corbisier, and Álvaro Vieira Pinto, who worked at the Instituto Superior de Estudos Brasileiros (ISEB) in Rio de Janeiro. Many of their ideas were influenced by such European sociologists and philosophers as Karl Mannheim, Karl Jaspers, Gunnar Myrdal, and

Gabriel Marcel. Politically, those were times of effervescence. At the policy level, Brazilian life was largely influenced by the legacy of national populism. This orientation was clearly manifest in the two governments of Getulio Vargas (1930–45 and 1951–54). The Brazilian northeast witnessed the emergence of a vibrant agrarian social movement led by a socialist lawyer named Francisco Juliao who had founded the first Peasant Leagues in the mid-1950s. The Peasant Leagues formed cooperatives and credit unions, and provided medical, legal, and educational assistance to peasants. The associational activities promoted by the leagues spread like wildfire, and at the beginning of the 1960s they had an active presence in 13 states and sparked a national movement for agrarian reform. At that time, some progressive groups of the Catholic Church that were close to Freire's circles started to support the Peasant Leagues. That sector of the Catholic Church experienced significant growth and became the liberation theology movement. Influenced by the writings of authors like Jacques Maritain, Thomas Cardonnel, and Emmanuel Mounier, and by their Brazilian interpreters Alceu de Amoroso Lima, Henrique Lima Vaz, and Herbert José de Souza (Gadotti 1994), this movement received a great impetus in 1958, when John XXIII, who advocated for a "church of the poor," and would later initiate Vatican II, was elected pope in Rome. Another important political development of that era was the 1959 Cuban revolution, which had significant influence on a wide spectrum of the Brazilian left, ranging from trade unions to national populist movements, and from radical student groups to socialist and communist parties. Partly in response to the increasing unrest arising throughout Latin America and with the background of the Cold War, in 1961 the United States created the Alliance for Progress to promote economic cooperation between North and South America, with the goal of increasing economic growth and reducing poverty. The Alliance for Progress established a US Agency for International Development (AID) office for Brazil in Recife, considered a security threat due to the expansion of the Peasant Leagues (Facundo 1984).

It was in this political, social, and intellectual context that, in 1961, a 43-year-old affluent lawyer named Joao Goulart became the twenty-seventh president of Brazil. Ideologically progressive and highly popular among unions and the poor, Goulart quickly established alliances with left-of-center political groups and implemented a series of national reforms and redistributive policies, such as the expropriation of uncultivated land and the establishment of state-run cooperatives. It was also in this context that in 1960 Paulo Freire founded Recife's Popular Culture Movement. The following year, Recife mayor Miguel Arraes (a progressive lawyer who would become governor of Pernambuco), appointed Freire as director of the Division of Culture and Recreation. Freire's team, which included members from different political orientations, managed to work together well. By 1963, Freire became the first director of the University of Recife's Cultural Extension Service, which brought literacy programs to thousands of peasants in northeast Brazil. When Freire assumed this position, northeast Brazil was one of the poorest and most unequal regions of the planet. Half of the land was owned by 3 percent of the population, the per capita income was only 40 percent of the national average, life expectancy was 28 years for men and 32 for women, and the illiteracy rate was about 75 percent (Elias 1994). Because literacy was a requirement for voting in presidential elections, the law excluded millions of Brazilians from electoral participation. One of the goals of the Goulart government was to introduce universal suffrage. This required people to acquire literacy skills that, in turn, called for appropriate adult education services.[7]

At that time, literacy training and adult education in Brazil (and elsewhere in Latin America) was typically a mere replication of the same contents and methods used to educate children. More often than not, adult classes were conducted in school settings, so adults had to fit in the evening in the same small seats where their children had sat in the morning and to copy similar words from the blackboard. Freire had a different understanding of adult education. In his view, education should not be just about the transmission of content from teacher to students. He believed that the traditional education aimed at domesticating learners into accepting oppressive structures, and started to develop an alternative educational approach aimed at liberation that combined study circles (called "culture circles"), lived experience, work, pedagogy, and politics. Freire was not the first to argue that adult literacy approaches should be different from the ones used in children's literacy. Others have advanced the argument before. However, Freire was the first one to develop, implement, and systematize a literacy method designed exclusively for adult education (Gadotti 1994). Moreover, for Freire, the challenge was not just to teach literacy skills, but to give voice to the people so they could transition from a culture of silence, oppression, and colonialism to one of pride and active political participation in which they would become masters of their own destiny.

Freire had the first opportunity for the widespread application of his educational theories in 1962, when he took a leading role in the literacy program "Bare feet can also learn to read" in the neighboring state of Rio Grande do Norte. In the small village of Angicos, Freire and his team pioneered his psychosocial approach to literacy, and surprised everyone when 300 sugarcane workers learned to read and write in only 45 days while they engaged in a critical analysis of their own social reality. When President Goulart became acquainted with the unprecedented success of this approach, he approved the creation of thousands of cultural circles across the country, appointed Freire as president of the National Commission on Popular Culture, and invited him to implement a national literacy campaign.[8] Then, in 1963, the Ministry of Education undertook a literacy campaign using Paulo Freire's method. That year, Freire issued a call in Rio for 600 students to serve as literacy tutors. When 6,000 volunteers showed up, the interviews had to be conducted in a soccer stadium. In dialogue with Ira Shor, Freire remembered that ebullient era: "It was a time of fantastic popular mobilization, and education was part of it" (Shor and Freire 1987:32). From June 1963 to March 1964, his literacy teams worked throughout the nation, starting with training courses for coordinators in every state.

Freire's team claimed success in teaching adult illiterates to read and write in only 30 hours. The key of this accomplishment was not so much a particular method or technique, but precisely Freire's departure from instrumental and decontextualized ways of teaching literacy to adults, and his emphasis on reading the word while also "reading the world." The main goal for the first year of the campaign was that 5 million adult Brazilians should become literate, politically aware, and civically engaged. This generated resistance from landowners, who felt threatened by the possibility that peasants organize in associations, become educated and exercise their right to vote, thereby creating conditions for land reform. Moreover, the Brazilian oligarchy, having overseen the fate of the country for decades, perceived the risk of losing control of the electoral college (Lownd 2001). The massive literacy campaign also received criticism from the influential daily *O Globo*, which charged that the method was subversive because it agitated people and gave them ideas about changing things (Kadt 1970, Monteith 1977, Taylor 1993, Sanders 2004).

In the meantime, Goulart signed decrees expropriating oil refineries and uncultivated land owned by foreign companies, including those that used to keep arable land unfarmed to drive up the price of produce. He also took a neutral stance in the Cold War between the United States and the Soviet Union. In reprisal, the Brazilian military, with support from the CIA and active participation of the US Embassy in Brazil, overthrew Goulart in a coup d'état in April 1964 and started to persecute progressive movements and leaders. The military junta, which would remain in power for two decades, arrested Freire and put him in jail for his literacy programs; he was charged, among other things, with having "absolute ignorance" and for being "an international subversive, and a traitor to Christ and the Brazilian people." The military had a particular understanding of Freire's "crimes" insofar as when he was arrested, one of the judges asked him: "Do you deny that your method is similar to that of Stalin, Hitler, Perón, and Mussolini?" (Gadotti 1994:34). In confinement, Freire began to work on his first widely circulated book, *Education as the Practice of Freedom*, in which he examined his failure to affect change in Brazil. After being imprisoned for 70 days in Olinda and in Recife, he managed to find refuge in the Bolivian embassy in Rio, which granted him political asylum. Now in his mid-forties, Paulo Freire was about to embark unknowingly upon a long and productive exile that would last more than 15 years.

Exile: The "pilgrim of the obvious" becomes an international figure

In Chinese, the word "crisis" has two meanings: "danger" and "opportunity." On the one hand, the 1964 coup d'état interrupted Freire's educational projects and displaced him from his beloved Brazil, causing considerable suffering and hardship to him and his family. On the other hand, this otherwise unfortunate situation allowed him to travel to many countries, which in turn gave him the opportunity to gain new insights and to further disseminate his proposals for educational and social change. During his 15 years in exile, Freire worked and traveled in several parts of the world. However, he established residence in only three places: Santiago, Chile (1964–69); Cambridge, Massachusetts (1969–70); and Geneva, Switzerland (1970–79). What follows is an account of those years away from Brazil and an exploration of some of the factors that influenced his contributions to the field of education.

After being expelled from Brazil, Freire traveled to Bolivia. He and his family had been there less than 3 weeks trying to settle down and recover from their abrupt departure from Brazil when they witnessed yet another coup d'état, this time against President Victor Paz Estensoro. Given these adverse circumstances, and Freire's health difficulties with the altitude of La Paz, he moved with his family to Chile, where a populist alliance led by Christian Democrats had just been elected. From 1964 to 1970, the administration of Eduardo Frei advanced progressive reforms and initiatives for community development, social promotion, and local associationism. Among those initiatives were literacy programs that attracted international attention, to the extent that United Nations Educational, Scientific and Cultural Organization (UNESCO) recognized Chile as one of the five nations of the world that had managed best in overcoming illiteracy. Several of the reforms initiated by Frei, particularly land reform, required that many government agencies move from urban to rural areas. The goal was to establish a new infrastructure, to expand the provision of services (health, education, credit, technical assistance, transportation, etc.), and to operate them efficiently. To meet this challenge, the newly elected Chilean government needed more professionals and technical cadres to support local development in rural areas. It was in this context that Paulo Freire was invited to assist with the training of these new technical cadres. Although Freire lived in Chile for less than 5 years, from November 1964 to April 1969, these were very intense years that played a significant role in his pedagogical, political, and ideological development (Paiva 1980, Austin 1997, Kirkendall 2004, Holst 2006). During that period, Freire worked in the Ministry of Education and in the Ministry of Agricultural Development, including the Chilean Institute for Land Reform (ICIRA: Instituto de Capacitación e Investigación en Reforma Agraria). He was also an acting professor in the Catholic University and a consultant for UNESCO on adult education, although he did not agree with the concept of "functional literacy" advanced by UNESCO at that time. During his Chilean period Freire was also invited to give lectures in the United States and to collaborate with the World Council of Churches.

In Chile, Freire found a dynamic and ebullient social and intellectual climate that challenged some of his ideas and helped him to become familiar with new bodies of literature, to reexamine and reformulate his educational theories, and to link those theories with concrete practices. Moreover, the high level of political mobilization that was part and parcel of Chilean society during the mid-1960s also helped Freire to connect his pedagogical theories to serious debates about social reproduction and social change. The Chilean experience was fundamental for the consolidation and reformulation of the pedagogical-political proposals that Freire had started to develop in northeast Brazil in the early 1960s and, ultimately, for the radicalization of his ideas (Gadotti 1994, Torres 1998b, Holst 2006). During his years in Chile, Freire interacted closely with the progressive groups of the Christian Democratic Party and became familiar with Marxist thought. He also became familiar with the postulates of dependency theory proposed by the Economic Commission for Latin America and the Caribbean (ECLAC)[9] that were articulated in the work of Raul Prebisch and others, especially Fernando H. Cardoso (a Brazilian sociologist exiled in Chile who became Brazil's president in 1995) and Enzo Faletto, a Chilean sociologist.[10] During this period, Freire's thought was particularly influenced by his own coworkers at ICIRA, especially by a young researcher and popular educator named Marcela Gajardo, who introduced him to the writings of twentieth-century Marxist thinkers like Antonio Gramsci and who would later become his editor in Spanish.

The Chilean influence resulted in a significant shift in Freire's conceptual framework and analytical tools, as evidenced by contrasting *Education as the Practice of Freedom* with *Pedagogy of the Oppressed.* Whereas the former, written in the mid-1960s, was influenced largely by his Brazilian experience and informed by a liberal developmentalist perspective, the latter, written in the late 1960s, was profoundly influenced by the Chilean context and largely rooted in Marxist humanism (Elias 1994, Gajardo 1998, Holst 2006).[11] In Chile, Freire's work concentrated in rural areas. He was critical of the Alliance for Progress (1961–63), arguing that this initiative was promoted by the United States to create favorable conditions for foreign investment in Latin America and that behind a façade of "technical assistance" there was a plan for political, ideological, and economic domination. This is the context that explains the concept of "cultural invasion" that Freire used in his Chilean writings. During the same period, and as a result of his experiences in the countryside, he questioned the theory and practice of rural extension. He elaborated his critique to this approach in a short book entitled *Extension or Communication*, published in 1969 in Spanish. Freire's two early essays on his approach to adult education (*Education as the Practice of Freedom* and *Extension or Communication*) would be published in English together in one volume—in 1973—as *Education for Critical Consciousness*.[12]

In Chile, Freire's educational perspective received the support of the progressive wing of the Christian Democratic Party, but the conservative forces of that party accused him of intervening in Chilean politics, a charge that Freire (1994b) vehemently denied. He stated that one of his ethical duties as a political refugee was to respect the host country, and when he heard of the first rumor, he made the decision to circulate in advance the texts of his talks. Soon thereafter the attacks escalated, and Freire was accused of writing a "violent book" in reference to *Pedagogy of the Oppressed*, which he finished in 1968. The tensions created by this situation were a key factor in Freire's decision to leave Chile in 1969 (Gadotti 1994). At that time, thanks to the positive reception of *Education as a Practice of Freedom* in many educational circles, Freire was invited to Harvard University to work as a visiting professor at the Center for Studies in Education and Development and to collaborate as a fellow at the Center for the Study of Development and Social Change. The following year, in 1970, *Pedagogy of the Oppressed* was published simultaneously in English (Continuum) and Spanish (Tierra Nueva) and in a short time it was translated into several languages, reprinted many times, and widely read around the world.[13]

The context that surrounded Freire in the United States was different than Chile, but it was equally intense. The late 1960s and early 1970s in the United States were characterized by deep social and racial conflicts, rising social movements, and youth rebellion. At that time, the student movement took an active role in politics, largely inspired by the Port Huron Statement of the Students for a Democratic Society (which argued for peace, participatory democracy, and racial equality, and presented itself as "an agenda for a generation") and by the free speech movement that originated at the University of Berkeley. Poverty, urban decline, segregated housing, unemployment, and police harassment led to massive unrest in several cities, including the turmoil in July 1967 in Detroit and Newark that ended with 69 people dead, more than 3,500 injured, and almost 10,000 arrested. In 1968, Martin Luther King Jr., the leader of the civil rights movement, was assassinated, and thousands of Chicano high school students launched a protest (known as the East Los Angeles Blowouts) that would eventually lead to significant educational reforms in bilingual and multicultural education. In 1969, half a million young people crowded at Woodstock for a radical concert that embraced the counterculture of the 1960s. In 1970, the military attacked a student demonstration against the Vietnam War at Kent State University, leaving four students dead, eight wounded, and one paralyzed. Women and gays joined African Americans and students in justice-oriented coalitions, numerous alternative communes flourished, Nixon became the first president in US history to resign from office after the Watergate scandal, and minority spokespersons and war protesters were actively engaged in making their opposition known.

Those were indeed turbulent years, and these social, political, and cultural dynamics influenced Freire profoundly. Wherever he looked, minority leaders and war protesters were giving speeches, publishing their views, and teaching. Faced with this new reality, Freire was surprised to find that the repression and exclusion of oppressed members of society from economic and political life was not limited to developing countries. As a result of this, he extended his definition of periphery from a geographical to a political concept, understanding there to be a "third world" within the "first world," and became interested in acquiring a better understanding of the dynamics of violence. He was also exposed to feminist and antiracist theories, and he thus began to integrate gender and race analysis into his own thinking, which, until then, had focused on class issues. At that time, Freire began to grow a beard that would become a lasting trait for the rest of his life. Although in those days beards were regarded as a symbol of rebellion, the reason for letting his beard grow was neither an ideological choice nor a political statement. It was a more practical one: the cold climate of Boston. During those last years of the 1960s Freire spent two summers in Cuernavaca, Mexico, at the Center for Information and Documentation (CIDOC). He was invited by CIDOC's director Ivan Illich, a former priest who at that time was working on the soon-to-be-famous book *Deschooling Society*.[14] Illich and Freire had interesting discussions on education that included agreements and disagreements about the potential role of educational institutions to democratize society (Freire and Illich 1975). Although both were highly critical of the educational establishment, they had different proposals to address the antidemocratic nature of schools. As we shall see later, Illich had little hope about the possibilities of democratizing the educational system and called for its elimination, whereas Freire proposed to democratize it as part of a broader program to democratize society. When Freire was in Boston, he wrote two academic papers on his educational theories for the *Harvard Educational Review;* they were published in 1970 as the first issue of a monograph series under the title *Cultural Action for Freedom*. In these papers, he argued that the situation of illiterates in developing countries is characterized by emptiness, marginality, and silence, and proposed a pedagogical intervention (cultural action) based on dialogue and awareness-raising (Freire 1970a).

In 1970, Freire was invited to work as a special educational advisor to the World Council of Churches in Geneva. By then, he had completed a transition toward a more radical conception of educational and social action, one that was grounded in the principles of liberation theology and in a deeper commitment to the oppressed. In his letter of acceptance to the World Congress of Churches, where he would work throughout the entire decade, he made this position explicit: "You must know that I made a decision. My case is the case of the wretched of the earth" (cited in Gerhardt 1993:546). Although Freire's official residence was in Switzerland, he spent most of that decade traveling, especially in Africa and Latin America, and identified himself as "a man from the Third World" (Kirkendall 2010). In 1971, with his wife Elza and a group of other Brazilians exiled in Switzerland, he founded the Institute for Cultural Action [Instituto de Açao Cultural, IDAC] to provide educational assistance to countries of the south that were struggling for full independence. Freire was elected president and served as chair of its executive committee. At the center of IDAC's approach was the use of the "conscientization" method[15] as an instrument of liberation in the educational process for social transformation. Almost immediately, IDAC was flooded with requests for publications, booklets, courses, workshops, and seminars from many parts of the world. In 1971 Freire visited Tanzania for the first time, invited by President Julius Nyerere, known as "Mwalimu" (teacher) because he was an educator before becoming involved in politics. Freire's visit to Tanzania was coordinated by Budd Hall, a young and energetic North American adult educator who later became the secretary general of the International Council of Adult Education. Freire visited several communities and became exposed to the ideas and the practices of "ujamaa (communitarian) socialism" proposed by Nyerere. Freire and Nyerere found many areas of agreement on education and development, and Freire proposed to establish a center based on those ideas. Nyerere responded, in somewhat ambiguous terms, that Freire should always feel at home in Tanzania and was welcomed to spend as much time in the country as he wanted. Freire did not follow up with a concrete proposal, probably because, as he often claimed, he was not good at fund-raising (Hall 1998:98). Although Freire did not directly advise any literacy program in Tanzania, his ideas had an impact on the approaches and strategies used by community development programs (Kirkendall 2010:105).

During January and February of 1973, following an invitation from religious leaders with the World Council of Churches, Freire toured 12 states of the United States. On weekdays, he held meetings with educators, social workers, and leaders of social movements to discuss their practice, usually in relation to the ideas advanced in *Pedagogy of the Oppressed*. On weekends, he participated in large seminars on topics previously defined. On the last weekend, representatives of the 12 seminars brought reports of each to a large meeting held in New York. In the weekend seminar held in Chicago, Freire came up with the "unity in diversity" argument as a response to the divisive results of identity politics. In *Pedagogy of Hope* he recounted that, at the beginning of that seminar, various groups (blacks, Indians, Mexican Americans) proclaimed that they wanted to meet only among themselves to discuss their issues. Freire responded that he respected their position, but he was convinced that as long as the "minorities" (who are ultimately the majority) are disconnected from each other, the only real minority (the dominant class) would continue ruling without restraint. After building his argument for a few minutes, he concluded that the only way forward was to create unity in diversity. Freire (1994b:154) lamented that his argument did not prevail. Some participants contented that the "unity and diversity" argument was "white talk," and the groups divided up and held their discussions separately.

In 1973 Freire visited Argentina for the first time. He had wanted to see Buenos Aires since childhood. When he lived in Chile in the late 1960s he was disallowed to enter Argentina by the 1966–72 military regime, but the newly elected democratic government invited him through the Ministry of Education. Freire put three conditions on accepting the invitation. The first was that, even if he had a full workload, he could have the opportunity to attend an evening of tango (Freire was passionate about Brazilian music and tango). The second was to avoid massive public lectures, and the third was to work intensely with popular education groups. The three conditions were met. Freire also held meetings with university presidents, most of them younger than him, and engaged in a long conversation with Rodolfo Puiggrós, a noted intellectual and historian who at that time was the president of the Universidad de Buenos Aires. In 1974, sponsored by the Australian Council of Churches, Freire traveled to Australia and New Zealand, engaging in meetings and giving public lectures. Some of these were recorded and disseminated in a series of videotapes entitled *Thinking with Paulo Freire.* In September 1974, he engaged in a discussion on the connections between education, peace, and social justice with European peace educators at the first Conference of the World Council for Curriculum and Instruction (Curle, Freire, and Galtung 1976). By the mid- and late 1970s, mostly through his involvement with IDAC, Freire assisted several newly independent African countries (Guinea-Bissau, São Tomé and Principe, Cape Verde, Mozambique, and Angola) in the implementation of adult education and literacy initiatives. In these programs, Freire for the first time connected educational projects with community economic development projects promoted by the new governments.[16] One of the most serious challenges he faced in Guinea-Bissau related to multilingualism, an issue that he had never faced before. A key pedagogical and ethical dilemma emanating from this situation was the choice between Portuguese and one of the many native dialects as the main language of the literacy campaign, which was connected to a political decision made by the national government on the lingua franca to be used in the country.

During the second half of the 1970s, Freire continued traveling to other countries to engage in dialogues, lectures, and seminars on his ideas and experiences. For example, in June of 1976, he participated in the first Assembly of the International Council of Adult Education, which was held in Tanzania and constituted the first attempt to link the discourses of adult education and international development at a world level (Hall 1998). In July and August, he spent several weeks at the Ontario Institute for Studies in Education (OISE) of the University of Toronto where he gave seminars and engaged in conversations with professors Roby Kidd and Alan Thomas. Those conversations are preserved in three videos: "Becoming Christian," "Guns and Pencils," and "Letters in the Earth." In that summer of 1976, a young Canadian adult educator named D'Arcy Martin asked Freire if he could interview him for a film he was making about popular education in Canada. By then, Freire and Martin had already met (through their common friend Betinho) and Freire had read Martin's thesis on the potential and limits of conscientization (Martin 1975). Initially, Freire contemplated the request with reluctance, because he had never done a film or TV interview alone, and was concerned about the power of media to manipulate content through careful editing of footage. Then, unexpectedly, Freire enthusiastically exclaimed: "Don't you see the opportunity this gives us, D'Arcy? The American and European TV people chase me now precisely because I refuse their offers. So if you interview me, that film will be worth money for resale. It could be my contribution, not just to your film, but to the financing you need to make it" (cited in Martin 1998:121). A few weeks later, a producer called Martin from Frankfurt to say that Freire declined to appear on German TV and mentioned that the only available interview was in Canada. The producer flew to Toronto and purchased the rights, and with the proceeds Martin and his colleagues edited the documentary *Starting from Nina: The Politics of Learning*.[17] Reflecting on this, Martin said that he learned from Freire that political capital could be a privilege to denounce but also a resource to use for collective benefit (Martin 1998:122). During the late 1970s, Freire's services were also sought in Central America and the Caribbean, where he provided advice to the literacy campaigns carried out in Nicaragua and in Grenada, invited by the Sandinistas and by the New Jewel Movement, respectively. By the end of the decade, the political situation in Brazil had begun to change, and Freire started to explore the possibility of returning home with his family.

Back in Brazil: Politics, public service, and books

At the end of the 1970s, the military dictatorships of Ernesto Geisel and Joao Figueiredo introduced a gradual plan to democratize the country. Amnesties were granted to thousands of exiled Brazilians. Following a short trip to Brazil in August 1979, Freire had discussions in Geneva with his family, his colleagues at IDAC, and the World Council of Churches about a potential permanent return to his home country. A visit from his friend Paulo Evaristo Arns, then archbishop of Sao Paulo, convinced Freire that it was time to move back, and after 15 years of absence he returned to Brazil in March 1980. In this final period of his life we identify three main elements. The first was his active participation in the Workers' Party, of which he was a founding member in 1980. The second was his involvement in the state, accepting an appointment as secretary of education of Sao Paulo in 1989. The third was his continuing engagement with books, not only through academic positions but also through writing: in the last 17 years of his life he produced more publications than in the previous six decades.

Upon his return to Brazil, Freire had the opportunity to resume his position at the Federal University of Pernambuco, where he had been senior professor until the coup d'etat of 1964. However, he did not take up that position because, according to the terms of the 1979 amnesty, the Brazilian government demanded that those returning to the country from exile had to take a sort of "test of dangerousness" given by a commission appointed by the military. Freire's refusal to take the test affected him financially for many years (Gadotti 1994).[18] Eventually, he was appointed a professor at the Pontifícia Universidade Católica de São Paulo (PUC) and a visiting professor at the Universidade Estadual de Campinas (UNICAMP); he also supervised the adult literacy project of the Workers' Party. After so many years abroad, Freire said that his first task was to "re-learn" Brazil, and for this purpose he traveled the country, participating in seminars and meetings with a variety of publics. He also kept writing and published *The Importance of the Act of Reading* and *The Politics of Education: Culture, Power and Liberation*. In 1983 and 1984, he visited Mexico in two opportunities, invited by the Instituto Nacional de Educación de Adultos (INEA), to participate in internal seminars on the theory and practice of literacy aimed at improving the literacy programs carried out by the institute. On those occasions he also delivered public lectures on adult education and gave some interviews (Freire 1984b). In 1985, Freire and his wife Elza jointly received the Outstanding Christian Educators Award for their lifetime contributions to the field of education. Also in 1985, Freire gave the keynote address at the World Assembly of Adult Education in his role of president of the Latin American Adult Education Council. The assembly was held in Buenos Aires (Argentina) after the return to democracy, and was attended by 500 popular educators from over 100 countries.[19]

In 1986, Freire was awarded the UNESCO Prize for Peace Education, and the same year he suffered the loss of his wife Elza, with whom he shared 40 years of marriage in Brazil and in exile. After the death of Elza, Freire experienced a deep depression. A year later he visited Bolivia, where he participated in debates on popular education, the role of universities in developing countries, and pedagogical ideas in Latin America; and in 1988 he married Ana Maria Araujo, an educator, scholar, and long-term friend[20] whom Paulo affectionately called "Nita" (a short form of Anita). The marriage with Nita helped Paulo overcome his sorrow and recover his enthusiasm for living. As he used to say: "When I fell in love with Nita, I fell in love with the world and with life again" (Vittoria and Araujo Freire 2007:10). Nita had known Paulo since she was 3 years old and he was a teenager attending the Oswaldo Cruz secondary school. Nita's father, Aluizio Pessoa de Araujo, was the school director and his teacher, and granted young Paulo a scholarship to attend the school when his father died and his family suffered economic hardship. Freire later returned to the school a few years after graduation to teach Portuguese classes. Freire and Nita met again at the university in the 1980s, when she was pursuing a master's degree and he returned as a professor and both were widowers. Nita and Paulo worked together on several projects until he passed away.[21] During the 1980s, Freire began to write books in conversation with others, inaugurating a series of "dialogue books" in Portuguese, Spanish, and English. In 1987, Freire visited the Highlander Folk School, a popular education center in Tennessee founded by Myles Horton in 1932 that was part of the progressive labor movement and played an important role in the civil rights movements of the 1950s, including a successful voter education strategy connected to a literacy program, similar to Freire's initiatives in northeast Brazil in the 1960s. In their lively exchanges, Freire and Horton shared a belief that liberation is achieved through popular participation and that participation is achieved through an educational practice that is itself both participatory and liberatory. At Highlander, Freire and Horton also discussed social and educational issues with local students and adult education workers; these discussions were recorded in the film *Myles Horton, Paulo Freire and Friends Gather at Highlander.*

Immediately upon his return to Brazil, Freire also involved himself in political affairs. In 1980, he became one of the founding members of the Workers' Party of Brazil, together with several other workers and intellectuals, including then-union leader and later Brazil's president Luis Inácio da Silva (Lula). A few years later, he cofounded *Instituto Cajamar,* a residential education and leadership development center in the outskirts of Sao Paulo connected to the labor movement, popular organizations, and the Workers' Party. At *Cajamar* he participated in course design and taught classes, and soon thereafter became the president of its council. He also joined a small organization of committed popular educators called *Varela* and established connections with neighborhood groups, environmental associations, feminist movements, and religious grassroots communities inspired by liberation theology. Through these activities with educational, political, and community organizations Freire had a great opportunity to combine the theory and practice he proposed in his own writings (Gerhardt 1993). In 1987, he was invited to join the UNESCO International Jury, a body that meets annually in Paris to select the best literacy project from submissions from around the world. He served in this capacity until 1995. Although during the 1980s Brazil was still under military rule, it continued its slow return to electoral democracy that had started in the late 1970s. This transition to democracy, a transition that eventually resulted in gradual opening of the political process and withdrawal of the military dictatorship, would take the entire decade, but speeded up in the late 1980s due to a combination of factors, most prominently the pressure of domestic social movements and the end of the Cold War. In 1988 a new democratic constitution was passed, and in 1989, general elections were held, with Fernando Collor de Melo becoming the first president to be elected by direct popular ballot since the 1964 military coup. In the municipal elections that then took place, the Workers' Party won the municipal governments of several medium-size cities and also of Sao Paulo, Brazil's largest city.

This electoral result had a direct impact on Freire's professional trajectory because the newly elected mayor of the city of Sao Paulo, Luiza Erundina de Sousa, invited him to become the secretary of education of her administration. She and Freire were both from Pernambuco and had known each other for a long time. Freire said that he accepted the offer in order to be consistent with all he had done, said, and written in the past: "If I had not accepted the honorable invitation by Erundina, I would have to, for a matter of coherence, pull all of my books out of press, stop writing, and be silent till death" (Freire 1993b:58). In his view, he had no other choice. As a result, Freire took office as secretary of education of Sao Paulo on January 1, 1989. A year later, he explained to a group of Uruguayan educators: "If I die, for instance, this year, I would not have written the four books I wanted to write, but I proved myself in a job that I needed to perform before dying. Much more necessary than writing those four books was to know how I would behave holding power, and I would like to tell you that I behave well, with a relative coherence"(CIDC 1990:32). When Freire was appointed secretary of education of Sao Paulo, some people expressed concerns about his qualifications to perform this job adequately. They complained that he had little administrative experience in the school system, and that his work with pre-literate adults in the 1960s in nonformal settings was perceived as largely irrelevant to the challenges of a massive formal educational system at the end of the twentieth century (O'Cadiz et al. 1998). Those preoccupations were somehow warranted, but Freire was not totally unfamiliar with the formal education system.

Among other things, he had worked as a secondary school teacher for many years, and during his tenure at SESI in the 1940s and 1950s he organized dialogue circles with parents to discuss issues related to the education of their children. Interestingly, one of his first articles, written in 1955, is a reflection about this experience. In this article, which is the oldest one available at the Paulo Freire Institute, he dealt with models and processes to nurture the participation of parents in public and private schools. Moreover, in the 1970s, he provided advice on the educational systems to former Portuguese colonies in Africa (Gadotti 1996).

The social and educational landscape of Brazil when Freire became secretary of education was characterized by serious problems. Almost two-thirds of the economically active population lived in poverty. Over one-third of children aged 7 to 14 (7.6 of 23 million) were unschooled; 46.3 percent of all Brazilians had an average of two or less years of schooling, and 25.5 percent of Brazilians 10 years and older were illiterate. When Freire became secretary of education, he proposed a program based on five policy objectives: (1) increased access to schooling (about 1 million children could not enroll in schools due to limited school capacities); (2) democratization of school administration; (3) improved quality of instruction; (4) education for working youths and adults; and (5) the development of critical and responsible citizens (Freire 1993b; O'Cadiz et al. 1998). These ambitious goals were soon challenged by difficult circumstances. Freire encountered a massive municipal educational system (more than a million children) and a significant proportion of teachers that used authoritarian and traditional pedagogical methods in rundown schools. Sixty-seven percent of the schools required major repairs due to collapsed ceilings, exposed electrical wiring, and defective plumbing. Many had unusable desks and chairs.[22] School vandalism (including break-ins and looting) was rampant. Dropout rates (or, in Freire's terms, "push-out" rates) were high,[23] and 1.5 million residents of Sao Paulo were illiterate (Torres 1994, Stromquist 1997, O'Cadiz et al. 1998). A junior teacher earned slightly more than a domestic servant, and staff turnover was high. These challenges did not diminish Freire's determination to make a difference. Upon taking office, he said that he had more political and pedagogical understanding of what needed to be done to bring more rigor, happiness, and democracy to public schools. He confessed that it was not going to be easy to put into practice all the ideas that he discussed in his many books, but at the same time, he was enjoying the challenge because it gave him a new sense of purpose: "It is one thing to write down concepts in books, but it is another to embody those concepts in praxis. Those things are showing themselves to be very challenging, but they continue to give me a sense of joy and satisfaction. It is not perchance that I find myself even younger now" (Freire, in Torres 1990:3).

As secretary of education, Freire ignited a variety of initiatives. At the beginning, he devoted significant time, energy, and resources to fixing the derelict infrastructure of the K–12 schools that served almost a million children. As a result of this effort, by the end of his administration the number of students enrolled in the public school system increased by over 15 percent, 77 new schools were constructed, 60,000 new desks were purchased, major maintenance and repair work was done in most schools, and arrangements were made to maximize the use of existing school buildings and to open them for community activities. Audio-visual equipment, computers, and children's books were purchased, as well as school supplies for poor children. He also launched an adult literacy education program (MOVA, or Movimento de Alfabetização) that followed many of the pedagogical principles that had framed his adult education projects in Angicos two decades earlier. To implement this program, Freire established partnerships with nongovernmental organizations and neighborhood groups. Probably the most significant initiative put in motion by Freire and his team at the Secretary of Education was a curriculum reform movement based on an interdisciplinary and participatory approach to knowledge production. The curriculum used generative themes related to real situations and issues relevant to the learners and their communities (e.g., relations among students, transportation, pollution). The curriculum reform project was complemented by system-wide initiatives to replace the prevailing authoritarian model of education with classroom relations involving dialogue and more democratic forms of management, including partnerships with local groups and parents for participatory decision-making processes regarding planning, implementation, and resource allocations. This open system was intended to create more school autonomy and community responsibility; to ensure more transparency, accountability, and sustainability of educational reforms; and to allow schools and government the opportunity to cooperate on the formulation of education policies. As secretary of education, Freire also introduced a more democratic and decentralized structure for school supervision, technical assistance, and support. As part of the latter, he instituted a new model of in-service teacher training consisting of professional development groups in which teachers—through facilitated meetings—could reflect upon their pedagogical knowledge and practice, explore educational theories, and develop skills in a collective and continuous process (O'Cadiz et al. 1998, Gadotti 2003).

A related initiative was the "Citizen School," understood as one that promotes the exercise of citizenship by all those who participate in it: "It is a school of community and camaraderie for collective production of knowledge and freedom, a space that articulates rights and obligations and lives the tense experience of democracy" (Freire 1997).[24] The Citizen School project of São Paulo made some modest accomplishments, but the process was interrupted in 1992 when the progressive coalition lost the municipal elections. However, its more important contribution was to open the path for other Citizen School projects to emerge and gain momentum, not only in Sao Paulo but also in other parts of Brazil.[25] During Freire's tenure as secretary of education the World Bank sent a mission to Sao Paulo to persuade his administration to accept a loan to carry out projects of curriculum reform and teacher training. In a conversation with Carlos Torres, Freire revealed that he felt so aggravated with the bank's suggestions that he suggested the mission return to the United States and once they solved the educational problems there he would be happy to talk with them about their suggestions to improve Brazilian education. Freire told the mayor that he was ready to resign from his post if the World Bank's loan was accepted. He argued that something was wrong with priorities if a country like Brazil had to depend on foreign loans to educate its children. His position prevailed, and during the administration of the Workers' Party in Sao Paulo, no World Bank loan was negotiated (C. A. Torres 2002:379–80).

In evaluating his performance as secretary of education, O'Cadiz et al. (1998) argue that, overall, Freire was able to rise up to the challenge by adding new ideas to his repertoire while being consistent with his original educational and philosophical ideals. Among the elements of that original framework that remained in Freire's work as secretary of education were the notion of education as a tool for social and cultural emancipation, the role of students and teachers as subjects of their own learning process, the importance of "reading the word" through "reading the world," the democratization of student-teacher relations, the recognition of education as a political-pedagogical project, the emphasis on dialogue, the interaction between popular and scientific knowledge, and a curriculum construction process that starts from local reality. Despite its enthusiasm and the innovative reforms, the Freire administration was not totally successful in achieving its goals. Perhaps one of the problems was that he tried to implement too many new initiatives at the same time in too many schools. The ambitious scope and speed of the project, coupled with the low administrative experience of his team, the inadequate professional preparation of teachers to understand and implement creatively complex and innovative approaches, the limited resources for compensating personnel and teachers for their extra time devoted to the project, the resistance of educators belonging to opposition parties, and the criticisms of conservative media, created many obstacles and challenges. Moreover, some of his initiatives found resistance even among bureaucrats in the Secretary of Education and school administrators sympathetic to the municipal government of the Workers' Party.

One proposal that was particularly controversial was a governance reform that recommended giving more power to the school councils, to make principals and vice-principals elected positions (with parents and children accounting for 50 percent of the vote, and teachers and staff the other 50 percent), to allow only one reelection (which meant that administrators would have to return to classroom teaching after 4 years), and to force teachers to accept only one full-time job. This proposal was rejected. For Freire, the defeat of this initiative was not because it lacked merit but because of long-standing corporatist traditions and the political conservatism of the municipal educational system. Another controversial issue arose when two of his books were included in a bibliography (prepared by an independent committee) for a teachers' examination. These and other criticisms against Freire were publicly raised in local media by conservative academics and journalists. All these conflicts and the stress of managing a massive bureaucracy took its toll on Freire, whose health was deteriorating[26] and who wanted to devote more time and energy to academic endeavors. After almost three exhausting years as secretary of education of Sao Paulo (from 1989 to 1991), he decided to go back to his teaching and writing activities for the remaining years of his life, and he resigned from the post of secretary.[27] Insofar as he passed on his leadership role to a team of collaborators coordinated by Mario Sergio Cortella, a theology professor who became secretary of education for the remainder of the administration, the general orientation of the Secretary of Education was maintained. Freire agreed to continue collaborating with the municipal administration as a sort of "honorary ambassador" until the end of its mandate in 1992 (Torres 1994, Gadotti 1996).

From his resignation as secretary of education in 1991 to his death in 1997, Freire resumed his academic activities and wrote extensively. His intellect and his resolve were intact, but his health was failing. In those years, he used to say to his friends that his body was not keeping up with his mind (Cintra 1998). According to his widow Nita, "he died in full activity, at the height of his wisdom and of his ethical, political and pedagogic thought" (Borg and Mayo 2000). Indeed, probably feeling that he didn't have much time left, in that short period Freire wrote more books than in any other period of his life. Among those late books are *Pedagogy of the City* (an account of his work as secretary of education of Sao Paulo), *Pedagogy of Hope* (a reexamination of *Pedagogy of the Oppressed* 25 years later filled with anecdotes), *Teachers as Cultural Workers: Letters to Those Who Dare Teach* (an analysis of issues faced by teachers in building democratic schools), *Letters to Cristina* (a chronicle of his life and work in response to a request from his niece), *Pedagogy of Freedom* (a framework, based on 20 principles, that informs the professional practice of teachers), and *Pedagogy of the Heart* (a discussion of a wide range of topics connecting childhood reminiscences, social critique, educational theories, and political alternatives). At the time of his death, he was working on a book about neoliberalism and another on ecopedagogy.[28] A few years after Paulo passed away, Nita organized and published some of his unpublished writings.

Biographical addendum: The personal side of Paulo Freire

This chapter consists of an intellectual biography. As such, it is expected to deal solely with the ideas and the work of Paulo Freire. However, as we approach its conclusion, I would like to add a few lines about his personal side. This is relevant because it can provide more contextual elements to understand his ideas and his work. Many anecdotes have been told about Freire, ranging from friendly interactions with Canadian colleagues (Boshier 1999, Hall 1998, Martin 1998) to an uncomfortable walk with Latin American colleagues in the red light district of Hamburg after an education meeting or his experience with Thai food in New York (R. M. Torres 2010). Those anecdotes reveal different facets of his personality such as generosity, humor, humbleness, curiosity, creativity, love of Brazil, and an inclination to transform daily experiences into learning opportunities. For other brief comments about the personal dimension of Freire, I defer to three persons who have been close to him: Marcela Gajardo, who collaborated with him in Chile in the 1960s and remained a friend until his death; Ana Maria Araujo (Nita) Freire, who met him for the first time as a child in the 1940s and later shared a decade with him as his second wife; and Moacir Gadotti, who worked almost without interruption with Freire since they met in Geneva in 1974 and is the director of the Paulo Freire Institute.

In an article in *Convergence* (1998), Marcela Gajardo praised Freire's deep human qualities. She noted that, throughout his life, Freire never left a letter unanswered, and that the doors of his house (in Brazil, in Chile, in Geneva, or wherever he was living at the time) were always open for his friends and for the friends of his friends to talk about everything, to laugh and to analyze, to dream possible and impossible dreams, and to create. In those situations it was possible to know Freire in his immense humanity (Gajardo 1998:48). In the same issue of *Convergence*, Ana Maria Araujo Freire (1998) commented that Paulo had a combination of intelligence and humbleness, patience and stubborn rebellion, generosity and indignation, seriousness and playfulness, reason and emotion, realism and hope, political commitment to the oppressed and tolerance for those who disagreed with him. She added that he was a good and compassionate listener, and was passionately engaged with knowing, with dialogue, and with life. Moacir Gadotti (2001a) also commented on Freire's humility, openness, tolerance, and intellectual rigor, and highlighted two particular virtues: coherence and simplicity. Through his daily actions and his style of leading by example, Freire showed a high level of coherence between theory and practice, and always maintained a hopeful attitude, even in difficult times. Simplicity, noted Gadotti, is one of the most difficult virtues to accomplish because it requires not only wisdom but also the capacity to express complex ideas in clear (but not simplistic) terms, without falling into intellectual arrogance and without using unnecessary jargon. Another feature of Freire that was mentioned by all three is his disposition to engage in self-criticism and to permanently review his ideas. Indeed, since the publication of his first books, he never stopped disclosing publicly his mistakes and reformulating his thought.

Other people who interacted closely with Freire have also recounted many stories and anecdotes that made reference to his tenderness, solidarity, commitment, joyfulness, patience, and generosity. I will illustrate this point with two examples. Reflecting on a course on adult literacy that he took with Freire in Chile in the late 1960s as a young student, Calvo Muñoz (2006) reported that the impact of Freire on his life was so profound that after the course he abandoned his plans to become a psychologist and dedicated his life to education. Through a series of anecdotes, Calvo Muñoz described Freire as a gifted teacher who guided his students with love, humor, and hope, and who managed to discuss their mistakes while showing them their accomplishments and providing helpful suggestions for future interventions. Giroux (2010:3) stated that he has encountered many intellectuals throughout his academic career, "but Paulo stands out as exceptionally generous, eager to help younger intellectuals publish their work, to write letters of support, and to give as much as possible of himself in the service of others." Like Calvo Muñoz, Giroux reveals that he is now convinced that, had it not been for an encounter with Freire one evening in early 1980, he would have not stayed in the field of education. For Giroux, Freire's own life was a testimonial to his belief in democratic values and "to the notion that one's life had to come as close as possible to modeling the social relations and experiences that speak to a more humane and democratic future." (p. 4).

Summary and conclusions

In this chapter, Freire's biography has been broken down into three main periods: "Early Brazil" (from his birth in 1921 to the coup d'etat of 1964), "Exile" (particularly his work in Chile, the United States, Switzerland, and Africa, from 1964 to 1980), and "Late Brazil" (since his return in 1980 until his passing in 1997). Freire's educational ideas can be better understood in dialogue with his biography and, in turn, his biography cannot be isolated from the geographic and historical context in which he lived. First, the fact that Freire was born and raised in one of the poorest and most unequal regions of the world—coupled with the fact that his family experienced economic hardship—helps to explain his sensitivity to issues of social inequality and his orientation toward social justice. Second, his parents' pedagogical approach (teaching him to read and write starting from his own vocabulary universe) seemed to have had an impact on the development of Freire's methodology for adult literacy education. Third, initial influences on Freire's approach can be found in his parents' different religious orientations, his exposure to the liberation theology movement, and his engagement with particular readings during his youth. Fourth, meeting his wife Elza was a pivotal moment in Freire's life, because she was highly influential in his choice of the field of education and in the development of his ideas. Fifth, one of the most significant formative experiences in Freire's trajectory was his work from 1947 to 1957 at the Social Service of Industry (SESI), to the extent that in *Letters to Cristina* he refers to that decade as "the most important political-pedagogical practice of my life" (Freire 1995:81). Sixth, Freire's exile and travels to a variety of countries made an impact on his political and educational views, but probably the most important experience in the evolution of his intellectual biography was the Chilean phase (1964–69), because it was then that he moved from a more voluntaristic, developmentalist framework to a more structural understanding of social reproduction and social change that incorporated Marxist categories. Seventh, his return to Brazil coincided with the return to democracy and the creation of the Workers' Party, and the victory of this party in the municipal elections of Sao Paulo in 1988 gave Freire a unique opportunity to put his ideas on education and democracy into practice.

Freire was an original thinker who was inspired by different traditions. Structural Marxist analysis helped him to examine the role played
by the educational system in reproducing social inequalities, but he did
not fall into the trap of the overly deterministic and mechanistic theories of reproduction associated with "vulgar" or "orthodox" Marxism
(Mayo 2000, Morrow and Torres 2002, Aronowitz 1993, Roberts 2000).
His approach was more closely associated with the tradition of Marxist
humanism, which he combined, in an open and undogmatic way, with
elements of Christian humanism, emphasizing concepts like full human
development, agency, subjectivity, ethics, and democracy.

He was also influenced by existentialism and phenomenology, particularly in his first works. He built some of his pedagogical arguments
on the shoulders of thinkers like Rousseau and Dewey, and from them
he gained faith in the potential of education to build a better, more democratic society.[29] For this reason, he distanced himself from deschooling
advocates and throughout his life was willing to work within the educational system. Furthermore, Freire was a creative synthesizer and a dialectical thinker, and as such he contributed to overcome the false
dichotomy of the "pedagogism" of the 1960s and the "reproductionism"
of the 1970s. Pedagogism refers to the naïve optimism that placed excessive confidence in education as the main remedy for all social problems,
and reproductionism refers to the paralyzing pessimism that results from
arguing that schools are nothing else than tools of the capitalist state to
reinforce social inequalities (Gadotti 1996, Gadotti and Torres 2009).

Of interest, Freire did not write in a traditional academic style.
Indeed, his most influential and celebrated book, *Pedagogy of the
Oppressed*, would probably have faced significant challenges for approval
as a doctoral thesis in a traditional research university. He cites few other
scholars, makes few references to prior research, uses mostly anecdotal
evidence to support his claims, and does not include long bibliographies
in his books (Elias 1994, Roberts 2000). At the same time, his personal
style, combined with a powerful prose that combines denunciation and
annunciation, a great ability to present complex ideas and connect them
to real-life situations, and a language fueled with hope and possibility,
may explain the popularity of his work. Throughout his life, his ideas
evolved and changed, but the philosophical principles and ethical foundations of his approach remained essentially the same. As he noted

once, reflecting on his past, "If I were the same that I was 40 years ago, I would be profoundly disappointed, but at the same time, if I were nothing of what I was 40 years ago, I would be profoundly sad" (CIDC 1990:123). Toward the end of his life, Freire was concerned with market-oriented reforms promoted by the neoliberal model, and called for the development of a radical democratic citizenship education.

As one of the most influential and creative educational thinkers of the twentieth century, Freire marked a rupture in Latin American education, breaking with the elitist educational system and making a commitment to improving the living conditions of marginalized populations and to achieve social justice (Gadotti 2003). His educational ideas emerged in Pernambuco, but his message has universal appeal. He made important contributions to our understanding of the connections between theory and practice and between education and democracy. He argued that education can be used for domination but also for liberation, and examined key dynamics that are present in both situations. He developed an innovative approach to adult literacy programs that combined the reading of the word and the world. Last but not least, he influenced significantly the development of critical pedagogy and of a movement known as "popular education," and he established the foundations for the transformation of traditional public schools into "Citizen Schools." In 1997, Freire was looking forward to travel to Cuba in May, where he was going to receive an award from Fidel Castro, and was preparing a trip to Boston to teach a course at Harvard with Donaldo Macedo. He was also scheduled to attend the Fifth International Conference of Adult Education that was held in July 1997 in Hamburg, where he was expected to maintain a dialogue with German philosopher Jurgen Habermas. None of these trips materialized. Freire passed away on May 2, 1997, at the Albert Einstein Hospital of Sao Paulo, where he was admitted for heart problems. Since his death, his ideas have continued to be discussed, endorsed, criticized, adapted, co-opted, ignored, and misunderstood. How did Freire wish to be remembered after his death? In May 1990, in a video interview with Carlos A. Torres, Paulo Freire asked himself: "What is my legacy?" Then, without pausing, he answered his own question:

I think that it is possible to be said about Paulo Freire, when I die, that Paulo Freire was a man who loved, who could not understand life's existence without love and without knowing. Paulo Freire lived, loved and tried to know. Paulo Freire was constantly curious and asking questions to himself. (Freire 1995:181)

In this, his own epitaph, Paulo Freire reminds us of perhaps the two most important qualities of educators: love and intellectual curiosity.

Notes

1 Cited in C. A. Torres 1998a.
2 Critical pedagogy emphasizes a historical and social analysis that focuses on the relations between power and knowledge, bridges the gap between learning and daily life, and encourages the agency of teachers and students to intervene in the social world to challenge structures of domination and promote a more just society (Giroux 2010). Popular education is characterized by an ethical commitment to social justice, a political-pedagogical project that emphasizes the role of human agency in social change, and a participatory, dialogical pedagogy that focuses on the collective, departs from people's daily lived experiences, and promotes an integration of popular and scientific knowledge (Schugurensky 2000).
3 *Letters in the Earth.* Roby Kidd and Alan Thomas in dialogue with Paulo Freire. Videotape. OISE, 1976.
4 As we will see later, Aluizio Pessoa de Araujo would also play an important role in helping Paulo to obtain his first teaching job, and over time Paulo developed a friendly relationship with the Araujo family. Several decades later, Freire married Ana Maria (Nita) Araujo, Aluizio's daughter.
5 For a detailed biography of Elza Freire and her contributions to education, see Spigolon 2009.
6 Camara's famous dictum ("When I feed the poor, they call me a saint, but when I ask why the poor are hungry, they call me a communist") summarizes the challenges faced by members of the progressive Church in Brazil at the time Freire became involved in it.
7 Around the same time illiterate people in the United States faced a similar situation, because they were not allowed to vote by law. This challenge led to the creation of the citizenship school by the Highlander Centre in the Southern United States. In a striking parallel with Freire's work in northern Brazil, Highlander combined literacy training with critical analysis of social reality and social organizing, making a significant contribution to the civil rights movement.

8 In 1963, he also became one of 15 "Pioneer Council Members" chosen by Governor Miguel Arraes to preside over matters of education and culture in the state of Pernambuco (Lownd 2001).

9 Dependency theory emerged in Latin America in the 1960s as a response to modernization theory. Whereas modernization theory argued that Latin American societies were underdeveloped because they were still at the first stages of a common, universal path to development (and hence should be integrated into the world market in order to develop), dependency theory argued that Latin American economies were already integrated into the world system, but under unequal conditions of exchange.

10 In Chile, Cardoso and Faletto wrote their influential book *Dependency and Development in Latin America* (published in Spanish in 1969 and in English in 1971).

11 The books were also different in style and purpose. *Education for Critical Consciousness* provides a good introduction to Freire's approach to adult literacy, including a discussion of its philosophical principles; the social context in which the program originated; and a detailed, illustrated description of its methodology. *Pedagogy of the Oppressed* is a more theoretical work that provides a critique of mainstream approaches to education and advances the main principles of an alternative political-pedagogical approach.

12 Because Freire lost his original manuscript of *Education as a Practice of Freedom*, several years later he had to translate it back to Portuguese from the English translation.

13 Although there is disagreement in the literature on the date of the first Portuguese edition of *Pedagogy of the Oppressed* (Gadotti 1996:262, Araujo Freire 2008:433, Freire 1994b:51), there is strong indication that it was first published in 1974 by Paz e Terra.

14 Ivan Illich's proposals for deschooling society were not entirely new. For instance, similar arguments and proposals had been formulated before by Paul Goodman in *Compulsory Miseducation and the Community of Scholars*, published in 1962.

15 For a discussion on conscientization, see Chapter 2.

16 For a self-reflection on the work of IDAC in the 1970s, see Freire, et al. 1983. IDAC's main office was moved to Brazil in 1980, when Freire returned to his home country.

17 The title was taken from one of Freire's stories, about a man in a literacy class whose first written word was his wife's name, Nina.

18 He got his position back in 1985, but retired immediately to leave room for the younger generation (Gadotti 1994:139 and 1996).

19 Freire's keynote speech at the 1985 assembly dealt with a variety of issues, from Buenos Aires and tangos to the role of questions in pedagogy, censorship, virtues of adult educators, coherence, self-criticism, spontaneity and manipulation, democracy, theory and practice, and the presence of

Middle Age elements in the twentieth century. That lecture has been preserved in the booklet "Paulo Freire en Buenos Aires" (CEAAL 1985).

20 Nita had known Paulo since she was 3 years old and Paulo was a teenager attending the Oswaldo Cruz secondary school directed by her father. Freire returned to the school a few years after graduation to teach Portuguese classes.

21 Nita also wrote about her years living with Paulo—a "third age marriage—in *Nita e Paulo: Cronicas de amor* (1998) and in *Paulo Freire: Uma história de vida* (2006). For interviews with Nita about Paulo, see Borg and Mayo (2000) and Vittoria and Araujo Freire (2007).

22 When Freire became secretary of education of Sao Paulo, more than 650 schools were in poor physical condition, and there was a deficit of 35,000 student chairs and desks.

23 I was unable to find reliable data on drop-out rates for the city of Sao Paulo, but at that time 8 million Brazilian children had never entered school, and 6 million had left school after their first or second year (Mayo 2004:93).

24 Cited in Gadotti and Torres 2009:1263.

25 For an analysis of the Citizen School model in other jurisdictions, see, for instance, Gandin and Apple (2002, 2003), and Clovis and Schugurensky (2004).

26 Freire was a heavy smoker for most of his life. He quit smoking in his late years, but at that time his lungs had already suffered the damage.

27 Some close to Freire have argued that his departure had to do exclusively with personal plans, because he intended from the beginning of his mandate to serve for about 2 years and return to his writing projects (Gadotti 1994). Others have claimed that he left because he became frustrated with the internal opposition by the educational bureaucracy (Stromquist 1997). It was probably a combination of both factors, with the latter precipitating events.

28 Regarding the book on neoliberalism, see Borg and Mayo 2000. The claim on the ecopedagogy book was made by Gadotti at the Lifelong Citizenship Learning, Participatory Democracy and Social Change Conference, held at the Ontario Institute for Studies in Education, University of Toronto, October 16–18, 2003.

29 For an analysis of the continuities and discontinuities between Rousseau, Dewey and Freire, see Schugurensky 2002.

Chapter 2

Critical Exposition of Freire's Work

Introduction: "I write about what I do"

To encompass Freire's rich contribution to education in one chapter is difficult, partly because of the extent and variety of his published work (books, articles, interviews, dialogues, letters, etc.), but also because this work is not exempt from modifications and even contradictions. As a self-reflective intellectual, Freire was always open to new ideas that challenged him to reconsider his arguments. His production has an overall consistency, but it was dynamic and changed substantially throughout his lifetime reflecting his own evolution: his original humanist approach, rooted in the tenets of progressive education, phenomenology, existentialism, and developmentalism, was later enriched by other currents such as liberation theology, Marxism, postcolonialism, feminism, critical race theory, and postmodernism. If the study of his writings is a difficult task per se, it becomes even more difficult when it is complemented by an analysis of Freire's own practices as an educator and policymaker. Freire's work on education includes a spectrum of activities such as tutoring, school teaching, adult educator, literacy coordinator, international advisor, political activist, and educational administrator.

Freire was a prolific author. Throughout his life, he produced many publications, either alone or in collaboration. His ideas can be found in hundreds of works, including books, articles, lectures, prefaces, and conference presentations. Some materials, like taped interviews and letters, still remain unpublished. Freire's writings embraced many topics and issues. For instance, the *Dicionário Paulo Freire* (Streck, Redin, and Zitkoski 2008) discusses more than 230 themes covered by him. His most famous book (and also the one that generated more intense reactions) is *Pedagogy of the Oppressed*. However, this was not his first book and certainly not his last. This is a pertinent observation, because sometimes it is assumed that Freire's ideas and those in *Pedagogy of the Oppressed* are one and the same, overlooking that in later works he criticized and revised some aspects of his earlier ones. Although Freire wrote consistently, he did not consider himself a writer in the strict sense of the word. When asked if he identified himself as a writer, he replied that he would have liked very much to be one, but he only wrote about his praxis as an educator and hence did not create literature in the manner of novelists and poets who, in his mind, were the "real writers." And then he added:

> "Maybe I'm wrong; maybe I have a narrow understanding of being a writer. I also have to tell you that in thinking like this I feel sad because I would like very much to be a writer. Maybe in some moments of my books—a certain moment of the analysis I am doing, and so on—readers could think they are reading a 'writer.' This is when I become most happy in writing." (Freire, in Olson 1992)[1]

Beyond the opinions on the literary quality of Freire's writings, in reading his texts one may identify some recurrent themes and arguments, even some repetitions. To a certain extent, some repetition is unavoidable among prolific scholars whose writings span several decades. Having said that, it is worth noting that sometimes with Freire the same theme may appear in more than one publication but with different formulations and styles because he was addressing different audiences (e.g., educational administrators in Africa or elementary school teachers in Brazil) or different issues. Furthermore, sometimes the theme may be the same (e.g., directiveness in teacher/student interactions, relations between education and politics, or school democracy) but Freire's reflections on the theme could be different (even contradictory) because his ideas were not static and he modified some of his positions over time. As he pointed out in *Mentoring the Mentor*, his ideas were never frozen: "My thinking has been evolving, and I have been constantly learning from others throughout the world" (Freire 1997b:312). For this reason, it is important to read his life's work in a holistic and dynamic way.

Reading Freire's lifetime work presents two challenges to English-speaking readers. First, only a portion of his texts and interviews has been translated into English. Second, some meaning may be lost in translation. In an interview with Borg and Mayo (2000), Nita Freire claimed that those who read Freire only in translation miss much of the beauty, poetry, aesthetics, political force, cultural richness, and emotional resonance of his writings.[2] Brazilian readers not only have the opportunity of reading Freire's text in their original language, but also to purchase some of those books at affordable prices.[3] In the first part of this chapter I discuss the main ideas and arguments put forward by Freire in his different publications, seeking to establish connections to the personal and historical context in which those works were written and to the activities in which Freire was engaged at that time. This I believe to be appropriate because most of Freire's texts draw heavily on his own practice. As he pointed out in an interview with Carlos A. Torres, "I write about what I do … my books are as if they were theoretical reports of my practice" (Torres 1990:102). In the second part I outline the main dimensions of his work and discuss three tensions that arise from his arguments. In the concluding section, I provide a summary of Freire's ideas.

The 1940s and 1950s: From SESI to doctoral dissertation

Although Freire was not formally trained as an educator, he had an intense desire of becoming one since his childhood, and by experimenting teaching other children and youth, he became sure that this was his calling. Freire's formal university training was in law, but at that time he was more interested in reading philosophical, sociological, and theological works. Although he worked as a tutor during his youth and briefly taught language courses in a secondary school, when he started employment in the educational department of Social Service of Industry (SESI), he had not yet engaged in any systematic reading of educational theory and methods. However, his interest in pedagogy was sparked after his marriage to teacher Elza Oliveira, with whom he became involved in educational and cultural activities of Catholic groups in Recife.

Little has been written about Freire's decade at SESI (1947–57), but it is clear that those formative years were important in the development of his educational ideas, to the extent that without the lessons learned from this experience (especially from his mistakes), he would not have been able to write *Pedagogy of the Oppressed* in the late 1960s (Taylor 1993). Moreover, his theories of knowledge, human development, dynamics of oppression and liberation, and the role of education in those dynamics can be better understood in the context in which they originated: the Brazilian Northeast. At that time, most of the adults who lived there were illiterate and immersed in what Freire called a "culture of silence." In that context, marked by colonialism and exploitation, Freire aimed at giving the victims of that culture their own voice and the opportunity to participate actively in an independent and democratic Brazil (Gadotti 1996, Romao 2001, Rosas 2001).

At SESI, Freire had his first encounter with adult education, became familiar with issues of popular culture and adult illiteracy, and began to see the possibility of self-governance and dialogue for overcoming the culture of silence. For him, dialogue was not just a strategy to achieve better educational results or a tactic used by educators to manipulate students, but part of human nature, because human beings are essentially communicative. He recognized that the learning process had an individual dimension, but argued that discovery was a social process that relied on dialogue. For him, dialogue is the moment when people meet to discover and transform reality (Gadotti 1994, Flecha 2004). Several of Freire's pedagogical proposals began to take shape during the decade at SESI, when he tried to demonstrate that the principles of dialogue, democracy, and self-governance could be implemented in institutions, and hence involved children and parents in discussions about educational and social issues, and promoted adult learning circles in "workers' clubs." Moreover, as SESI's director, Freire established an open and horizontal style of administration, which generated criticism and eventually led to his resignation (Gerhardt 1993). The educational ideas that had been germinating in Freire's mind during his time at SESI were first expressed in an unpublished article written in 1955 that dealt with parental participation, and soon thereafter in the 1958 report *Adult education and marginal populations: the problem of the mocambos.*[4]

In this text, Freire discussed five seminal ideas that he would continue developing and refining throughout the rest of his life. First, he suggested that adult education must begin with the knowledge, the experience, and the daily lives of learners. Second, he argued that literacy programs should go beyond the mere act of reading letters, sentences, and paragraphs and should also include the critical analysis of social reality. Years later he would summarize this idea as "reading the word and reading the world" or "reading the text and context" (Freire 1984c). Third, he proposed that educational processes should be horizontal and dialogical. This did not mean that educators should abdicate their role. Educators are, of course, expected to teach and to orient their students, but at the same time, Freire claimed, they should listen to their students' ideas, recognize their knowledge, and learn from that knowledge. This was an unusual proposal, contrary to the hierarchical educational practice of the time in Latin America. Fourth, he suggested that adult education should not be just an instrument to obtain a diploma, but also a process to nurture the sociopolitical consciousness of learners and their participation in public life. Fifth, he contended that adult learners could—and should—participate in selecting the content of their own learning[5] (Trilla 2001, Gadotti 1996, Romao 2001). In the following months, Freire would further elaborate and expand these ideas in his doctoral dissertation, which could be considered his first treatise on education. Freire completed this thesis in 1959 as part of his application for a position on History and Philosophy of Education at the University of Pernambuco. According to one biographer (Gerhardt 1993), the university committee did not approve the thesis.[6] Freire was ranked second among the applicants, and therefore was not hired for that position. It has been argued that had he won and joined the university ranks, he probably would not have continued working in adult education, not faced the challenges of exile, and not made the lifetime contributions that he would eventually make (Romao 2001). Freire himself recognized that episode as a crossroad in his life: "I lost a university position, and I gained a life."[7]

Freire's doctoral thesis became his first book when he self-published it in 1959 under the title *Educação e atualidade brasileira* (Present-day education in Brazil). Since only a limited number of copies circulated, it was almost impossible to have access to its content for several decades, until Cortez published it in 2001. *Educação e atualidade brasileira* was based on his 10 years of experience at SESI and emphasized a dialectical approach to comprehend the contradictions of social forces. Such approach allowed Freire to examine the tensions between a paternalistic and fatalistic culture, on the one hand, and a political-pedagogical project for democratization and social transformation through dialogue, critical reflection, and collective action, on the other. In this book, Freire engaged with some of the main debates on social change of that period (e.g., modernization, development, industrialization) and related them to democracy and education. For instance, although he shared the optimism of the time about the positive potential of industrialization, he also cautioned that repetitive, mechanized work could lead to the massification of human beings. To counteract that risk, he suggested such "democratic solutions" as workers' participation in decision making in their enterprises. These two concerns—humanistic development and institutional democratization—would continue to occupy Freire's attention during the next 40 years. In *Educação e atualidade brasileira*, it is possible to identify the influence of the progressive school, and particularly of the educational philosopher John Dewey.

As mentioned in Chapter 1, Freire became familiar with Dewey's ideas through Anixio Teixeira, a leader of the New School Movement in Brazil. Drawing on Dewey and Teixeira, Freire criticized in his first book the centralization, authoritarianism, and elitism of the Brazilian education system and argued for active participation of learners in their own learning process, for cooperative learning, and for closer connections between the subject matter and the local environment. Moreover, he argued that education for democracy cannot be separated from the practice of democracy and that democracy can be learned more effectively through direct and active participation in social and political life, including neighborhood associations, community groups, unions, educational institutions, and recreational clubs (Freire 1959). A few years later, when he reflected on this experiential approach, Freire said that he firmly believed that people could learn social and political responsibility only by experiencing such responsibility . . .

> through intervention in the destiny of their children's schools, in the destinies of their trade unions and places of employment, through associations, clubs and councils, and in the life of their neighborhoods, churches and rural communities by actively participating in

associations, clubs and charitable societies. They would be helped to learn democracy through the exercise of democracy; for that knowledge, above all others, can only be assimilated experientially. (*Education for Critical Consciousness*, 1973:36)

In Freire's doctoral thesis it is also possible to identify the impact of the *Instituto Social de Estudos Brasileiros* (ISEB),[8] a think tank connected to the project of national development created by the government of Juscelino Kubitschek. This influence can be found not only in the arguments on independent paths to development, but also in one concept (*conscientization*) that played an important role in Freire's pedagogical approach. This term, which refers to the development of a critical consciousness and could be translated as "consciousness raising" or "awareness raising," has been often—and wrongly—attributed to Freire. The concept was coined in the early 1960s by members of the ISEB team and was popularized by Bishop Helder Camara. As Freire explained:

It is generally believed that I am the author of this strange term, conscientization, because it is at the core of my educational ideas. In reality, the term was created around 1964 by a team of ISEB, among them philosopher Álvaro Pinto and Professor Guerreiro. When I heard this word for the first time, I immediately realized the depth of its meaning, because I am absolutely convinced that education, as a practice of freedom, is an act of knowledge, a critical approximation to reality. Since then, this word is part of my vocabulary, but it was Helder Câmara who was responsible for popularizing it and for translating it into English and French. (cited in Vittoria and Araujo Freire 2007:112)

Although his ISEB colleagues coined the concept and Bishop Camara popularized it, it was Freire who filled it with meaning. As Nita Freire observed, it was Freire who elaborated on this concept and who developed and applied a methodology to put it into practice in educational initiatives aimed at social change. In his elaboration of the term, Freire conceptualized *conscientization* as a process by which the oppressed develop the capacity to read critically the social world and become subjects of history (Vittoria and Araujo Freire 2007). Then, he formulated an educational strategy that he used in a mass literacy campaign to help peasants and agricultural laborers develop a critical understanding of their own reality and to become political subjects capable of transforming that reality. *Conscientization* was a central component of this pedagogical-political project aimed at social change, as Freire argued that the oppressed could participate better in an emancipatory project when they understood themselves, in relation to the oppressors, in historical and social terms.

Early 1960s: The literacy circles, a Copernican revolution in adult education

In the early 1960s, Freire became involved in a literacy program with sugarcane workers in the town of Angicos (Rio Grande do Norte) in northeast Brazil. The workers lived in poor conditions. Not only were they oppressed by unequal economic structures and governmental policies, but also they were denied the possibility of bringing about change through democratic elections: at that time, illiterate people were not allowed to vote. In response to this situation, Freire developed an innovative approach to teaching literacy that aimed at transforming participants' social situations by simultaneously developing their reading and writing skills, their critical consciousness, and their human agency (i.e., their capacity to act as agents in the world). At that time, most literacy programs used a linguistic approach. Literacy was understood to be the cracking of a linguistic code, and sociological or ethnographic factors related to literacy learning were largely ignored (Alim 2004). More often than not, adults were taught in the evenings in the same classrooms (and in the same seats) where their children had attended school during the day, frequently using the same primers and the same vocabulary. Freire's practical experience with adult literacy taught him that this method did not work. For instance, he noted the frustration experienced by adults who, after a long and tiring day's work, were asked to repeat such sentences in a reader as "Eva viu a uva" [Eva saw the grape] or "A ave é do Ivo" [the bird is Ivo's].

Instead, Freire proposed a different approach. His inspiration came directly from his previous experience with culture circles in Recife. Those circles were based on three elements: a coordinator instead of a traditional teacher, a dialogical methodology instead of lecture-based classes, and a curriculum that related to the lives of the learners instead of decontextualized and irrelevant content. In the culture circles, participants were regarded as adults with experience, knowledge, and wisdom, who deserved respect and dignified treatment (Bhattacharya 2008). In the culture circles, the topics of the dialogues were proposed by the groups themselves and ranged from the political history of Brazil to the vote for illiterates, and from national development strategies to the role of multinational corporations. After the exciting experience with the culture circles, Freire's team wondered whether it would be possible to adopt a similar approach to the field of adult literacy. The so-called Freire "literacy method" thus emerged from the previous experience with culture circles and combined teaching how to read with the development of a critical consciousness and the democratization of knowledge. The notion of dialogue was central to the literacy-circle model: "Whoever enters into dialogue does so with someone about something, and that something ought to constitute the new content of our proposed education" (Freire 1973:46). Freire's literacy circles usually numbered 25 to 30 participants. One of the guiding principles behind the circles was that learners should be able to distinguish between nature and culture, to understand culture as a human creation, and to recognize their own capacity to create culture and to act as subjects (as opposed to objects) in the world. For Freire, such a process should include a range of activities in which participants are engaged in their daily lives and which could be enhanced through literacy. Hence, participants were encouraged to make a connection between reading and writing, on the one hand, and their role as agents of social change, on the other. Since the literacy teaching/learning process was premised, according to Freire, on the acts of creation and re-creation, participants' confidence to intervene in the world—and the sense of human agency that this implies—was expected to increase over time. Freire summed up this idea in his conceptualization of educational processes: reflection and action of women and men upon the world in order to transform it.

A Copernican revolution

In adult literacy, Freire's approach represented the equivalent of a Copernican revolution. I make this claim for four reasons. First, whereas previous models of adult literacy conceived the learner as a passive consumer of knowledge, Freire's model, through decodification and cocreation of words, conceived learners (called "participants") as active subjects of the learning process and placed them at the center of that process. Second, unlike previous adult literacy programs, which were decontextualized and which often replicated primers designed for children, Freire's model put the social reality, the vocabulary, and the experience of the learners at the center of the literacy curriculum. Third, while in previous models the methodology tended to consist of a teacher speaking in front of a class ("banking education"), Freire's model emphasized questioning, group projects, dialogue, and discussion (problem-posing education). Fourth, whereas previous models had solely an instrumental logic, did not question social inequalities, and aimed at the adaptation of learners to the existing world, Freire's model was based on an emancipatory rationality, nurturing both critical awareness and learners' capacity to liberate themselves from oppressive situations and to affect social change. In other words, Freire understood illiteracy not as an individual problem to be solved through technical interventions but as a social problem that must be addressed through mass social mobilization.

Freire's approach to literacy teaching (known as psychosocial or sociolinguistic) was likewise predicated on four main premises. First, adults learn to read more effectively with words that are familiar and relevant to them. Second, it is possible to organize the literacy process around a few words that contain all the phonemes, and these words (which Freire labeled "generative") allow readers to create new words. Third, the literacy process should take place in literacy circles and not in school classrooms organized in rows. Fourth, the process should enable participants to acquire reading and writing skills together with critical analytical skills: Freire refers to this as "reading the word and the world" or "reading the text while reading the context." For Freire, reading the word is always related to (and preceded by) the reading of the world:

"Reading the world always precedes reading the word, and reading the word implies continually reading the world . . . this movement from the word to the world is always present; even the spoken word flows from our reading of the world . . . we can go further and say that reading the word is not preceded merely by reading the world, but by a certain form of writing it or rewriting it, that is, of transforming it

by means of conscious, practical work. For me, this dynamic movement is central to the literacy process." (Freire and Macedo 1987:35)

The main difference with traditional (linguistic) approaches was that
Freire paid attention to sociological, ethnographic, and psychological
factors in the process of literacy acquisition (Al-Kahtany 2006, Alim
2004). The linguistic approach understands literacy as cracking a linguistic code, whereas, for Freire, it is about developing the critical capacity to read texts and contexts. Hence, Freire's method, unlike previous
approaches, used the existing vocabulary of the illiterates to teach them
to read the word, to gain a better understanding of their world, and eventually to transform it. The Angicos experience demonstrated the success
of this approach with 300 sugarcane workers learning to read and write
in 45 days. It was then that President Joao Goulart invited Freire to
coordinate a national literacy campaign with the objective of teaching
literacy to 2 million people through 20,000 cultural circles. Whereas the
core of his original contribution to adult literacy was developed in the
early 1960s in northeast Brazil, Freire was unable to perfect and expand
that model due to the coup d'etat of 1964. However, in exile, he would
have the opportunity to engage in other aspects of adult literacy
(particularly in Chile and in Africa) and to further refine his approach.

The stages of the literacy method

Typically, Freire's literacy method involved three stages: research, thematization, and problematization. These three stages, together with
examples of images used to depict situations and of words discussed in
the literacy circles, are clearly described by Freire in the appendix to
Education as the Practice for Freedom (Freire 1973:61–84).

Stage 1: Research

The first stage consisted of a socioanthropological investigation of the
material, social, and cultural context in which the illiterates lived. Before
starting this research, Freire contacted municipal and state authorities
(mayors and governors) to inform them about the project and to request

technical independence for his team, without any type of partisan interference. When Freire's teams visited a community for the first time, they explained the reasons for their presence and invited community members to participate in the inquiry by becoming volunteer coinvestigators.[9] This inquiry—which consisted of interviews, observations, and informal interactions with local residents in the places where they congregated—aimed at better understanding the social, cultural, economic, and political dynamics in that community. Freire asked investigators to take notes of everything, including seemingly insignificant details such as people's attitudes in different contexts and their expressions, vocabulary, and syntax:

> It is essential that the investigators observe the area under varying circumstances: labour in the fields, meetings of a local association (noting the behavior of the participants), their language used, and the relations between officers and the members), the role played by women and by young people, leisure hours, games and sports, conversations with people in their homes (noting examples of husband/wife and parent/child relationships). No activity must escape the attention of the investigators during the initial survey of the area. (Freire 1970b:104)

Through this study, Freire's team members and their local coinvestigators identified the most frequent activities and main issues affecting the community and compiled a lexicon of the most significant words used in that community, including local sayings and words connected to the daily experience, frustrations, and hopes of the people. This first list of words had different degrees of social, political, cultural, and existential relevance in that particular context, but not all of them would be appropriate for teaching literacy. Therefore, from this large universe of words, the team would select a shorter list (usually between 15 and 18 of them) according to their phonemic richness; their level of phonetic difficulty; and their potential in confronting social, cultural, and political reality. These 15 to 18 words were called *generative words*, and represent the heart of the Freirean method. Generative words included the basic sounds of the language and were used to help learners move from simple letters and sounds to more complex ones. Another criterion to select generative words was to avoid unnecessary complications that could result in confusion and frustration among learners.[10] Likewise, words that referred to concrete and familiar objects came early on the list, while words referring to abstract social and political realities came later (Brown 1974). Although sometimes the same generative words appeared in different contexts,[11] others varied according to the characteristics of each locality. For instance, in Pernambuco, Freire's team identified such words as brick, earth, employment, vote, pain, ashes, straw, crab, hoe, ingenuity, machine, chore, and mangrove. In the favelas of Rio de Janeiro, they encountered similar words such as brick, and also different ones such as slum, rain, job, land, bicycle, wage, food, well, government, and wealth.

Stage 2: Thematization

In the second stage, thematization, each generative word was complemented with an illustration that depicted a social situation related to that word. These words and their companion images were presented to the study circles in the form of slides (whenever a slide projector was available), flipchart paper, or cards. Because the generative words were multisyllabic, it was possible to "generate" many new words from their syllables or from variations of their syllables. Once the group identified the generative word in the poster, the word was analyzed through its syllabic division, a relatively clear task in such syllabic languages as Portuguese or Spanish. The first generative word was always trisyllabic, and each of the three syllables consisted of one consonant and one vowel, like "favela" or "tijolo" (brick). In the literacy circle, each syllable of the word was unfolded in its respective syllabic family, leaving the consonant but changing the vowel. In the first syllable of "tijolo," for instance, it would be TA-TE-TI-TO-TU. Given that the Portuguese language has five vowels, the three consonants of the word "tijolo" can be combined with these vowels to produce 15 syllables:

TA	TE	TI	TO	TU
JA	JE	JI	JO	JU
LA	LE	LI	LO	LU

By engaging in a horizontal and a vertical reading, learners began to discover the different sounds resulting from combinations of vowels and consonants. Then, using all these new syllables, participants in the literacy circle started to generate new words. For instance, by reconstructing from the original word (tijolo), they "created" others, such as tatu (armadillo), luta (struggle), tela (screen), juta (jute), lajota (tile), lote (lot), and loja (store). Moreover, participants were often highly inventive and, by combining syllables and vowels, created words such as tio (uncle), lua (moon), and leite (milk), or even phrases such as "tu ja les" ("you now read"). Likewise, with the word favela, learners created words such as fala (speech), vela (candle), vivo (alive), luva (glove), vovo (grandpa), leve (slight), fila (queue), and vila (town). This process of decodification and codification, of collective problem solving and discovery, constitutes a key component of Freire's literacy method because it allows learners to develop the tools to teach themselves how to read and write. Sometimes learners formed combinations of syllables that were not real words, but Freire was unconcerned. For him, what was important was the discovery of the mechanism of phonemic combination together with the active and creative process of producing words. Even more important than the words themselves was the group discussion that followed each generative word (Janmohaded 1994, Roberts 2000, Brown 1974). For generative words are generative in two ways: the linguistic dimension and the social dimension. The linguistic dimension of generative words refers to the fact that learners, by reorganizing the syllables of the words, can cocreate new words. The social dimension refers to the fact that these words together with the attendant drawings generated intense discussion about social and political aspects of the learners' communities; this dimension of the generative word gave rise to the third stage, known as problematization.

Stage 3: Problematization

In the problematization stage, learners were encouraged to think about the situations presented in the drawings and to discuss issues affecting the community related to the generative words and the companion illustrations. These issues ranged from housing to health, urban reform, food, education, employment, natural resources, and domination. The main objective of the third stage—and of the overall method—was conscientization, which involved the transit from a magical or naïve vision of the world to a critical awareness of social reality. Freire (1985a) identified three stages in the development of a critical consciousness. The first stage, which he called "semi-intransitive consciousness,"[12] is characterized by a limited perception of reality, that is, a focus on matters related to survival and biological needs. The second stage of consciousness, which Freire called "naïve transitivity," is manifest when people move from basic needs to broader contexts and is characterized by simplistic explanations of social problems, conservatism, an underestimation of ordinary people, a disinterest in inquiry or politics, and little disposition for genuine dialogue. The third stage, "critical transitivity," is characterized by curiosity, dialogue, a deeper interpretation of social problems, the capacity to test hypotheses and connect facts, and an open attitude to reviewing preconceived notions and to accepting new ideas without rejecting the old. In Freire's political pedagogy, then, a critical consciousness included both an understanding of the causes of political, social, and economic domination, and the recognition that these domination structures are not natural phenomena but social processes that can be challenged and overcome through collective action. This was, for Freire, the essence of a liberating education.

The drawings of existential situations of the group focused on problems and contradictions, with the intention of encouraging reflection and debate. It was also expected that discussion of local issues would open the door to broader perspectives, linking those issues to regional, national, and international issues. Freire strongly advised that images should never present situations unfamiliar to the participants. He also recommended that the images should reflect different elements interacting in situations, but without being too explicit (because this could degenerate into mere propaganda) or too enigmatic (because this ran the risk of appearing to be a puzzle to trick learners): "Codifications should be simple in their complexity and offer various decoding possibilities in order to avoid the brainwashing tendencies of propaganda. Codifications are not slogans; they are cognizable objects" (Freire 1970b:107). Freire also argued that the literacy method helped participants understand that it is possible to symbolize real-life situations through words and images, to make connections between the concrete and the abstract, and to engage in processes of decodification and codification. At the same time, he emphasized that teaching literacy should not be limited to codification and decodification, and should include a better knowledge of social reality, an awareness of the causes of daily problems, and the collective search for solutions. The drawings helped to generate discussion and enhance participants' meaning-making about their own existential reality. He emphasized that starting the discussions with abstract situations gave participants the necessary emotional distance to "re-admire" their own reality and to analyze the situation presented (Fletcher 1970, Gadotti 1994). In *Pedagogy of the Oppressed,* Freire noted that such emotional distance is important because for many learners, alienated by a culture of personal achievement, to recognize their situation as objectively unfavorable could hinder their possibility of success.[13]

Freire observed that when learners reconstructed words from independent syllables and as they experienced a shift from illiterate to literate individuals, an important transformation began to occur. Then, at a pace much faster than in previous literacy approaches, they started writing about their own experiences, reading each other's writings, and seeking solutions to their problems as a collective. Although in Freire's approach there is no direct transfer of knowledge through a primer from teacher to learner, this does not mean that the method does not pay attention to content, which was carefully developed, grounded in the experience and realities of learners, and paid due consideration given to linguistic complexities. Session after session, generative words would be presented in sequential order and participants would be invited to form new words, to practice reading and writing, to express opinions, to write them down, to read newspapers and magazines, and to examine local problems and find solutions to them (Brown 1974, Fletcher 1979, Gadotti 1994). In this process, teachers were not just transmission belts between the primer and learners, but were expected to play a formative and creative role throughout all its phases. Moreover, the method was organized in such a way that it enabled learners to take increasing control of the content and to develop a sense of agency. This constituted a crucial aspect of Freire's literacy circles because the impoverished peasants of northeast Brazil, suffering the stigma attached to illiteracy and centuries of colonialism, did not believe in their own capacity to create culture, to make decisions, or to intervene actively in society. The discussions on social reality were not unstructured: they were guided by certain themes or issues developed by Freire's team and introduced by the circle coordinators.

For instance, in one case, the "wealth" included several topics for discussion: Brazil and the world, the relationship between wealth and poverty, development and underdevelopment, and national emancipation (Freire 1973:84). Freire argued that a precondition for social action was an educational process that treated learners with respect and nurtured their critical capacities so that they were able to examine the structure of their own oppression and to recover their sense of agency. Regarding the development of critical consciousness, the decodification of images with social situations and the ensuing discussion provided learners with an opportunity to reflect on their understanding of the world, to raise their awareness before decoding words, and to challenge some of their assumptions.[14] By examining pictures depicting familiar realities, people revisit their understanding of culture: "the pictures of concrete situations enable the people to reflect on their former interpretation of the world before going on to read the word" (Freire and Macedo 1987:36). Regarding the development of agency, it started with literacy circle coordinators not referring to participants as illiterates. Then, the discussions of pictorial depictions highlighted the participants' role in transforming nature through their work, and hence enabling them to think of themselves as creators of culture and as potential subjects of history. To sum up, the problematization stage allowed learners not only to appropriate tools to access the written world but also to analyze critically their own reality and make collective plans for change.

Late 1960s: From *Education as a Practice of Freedom* to *Pedagogy of the Oppressed*

Despite the unprecedented success of his literacy method, the militaries that took power in 1964 jailed Freire and sent him into exile. When revisiting that period, Freire claimed that his only crime was to treat literacy as more than a mechanical problem by linking it to critical awareness of social reality. After being released from jail Freire spent a short time in Bolivia and then moved to Chile where, in 1965, he received governmental support to apply his literacy approach to a historical circumstance characterized by significant social, cultural, and political dynamism and by the active participation of rural workers in national agrarian reform. Freire's educational work for the Chilean Research and Training Institute for Agrarian Reform (ICIRA) helped him to reevaluate the practice of his literacy method and to reconsider its theoretical foundations (Sanders 2004, Gadotti 1994). In those years, Freire had the opportunity to reflect on his Brazilian and Chilean experiences and to put these reflections in writing. This resulted in four publications that would be released around the same time: *Education as a Practice of Freedom, Extension or Communication, Cultural Action for Freedom,* and *Pedagogy of the Oppressed.* In these publications, it is possible to identify changes in Freire's conceptual framework. When he arrived in Chile, he was still influenced by the ideas of developmentalism, phenomenology, Hegelianism, and liberation theology. But as he became exposed through his Chilean friends and colleagues (like Marcela Gajardo), and other Brazilian exiles (such as political scientist Francisco Weffort and future Brazilian president, Fernando Henrique Cardoso), to other schools of thought such as Marxist humanism, dependency theory, and postcolonialism, he began to refine further his theories. Toward the end of the 1960s, he became familiar with still more theoretical approaches through his interactions with other colleagues in Cuernavaca (Mexico) and in the United States. Over time, he would enrich his original Christian orientation with ideas from other traditions and create his own secular theology based on concepts such as authenticity, humanization, and self-emancipation (Aronowitz 1993).

In *Education as a Practice of Freedom,* Freire drew upon the main arguments of his doctoral thesis together with several articles and lectures reflecting his work with culture circles and literacy circles. As he noted, the proposal described in the book was the product of more than 15 years of experiences in marginalized rural and urban areas (Freire 1973:41). Freire started to write *Education as a Practice of Freedom* when he was in jail in Brazil, and published it in 1967 when he was in Chile.[15] In this book, Freire dealt mostly with the context of northeast Brazil, which exemplified a colonial culture and economic exploitation in which a small elite of landowners controlled most decisions and where ordinary people were reduced to the category of objects. He also described in detail the different phases and tools of his literacy method. The main ideas presented in this book deal with the transition from closed to open societies and from a magical to a critical consciousness. Freire discussed the role of education in these transitions, paying particular attention to the concepts of dialogue and conscientization (the liberation process that consists of supplanting the "dominated conscience" with a "critical conscience"). Years later, Freire said that at the time of writing *Education as a Practice of Freedom* he was still naïve in his understanding of the connections between education, politics, and social transformation, and this explained why he failed to make any reference to the political nature of education or to social class (Cuadernos de Educación 1972, Shor and Freire 1987:32).[16]

In *Extension or Communication*, Freire reflected on his work at ICIRA. He argued that the very concept of "extension" is in direct contradiction to a truly humanist outlook to education because it implies the existence of an active, superior, and knowledgeable agent (the extension worker) who transplants information in a passive, inferior, and ignorant recipient (the peasant). In contrast to extension, which is antidialogical, hierarchical, and includes practices of cultural invasion, he proposed communication, which implies mutual dialogue and recognizes the learner as a subject and not as an object of the educational process. He argued that government technical experts (agronomists and extension workers) should understand the worldview of the peasants and should focus not on imposing their ways of doing things but on establishing a genuine dialogue. One of the main arguments posed by Freire in this publication is that education is more than technical training because it involves the full development of the person, it has a humanistic orientation, and it uses dialogical and participatory methodologies.

Cultural Action for Freedom, written by Freire during his stay at Harvard, is organized in two parts. The first deals with the adult literacy process as cultural action for freedom, and the second with the relationship between cultural action and conscientization. In this book Freire also discussed issues related to the culture of silence, to the dual task of denunciation-annunciation, and to the understanding of education as cultural action for freedom. He reflected on neocolonial relations between First World and Third World countries (in particular, former empires and their former colonies) and on the replication of those relations of domination in Third World countries, which in his view have contributed to the perpetuation of the culture of silence:

> On the one hand, the culturally alienated society as a whole is dependent on the society which oppresses it and whose economic and cultural interests it serves. At the same time, within the alienated society itself, a regime of oppression is imposed upon the masses by the power elites that, in certain cases, are the same as the external elites and, in others, are the external transformed by a kind of metastasis into domestic power groups. (1970a:2–3)

In *Cultural Action for Freedom,* Freire also elaborated on the notion of dialogue. He argued that a dialogue between antagonists was impossible because genuine dialogue presupposes equality of conditions and reciprocity (Gadotti 1994). In this book he also used the image of a "nutritive" or "digestive education" (a metaphor he borrowed from Sartre) to refer to the teacher-centered and information-based education, in which students are "fed" knowledge by the teacher. As we shall see, in later writings Freire would refine this concept and reframe it as "banking education."

Pedagogy of the Oppressed

Of the four works written in Chile in the late 1960s, *Pedagogy of the Oppressed* deserves special attention because it became the most popular and enduring single work produced by Paulo Freire, and because in that text he put together his ideas on education in a more organized way than in any of his other publications of that period. Moreover, *Pedagogy of the Oppressed* reflected more clearly Freire's transition from a liberal, developmentalist approach to a more radical one that applied Marxist categories to the analysis of social and educational realities. Stanley Aronowitz argues that *Pedagogy of the Oppressed* could now be considered a classic because it has outlived its own time and its author's. The book was published in 1970 in Portuguese, Spanish, and English. A few years later it was translated into Italian, French, German, Dutch and Swedish, Chinese, Indonesian, Korean, and Japanese, and the English version started to circulate widely in Africa, Asia, and Oceania. In the ebullient Latin America of the 1970s, *Pedagogy of the Oppressed* became a "must read" in progressive intellectual circles and among adult education groups. As of today, it has sold more than 1 million copies worldwide, an unusual number for a book on education. Together with Illich's *Deschooling Society* (1971), *Pedagogy of the Oppressed* was one of the most widely read books on education during the 1970s. The two books challenged deeply held assumptions about the role of education in society (Roberts 2000). C. A. Torres (2008:3) stated that *Pedagogy of the Oppressed* should be considered, along with Dewey's *Democracy and Education*, one of the two most influential books of educational philosophy of the twentieth century. The magazine *The Christian Century* called it "an inspiring and inspired document . . . that will prompt the reader to reconsider his or her situation in an oppressive society." For Ivan Illich, the book was "truly revolutionary pedagogy." Not all reviews were as laudatory. As we shall see in Chapter 3, the book also received its share of criticism.

In *Pedagogy of the Oppressed*, Freire denounced the oppressive dynamics of capitalist education and proposed instead, as an alternative, an emancipatory education. Drawing on insights from different disciplines (including philosophy, sociology, and psychology), he revealed the political nature of education and argued that education can be used for the purpose not only of domination but also of liberation. He then related this contradictory role of education to pedagogical approaches in the classroom and made the distinction between banking education and problem-posing education. He also built on the concept of "conscientization" that he had discussed in his previous publications, providing further elaboration on the stages of consciousness. *Pedagogy of the Oppressed* is organized in four chapters. Originally, Freire conceived the book as containing only three chapters. He wrote those three chapters by hand in a single effort during a 2-week holiday in Chile. According to Nita Araujo Freire (in Borg and Mayo 2000), he was able to produce the book in such a short time because he already had it in his head. Freire gave the manuscript with the three chapters to his friend and philosopher Ernani Maria Fiori (a Brazilian who was also exiled in Chile at that time) and asked him to write the preface. Fiori read the text and suggested Freire add a concluding chapter to provide a political analysis of the issues discussed in the first three chapters. Freire accepted the suggestion and spent several months engaging with new readings (he was especially captivated by *Wretched of the Earth* by Franz Fanon) and writing the final chapter while traveling by car in dusty roads or in motels with inadequate lighting.

The first chapter of *Pedagogy of the Oppressed*, drawing on Hegel's dialectic between the master and the slave, examines the relationship between "the oppressor" and "the oppressed." Freire argued that this relation had led over time to dehumanization. Then, he contended that the task of the oppressed is not to become oppressors of their former oppressors, but to restore the humanity of both: "This, then, is the great humanistic and historical task of the oppressed: to liberate themselves and their oppressors as well" (p. 28). He identified freedom as the key precondition for this quest for human restoration, but acknowledged that the oppressed, having internalized the image of the oppressors and accepted their justifications for an unjust world, were fearful of freedom.[17] Based on his own experience in literacy circles, he also noted that the oppressed were immersed in a culture of silence and were more likely to attribute their situation to fate or to God's will than to social relations of exploitation (Freire 1970b:107). In the first chapter of *Pedagogy of the Oppressed*, Freire also discussed the importance of objective and subjective conditions in the struggle for social change. He argued against the dichotomization of objectivity and subjectivity because they exist in a constant dialectical relationship. He contended that to deny the importance of subjectivity in the process of transforming the world is naïve and simplistic, because it implies the impossibility of a world without people. The subjectivist position, however, falls into the opposite trap of postulating people without a material world. He concluded that the oppressed can only change reality through collective struggle, and this requires a critical awareness of oppression through praxis, understood as simultaneous reflection and action. From a pedagogical standpoint, he stated that an emancipatory, humanistic education must eschew propaganda, management, manipulation, and pseudo-participation (which are instruments of domination) and foster instead a permanent relationship of dialogue and respect between educators and learners, together with a committed involvement of all participants in unveiling reality and cocreating knowledge through reflection and action.

The second chapter of *Pedagogy of the Oppressed* is probably the most popular and influential text of Freire to the point where it has become a classic reference point for scholars and practitioners interested in the emancipatory potential of education (Roberts 2000). In this chapter, Freire criticized the "banking" approach to education and contrasted it with a "problem-posing," emancipatory approach. Freire argued that the teacher-student relationship, be it in schools or in adult education, was characterized by "narration sickness" that involves a narrating subject (the teacher) and patient, listening objects (the students). The task of the teacher is to "fill" the students with the contents of his or her narrations, which are often detached from reality and are static and compartmentalized. The students, for their part, are expected to memorize and repeat mechanically the narrated content (e.g., "four times four is sixteen"), and are considered to be nothing more than containers or receptacles: "The more meekly the receptacles permit themselves to be filled, the better students they are" (p. 58). Freire contended that banking education results in the dehumanization of both the students and the teachers. The "banking concept" is a metaphor used by Freire to suggest that, in this model, students are regarded as empty bank accounts that remain open to deposits made by the teacher. In this analysis, Freire returned to Sartre's concept of "digestive" or "nutritive" education to describe the type of education in which teachers "feed" students with knowledge,[18] but reformulated it. He adopted the "feeding" metaphor but developed the concept further, operationalizing the banking education model into ten attitudes and practices: (a) the teacher teaches, and the students are taught; (b) the teacher knows everything, and the students know nothing; (c) the teacher thinks, and the students are thought about; (d) the teacher talks, and the students listen; (e) the teacher disciplines, and the students are disciplined; (f) the teacher chooses and enforces his choice, and the students comply; (g) the teacher acts, and the students have the illusion of acting through the action of the teacher; (h) the teacher chooses the program content, and the students (who were not consulted) adapt to it; (i) the teacher confuses the authority of knowledge with his/her own professional authority, which she/he sets in opposition to the freedom of the students; and (j) the teacher is the subject of the learning process, whereas the students are mere objects.

Freire's concern about banking education was not only related to classroom dynamics, but also to its long-term implications for the development of human agency and ultimately for social transformation. He argued that the relations promoted by the banking education model reflect even broader oppressive dynamics. The more students focus on storing the deposits entrusted to them, the more they accept a passive role, the more they tend to adapt to the world as it is, and the more they acquire a fragmented view of reality. This means that the more banking education they experience, the less likely they are to develop the critical consciousness; the creative capacities; and the confidence, skills, and attitudes to intervene in the transformation of the social world. The alternative to the banking education model is "problem-posing" education, which Freire also called liberating or emancipatory education. His main argument in this second chapter is that the banking approach corresponds to a model that treats education as a practice of domination, whereas his problem-posing approach is part of an alternative model that regards education as the practice of freedom. Such education is not about the transfer of information but about communication, dialogue, and acts of cognition in which all participants teach each other, mediated by the world and by the cognizable objects that in banking education are the exclusive property of the teacher. Problem-posing education aims at a constant unveiling of reality and power structures (through the process of conscientization) and at the development of creative power to transform those structures. In this sense, Freire notes, liberating education involves both the denunciation of oppressive structures and the annunciation of a less oppressive world, and hence it is not only critical but also hopeful and prophetic.[19] Throughout most of the second chapter of *Pedagogy of the Oppressed*, Freire compares the features of banking education with those of problem-posing education by exposing their differences:

- Banking education emphasizes information transfer; problem-posing encourages acts of cognition, liberating both the teacher and the students.
- Banking education attempts to mythologize reality by concealing certain facts about social relations; problem-posing education aims at demythologizing and unveiling the different layers of reality.
- Banking education resists dialogue; problem-posing education treats dialogue as indispensable to the act of cognition.
- Banking education treats students as objects of assistance; problem-posing education regards them as critical thinkers.
- Banking education fails to recognize men and women as historical beings; problem-posing education starts with people's own history and experience.
- Banking education has a predesigned, fixed, and static curriculum; in problem-posing education, the content emerges from the reality and the dreams of the learners.
- Banking education's goal is the perpetuation of social inequalities; the purpose of problem-posing education is to nurture the development of consciousness and active intervention in the social world.
- Banking education is about reinforcing fatalism and domination; problem-posing education is about nurturing autonomy and transformation.

In sum, whereas banking education is about domestication, problem-posing education is about liberation. It is worth noting that Freire's critique of banking education embraced the entire ideological spectrum. Indeed, he criticized conservative education, but he also deplored the dogmatic approach of authoritarian revolutionary leaders who do not want to waste time in dialogue, arguing that such time could be better spent "revealing the truth." For him, such a "vanguardist" approach is as banking and reprehensible as the education model carried out by the elites.

In chapter 3 of *Pedagogy of the Oppressed*, Freire discussed in more detail the theory and practice of problem-posing education. A key concept in this education approach is praxis, which comprises action and reflection. Freire noted that when education fails to pay attention to action, it runs the risk of *verbalism*, that is, idle chatter and alienation. At the same time, he cautioned that when education focuses exclusively on action to the detriment of reflection, it runs the risk of *activism*: action for its own sake in which true praxis is negated and dialogue becomes impossible. This consequence is important because dialogue is another central concept in problem-posing education. For Freire, dialogue is not just a strategy to achieve better educational results or a tactic used by educators to conquer and manipulate students. On the contrary, it is part of human nature because humans are essentially communicative beings. Freire, then, recognized that the learning process has an individual dimension, but he also argued that we need each other to discover. For Freire, discovery is a social process, and at the core of that process is dialogue, understood as the moment when people meet to discover and transform reality. Dialogue is an act of creation and cocreation, and cannot exist without humility, love, hope, critical thinking, and an intense faith in the power of people to make and remake history. At the same time, dialogue is a prerequisite for trust and freedom (Freire 1970b, Gadotti 1994).

In this chapter Freire also put forward a key concept: "inédito viable," which was translated by Myra Bergman Ramos as "untested feasibility," and refers to the possibility of attempting something that was never tried before (Araujo Freire 2002). The first part of the concept alludes to the idea that the world is not in a state of being that can be taken for granted, and that a different world may be dreamt about. Such a notion challenges the fatalism and resignation of those who claim that "this is the way it is and it has always been," and hence nothing can be done. In short, the first word of the concept connotes the idea of grounded (not blind) hope. This connects with the second word of the concept (viable), which refers to the idea of agency and possibility, meaning that another world is not only desirable but also possible. In the remainder of the third chapter, Freire elaborated on these ideas, drawing on his experience with literacy circles in Brazil and Chile and providing examples to illustrate his arguments. The concept of "untested feasibility" is complemented with the notion of limit situations, another key category in the formulation of his political-pedagogical project as it relates to his understanding of human praxis. Freire became familiar with the concept of limit situations through Alvaro Vieira Pinto (1909–87), a philosopher and educator who was affiliated with ISEB and who had studied in Europe and, like Freire, went into exile in Chile after the 1964 coup d'etat in Brazil and worked there as an adult educator.[20] In *Pedagogy of the Oppressed,* Freire noted that Vieira Pinto used the concept of limit situations developed by Karl Jaspers but without the pessimistic slant of its original formulation.[21] Freire, following Vieira, argued that people respond to limit situations (i.e., situations that limit them) with "limit acts," (i.e., acts directed at overcoming those situations). By engaging in limit acts, people stop passively accepting reality as a "given," develop a more critical understanding of reality, locate the origins of their decisions in themselves and in their relations with the world and with others, and increase the belief in their own capacity to change things:

> As critical perception is embodied in action, a climate of hope and confidence develops which leads men and women to attempt to overcome the limit-situations. This objective can be achieved only through action upon the concrete, historical reality in which limit-situations historically are found. As reality is transformed and these situations are superseded, new ones will appear, which in turn will evoke new limit-acts." (p. 100)

The fourth and final chapter of *Pedagogy of the Oppressed* deals with theories of cultural action and with the role of education in processes of social transformation. In cultural action, Freire distinguished between oppressive and liberating cultural interventions. He referred to the former as antidialogical approaches and to the latter as dialogical approaches. Then he proceeded to discuss the four main characteristics of antidialogical action (conquest, divide and rule, manipulation, and cultural invasion) and contrasted them, one by one, with the four main features of dialogical action: cooperation, unity, organization, and cultural synthesis. Regarding the role of education in processes of social transformation, Freire connected the dialogical/antidialogical dichotomy to other dichotomies, such as colonizer/colonized, teacher/student, and the more generic one of oppressor/oppressed. In his discussion of this topic, Freire warned about revolutionary leaders who replicate the practices and methods of domination of the oppressors. He was particularly concerned about self-appointed revolutionary leaders who regard themselves as an enlightened vanguard, who ignore the experience and knowledge of the people, and who engage in antidialogic practices that may degenerate into propaganda and manipulation. He argued that such an approach inevitably results in a new elitist and bureaucratic leadership, whereas an authentic humanistic revolution should be based on genuine dialogue between the leaders and the people and in liberating educational efforts.

Furthermore, he contended not only that these dialogical cultural actions should not wait until a revolution occurs, but also that they are a fundamental in ensuring a social transformation process that is guided by the people and prepares them for their participation in power. With this argument, he was responding to those leftist leaders who claimed that it was impossible to carry out dialogical education activities before taking power and promised that once the revolution was won, they would develop a different educational model. Freire observed that they had a static view of the revolution, with an artificial separation between "before" and "after" (with the moment of taking of power as the dividing line), and that they ignored the revolutionary role of problem-posing education, dialogue, and cultural action. Along the same lines, he argued that a new society could not be built on mistrust and imperviousness, but on openness to and communion[22] with the people.

In chapter 4 of *Pedagogy of the Oppressed* Freire also returned to the relationship between reflection and action, providing further clarification to his earlier discussion about this relationship in the first chapter, where he had claimed that the pedagogy of the oppressed "makes oppression and its causes objects of reflection, and from that reflection will come their necessary engagement in the struggle for liberation" (p. 48). In this sentence, Freire seems to indicate that critical reflection is a necessary and sufficient condition for transformative action: if people develop awareness about a particular situation, action will naturally follow. In chapter 4, however, Freire explicitly states that this is not the case. He acknowledged that the relationship between reflection and action is more complex than that: "Let me emphasize that my defense of the praxis implies no dichotomy by which this praxis could be divided into a prior stage of reflection and a subsequent stage of action. Action and reflection occur simultaneously" (p. 128). Then he went one step further and claimed that a decision not to take action after carefully examining the different alternatives is also a form of action: "A critical analysis of reality may, however, reveal that a particular form of action is impossible or inappropriate at the present time. Those who, through reflection, perceive the infeasibility or inappropriateness of one or another form of action (which should accordingly be postponed or substituted) cannot thereby be accused of inaction. Critical reflection is also action" (p. 128).

Overall, *Pedagogy of the Oppressed* is a product of its time, and as such it engaged with the issues, controversies, and aspirations that were part of the political and social context of the late 1960s. At the same time, however, it provided a lasting contribution to debates on the relationship between education, social reproduction, and social change. Freire was also familiar with relevant contemporary literature, and in *Pedagogy of the Oppressed* it is possible to identify the influence of several books published in the 1960s, including *The Heart of Man* by Erich Fromm, *The Colonizer and the Colonized* by Albert Memmi, and the already mentioned *The Wretched of the Earth* by Franz Fanon. In writing *Pedagogy of the Oppressed*, Freire was influenced by a variety of schools of thought, including existentialism, phenomenology, Marxism, and psychoanalysis.[23] There is no shared-upon agreement among commentators about the relative impact of the different influences on Freire's theoretical framework. Consider, for instance, his theory of conscientization. For some (e.g., Gadotti 1994) the main roots of Freire's theory of conscientization can be found in Hegel. For others (e.g., Taylor 1993), the main influence can be found in the work on the stages of consciousness of French historian Lucien Febvre. To be sure, in *Pedagogy of the Oppressed* Freire credited both Hegel and Febvre, and he also acknowledged the ideas on consciousness advanced by French philosophers Lucien Goldmann and André Nicolai during the 1960s.[24] However, as already discussed, while Freire took elements from these thinkers, he managed to organize them in a coherent and original way, and to develop a somewhat unique theory of conscientization that had immediate practical applications. Likewise, the critique of banking education that

Freire presents in *Pedagogy of the Oppressed* was not totally new: it built on previous criticisms of traditional formal education such as those advanced by Rousseau, Dewey, and Sartre. However, he further developed them and, probably more importantly, connected them to broader dynamics of social and economic oppression, on the one hand, and to political and cultural liberation struggles, on the other. This was, at that time, a fresh and momentous contribution to the debates on education and social change.

The 1970s: International work and
The Letters to Guinea-Bissau

Reference to the 1970s as Freire's "international period" calls attention to two simultaneous developments: exposure and notability. First, through his intense travel schedule and his participation in many projects in different parts of the world, Freire became exposed to a variety of educational ideas and practices as never before in his life. Second, it was also during this decade that his work and his ideas came to be internationally acknowledged, his books translated into many languages and widely read, and he became to be recognized as a key figure in the world of education.[25] As discussed in Chapter 1, during the 1970s Freire experienced the second phase of his exile, which included a variety of international stop-offs. After 5 years in Chile, he worked at Harvard for 6 months and then moved to Geneva as educational advisor for developing countries of the World Council of Churches, which had played a role in the liberation struggles against colonialism in several African countries. Freire believed that this would be a better place for him to make a contribution and to learn than ensconced in the library of Harvard University: "At that time I was absolutely convinced that it would be fundamental for me to go around the world to expose myself to various situations, learn from the experience of others, and see myself in different cultural contexts. And this was what the World Council of Churches could give me more than any university" (Freire, cited in Gadotti 1994:41). These different cultural contexts provided Freire with a range of experiences that would be reflected in the works that he produced during the 1970s. On the one hand, he was invited to be visiting professor or lecturer at several universities around the world, including the Open University (UK), Louvain University, University of Toronto, University of Michigan, and the University of Geneva, where he conducted a regular seminar on popular education (Gadotti 1994), and he was also invited to participate in many conferences, such as the International Symposium for Literacy held in Persepolis in 1975, where he made a presentation entitled "Are literacy programs neutral?"

On the other hand, he collaborated with educational programs and literacy campaigns in several countries (Nicaragua, Grenada, Fiji, Peru, India) but particularly in some Lusophone African countries that had become independent after centuries of Portuguese colonization and painful national liberation struggles. Freire and his IDAC team were especially active in Guinea-Bissau,[26] where he served as an advisor to the literacy campaign as a result of an invitation from Education Minister Mario Cabral. During the second part of the 1970s, when Freire was active doing international work, he did not publish much. His main book of this period (*Pedagogy in Process: The Letters to Guinea-Bissau*) described his reflections on this initiative (Freire 1978b). In the foreword, Jonathan Kozol observed that not only was this Freire's most accessible book but also his most powerful and human. The publication contains 17 letters that Freire sent to Cabral and his team. In the first ones, he observed that he had not wanted to go to Guinea-Bissau as the "international expert" who was going to fix problems with recipes transplanted from other contexts, because that would be nothing less than another expression of neocolonialism. Instead, he made clear that to provide help with the reconstruction process, he had first to familiarize himself with the national reality, and his role should be that of one more collaborator in a collective project, with solutions emanating from the collective and not from foreign experts: "We will have nothing to teach if we do not learn from and with you" (p. 73). In the other letters, Freire repeated arguments that he had made before in *Pedagogy of the Oppressed* (e.g., education is a political act, people can be both illiterate and politically knowledgeable, banking education fosters dynamics of oppression, education programs should be connected to other areas such as production or health) but now applied to the specific context of neolocolonialism, independence struggles, and national reconstruction efforts in Guinea-Bissau. Three issues stemming from Freire's work in

Africa generated controversy in the adult education community. The first was related to supposedly antidialogical elements in his letters that contradicted the philosophy of dialogue he had proposed in previous writings. The second related to the mixed results of literacy campaigns. In her doctoral thesis, Linda Harasim (1983) contended that the Guinea-Bissau campaign was a total failure because practically none of the 26,000 students who had enrolled became functionally literate. In São Tomé and Príncipe, efforts were more successful: according to a letter sent by the Ministry of Education to Freire, 55 percent of all those who had enrolled and 72 percent of those who had finished became literate (Freire 1981, Gadotti 1994). The third had to do with choice of language for the literacy campaign, particularly in Guinea-Bissau: Freire was in favor of Creole, but the local leadership opted for Portuguese (Walker 1980, Leich 1982, Facundo 1984, Weiler 1996,[27] Roberts 2000, Wagner 1989, C.A. Torres 1993).

The 1980s and the "talking books"

In 1980, after 15 years of exile, Paulo Freire returned to Brazil, where he became active in politics and in academia. That year, he was one of the founding members of the Workers' Party, and he was appointed professor at the Pontifícia Universidade Católica de São Paulo. During the first part of this decade he published several short articles in which he reflected on different aspects of his lifetime experiences and developed theoretical insights from his educational practice. One of them was *The Importance of the Act of Reading*, which provides a good summary of his approach to literacy teaching.

A few years later, in 1985, Freire published *The Politics of Education: Culture, Power and Liberation*, a book that brought together in one collection in English a compilation of short articles that he had produced in Portuguese in the previous years. Donaldo Macedo translated the texts, and in the last chapter included an interview that he did with Freire about his life and his educational philosophy. The book filled some gaps in Freire's other works, although most of it repeats arguments and ideas (e.g., banking and liberating education, the literacy method and the generative word, culture of silence, and conscientization) that he discussed in previous publications. In the 1980s Freire also engaged in a series of dialogue books, a tradition that he had inaugurated in 1975 with Ivan Illich in Cuernavaca. In this decade he published at least 15 talking books in Portuguese, English, and Spanish with other colleagues. These collaborations took off in the second part of the decade, with at least a dozen books published in the short period between 1985 and 1990. Among the collaborative books of this decade are the following:

Vivendo e aprendendo: experiências do IDAC em educação popular (with Claudius Ceccon, Rosiska Dary de Oliveira, and Miguel Darcy de Oliveira, 1983)

Sobre educação: diálogos (with Sergio Guimaraes, 1984)

Por uma pedagogia da pergunta (with Antonio Faundez, 1985)

Essa escola chamada vida (with Frei Betto and Ricardo Kotscho, 1985)

Fazer escola conhecendo a vida (with Adriano Nogueira and Débora Mazza, 1986)

Apprendendo com a propia historia (with Sergio Guimaraes, 1987)

A Pedagogy for Liberation: Dialogues on Transforming Education (with Ira Shor, 1987)

Literacy: Reading the Word and the World (with Donaldo Macedo, 1987)

Freire for the Classroom: A Sourcebook for Liberatory Teaching (with Ira Shor, 1987)

Teachers as Intellectuals: Towards a Critical Pedagogy of Learning (with Henry Giroux and Peter McLaren, 1988)

Cultural Wars: School and Society in the Conservative Restoration 1969–1984 (with Ira Shor, 1988)

Pedagogía, Diálogo y Conflicto (with Moacir Gadotti, Sergio Guimaraes, and Isabel Hernandez, 1988)

Educación popular: un encuentro con Paulo Freire (Rosa Maria Torres 1988)

We Make the Road by Walking: Conversations on Education and Social Change (with Myles Horton, 1990).

In these books, Freire and his collaborators covered a range of topics, usually in the form of a structured conversation organized along themes.

Among these books, arguably *A Pedagogy for Liberation*, co-authored with Ira Shor, was particularly significant for three reasons: it was his first "talking book" in English, it was his first book dealing extensively with education in "First World" contexts, and it was his first book addressing the practice of problem-posing education in classrooms. Shor and Freire started to work on this book in 1984, and the text was based on careful editing of tapes from several conversations that Freire and Shor had in Canada and in the United States from 1984 to 1986. The book is both readable and profound in its examination of theoretical and practical issues related to liberatory education: in their conversations, the authors artfully combine personal stories with rigorous reflections.

We Make the Road by Walking, the last talking book of the decade, was of special interest for adult educators because Paulo Freire and Myles Horton were both "living legends" of twentieth-century popular education. Horton had founded the Highlander Center in Tennessee in 1932 and had a philosophical and political approach to adult education that was similar to Freire. Professor Budd Hall, who has been a leader in the adult education movement for several decades, said that "the Myles Horton/Paulo Freire talks represent one of the most important educational conversations of the twentieth century," and added: "This is the first book since Freire's *Pedagogy of the Oppressed* that I have said must be read." In this book, which was widely read in adult education circles around the world, Freire and Horton shared stories from their own experiences as educator-activists. This conversation gave Freire and Horton an opportunity to reflect on their experiences; to review their theoretical assumptions; and to elaborate on their main ideas about education, knowledge, and organizing issues, particularly the role of education in progressive social movements and in promoting social justice. The dialogue between Horton and Freire covered a variety of topics, including their formative years, the relationship between practice and knowledge and between conflict and consciousness, the political nature of education, the role (and different types) of leadership, the difference between education and organizing, participatory democracy, and the role of education in social change. Toward the end of the book, Freire made reference to the importance of humor, arguing that it is necessary to laugh with the people "because, if we don't do that, we cannot learn from the people, and in not learning from the people, we cannot teach them" (Horton and Freire, 1990, p. 247). This was not the only time that Freire talked about the role of humor in popular education. Indeed, on other occasions Freire referred to the pedagogy of the oppressed as a pedagogy of laughter (Gadotti, 1994:160, Lewis 2010).

As discussed in Chapter 1, by 1989 Freire's professional trajectory took a different path when the Worker's Party won the municipal elections of Sao Paulo and the newly elected mayor offered Freire the position of secretary of education of that city, the most populous in Brazil. Freire accepted the appointment, and with this acceptance came two new challenges. The first was to assume a new identity as a civil servant with heavy responsibilities in a large and complicated state bureaucracy, and to develop the attitudes and the competencies to fulfill that role successfully after years of working as an advisor, a professor, and an independent scholar. The second challenge was to engage productively, creatively, and efficiently in the daily work of the formal education system after many decades of working mainly outside schools in non-formal education, cultural circles, literacy programs, and the like.

The 1990s: From *Pedagogy of the City* to ecopedagogy

The work of Freire during the 1990s involved two main categories. On the one hand, he continued his administrative duties as secretary of education of Sao Paulo, which included both the daily management of the system and the development of a series of reform initiatives. On the other hand, he was involved in a variety of scholarly activities, including lectures, academic engagements, and publications. In 1991, he realized that these two sets of demands represented an excessive workload and, as he was approaching the age of 70, he decided to leave public administration in order to be able to dedicate the remaining years of his life to scholarly pursuits.

By that time, Freire's work as secretary of education had lasted 2 1/2 years, from January 1, 1989, to May 27, 1991. As pointed out in Chapter 1, when Freire took this position, his most urgent challenge was to repair the physical infrastructure of the educational system (Sieber 1997, O'Cadiz et al. 1998). He believed that his first task was to construct more classrooms and to keep them clean, joyful, and beautiful so as to create the preconditions for the second task: namely, to ensure competence in teaching, to nurture pleasure in learning, to promote the creative imagination, and to ensure the exercise of freedom. At the policy level, his main reforms were oriented toward the democratization of the educational system and the strengthening of the autonomy of schools. Freire argued that school autonomy was a precondition for allowing each school to develop its own pedagogical project. This should be complemented, Freire proposed, with new channels of participation such as school councils and student unions, continuous professional development for teachers, administrative support, an interdisciplinary curriculum, and the recognition of teachers as professionals and subjects of their own practice (Freire 1993b, Gadotti 1994).

All these proposals coalesced around his main reform initiative as secretary of education: the interdisciplinary curriculum. This reform was guided by four principles. First, curriculum reform should be generated collectively through an inclusive and democratic participatory process. Second, respect for school autonomy should also include respect for valid local practices and experiences. Third, the curriculum should value relations between theory and practice and include a constant cycle of action, reflection, and action. Fourth, the professional development of teachers should be permanent, and should include a critical analysis of the implementation of the curriculum at each school. Freire's portfolio as secretary of education also included adult literacy. Consistent with his theory that (a) effective, popular participation is a key component of adult education, and (b) the development of active citizens and effective popular participation cannot occur without the democratization of information, Freire established partnerships with popular movements as soon as he took office and gave them considerable decision-making power. He observed that an important challenge here was finding the best way to support and strengthen popular movements while respecting their independence and avoiding clientelistic relationships with the state.[28] His proposal was the creation of MOVA, or Movimento de Alfabetizacao de Jovens e Adultos [Youth and Adult Literacy Movement], which led to the organization of the First Adult Literacy Students Congress, held on December 16, 1990, with the participation of 3,000 adult learners. This innovative model of organizing adult literacy services in partnership with social movements and community organizations faced some limitations but overall was considered successful and eventually was adopted by other progressive municipalities in Brazil (Stromquist 1997, Borg and Mayo 2000).

From a pedagogical standpoint, a related issue was the commitment to methodological pluralism. Although the "Freire method" of adult literacy had been internationally recognized for a long time, the secretary of education did not impose any methodological approach on literacy teaching. The only approaches that were not accepted were those that were clearly authoritarian, racist, or antiscientific (Gadotti 1994). As mentioned before, at the end of May 1991, a few months before his seventieth birthday, Freire resigned as secretary of education to return to his academic activities and writing. In his farewell address, he said that, despite leaving, he remained committed to the educational project of the Workers' Party:

> Even though I will no longer be the Secretary, I will continue at your side in a different form . . . You can continue to count on me in the construction of an educational policy, of a school with a new face: more joyful, fraternal and democratic. (Freire 1993b:139)

Released from administrative responsibilities during the last years of his life, Freire was able to devote time and energy to several pending writing projects, some alone and some in collaboration with others. Among the books authored by Freire that were published during that period were *Pedagogy of the City* (1993), *Pedagogy of Hope: Reliving Pedagogy of the Oppressed* (1994), *Letters to Cristina: Reflections on My Life and Work* (1996), *Teachers as Cultural Workers: Letters to Those Who Dare Teach* (1998), and *Pedagogy of Freedom* (1998). As mentioned in Chapter 1, Nita Freire, Paulo's widow, organized some of his unpublished texts and published three posthumous books: *Pedagogy of Indignation* (2004), *Daring to Dream: Toward a Pedagogy of the Unfinished* (2007), and *Pedagogia da Tolerância* (2006), providing helpful annotations with contextual information.

The first book of this period was *Pedagogy of the City*, published in Portuguese in 1991 and in English in 1993. The main material for this book consisted of interviews conducted during the first part of Freire's mandate as secretary of education of Sao Paulo. The postscript, by Ana Maria Saul, discusses the main achievements and shortcomings of the reforms and initiatives undertaken by this administration. Overall, the book teaches some valuable lessons about the possibilities and limitations of educational reform at the municipal level. As an educational administrator, his philosophical approach to educational reform was that inflexible blueprints imposed on schools do not work and that the role of the secretary was to develop guiding principles and values; to provide adequate funding, technical assistance, and training; and to generate processes for authentic participation in deliberation and decision making. Although *Pedagogy of the City* does not bring any significant new element to Freire's philosophy of education, it includes stimulating discussions on teacher training, new technologies, relations between popular culture and dominant culture in the curriculum, leadership and educational decentralization, and school autonomy and system democratization that could be of great interest to those involved in progressive educational reforms, and particularly to those in programs of educational policy or educational administration (Roberts 1994, Mayo 2004).

In *Pedagogy of Hope: Reliving Pedagogy of the Oppressed*, Freire delivered on the promise made in the subtitle of the book and revisited his most celebrated book a quarter-century later, addressing some of the criticisms that the text received over the years. In this book, Freire also revealed interesting autobiographical information that provides a historical context for the development of his ideas over time. For instance, he revisited his own former practice as a banking educator and submitted to self-criticism: "it was as if my word, my theme, my reading of the world, in themselves, were to be their compass" (p. 22). In *Pedagogy of Hope*, Freire also described dialogues that he had with readers of *Pedagogy of the Oppressed* and observed that the responses from readers were often related to their particular geographic location. Freire distinguished three main "profiles" of readers. Students and professors from European and North American universities were more theoretically oriented and were especially concerned about the rigor and precision of the text, its internal contradictions and inconsistencies, and its relationship to the ideas of other thinkers that may have inspired the work. Those in developing countries were more interested in the political dimensions of the book and in its philosophical, ethical, ideological, and epistemological ramifications. Finally, workers—be they from developing or developed countries—displayed a particular interest in gaining more critical understanding of reality in order to improve future practice.

If *Pedagogy of Hope* contains some autobiographical elements, *Letters to Cristina: Reflections on My Life and Work* is eminently autobiographical. The book was Freire's response to a request from his niece Cristina, then a teenager, who asked him to write her letters about his life history and his professional evolution: "I would like for you to write me letters about your life, your childhood and, little by little, about the trajectory that led you to become the educator you are now" (p. 11). Freire confided that this letter from his niece represented a challenge for him, as it demanded him to organize the many files that he had collected over the years, to analyze that information by focusing on the main issues, and to write his ideas in such a way that a young person could understand. What Freire came up with was a book comprising 18 letters. In the first 12, he describes in detail the most relevant moments of his life, particularly his formative years in Brazil before going into exile. The last six letters are more conceptual in tone: in them, he discusses several topics that were central to his work as an educator such as progressive and authoritarian education, democracy, oppression, racism, sexism, class discrimination, conscientization, freedom, and the like.

Teachers as Cultural Workers: Letters to Those Who Dare Teach was published in English in 1998, 5 years after its publication in Portuguese. It is worth pointing out that in the original Portuguese publication, the first part of the title was *Professora sim, tia não* ("Professor, not aunt") in reference to the Brazilian context, wherein teachers are often reduced to the role of "aunts," thereby undermining their role as professionals and as cultural workers. The impetus for the book clearly originated in Freire's regular interactions with teachers when he was secretary of education. As Peter Mayo (2004:77) observed, "what this book places on the agenda is that there is no contradiction between a Freirean approach to an authentically dialogical education and the quest for professional recognition." Freire organized this book as one long introductory chapter (entitled "A Pedagogical Trap"), ten letters directed to teachers, and a concluding chapter. He argued that teaching is a profession (although not in the technical meaning of professionalization) that involves a specific task and a specific militancy (in the sense of advocating for students). In reference to the subtitle of the book, Freire claimed that those wanting to teach must be willing to dare. By daring he implied a loving search for knowledge, the predisposition to struggle for justice and for the conditions needed for a good learning environment, and the recognition that teaching can be both a joyful and an intellectually rigorous activity (p. 8). In this book, Freire also argued that teachers should be role models "setting forth the values of democracy," and this required three basic conditions. The first is that democracy must never be seen as a personal struggle of one or a few teachers. Second, as a consequence of the first condition, teachers must stick together when they challenge the system and propose more effective alternatives. Third, he encouraged teachers to demand continuing professional development, in particular activities that promote theoretical reflections on their own practice and that evaluate practice as a means of learning and growth—not merely as a tool to punish teachers (p. 12). The ten letters deal with a range of issues (some theoretical, some concrete) that are relevant to teachers who want to engage in progressive education practices and to progressive people who might consider entering the teaching profession. Among the various issues are the relations between reading the word and reading the world, the paralysis that sometimes results from fear and difficulties, the reasons to become a teacher, the first day of school, the teacher/learner relationship, discipline, and understanding the context. In the fourth letter, Freire identifies some indispensable qualities of progressive teachers: humility, lovingness, courage, tolerance, awareness of the tension between patience and impatience, joy of living, and verbal parsimony. He argues that these qualities are not innate but are developed over time, and that they are necessary to create a school that is a collective adventure of cocreation, that rejects immobility, and that is not afraid to take risks. In the 1990s, Freire also continued with "talking books" and other writings produced in cooperation with colleagues. Among the dialogue books of this period were *Paulo Freire on Higher Education: A Dialogue at the National University of Mexico* (with Miguel Escobar and Gilberto Guevara Niebla, 1994), *Mentoring the Mentor: A Critical Dialogue with Paulo Freire* (with James Fraser, Donaldo Macedo, Tanya McKinnon, and William Stokes, 1997), and *Critical Education in the New Information Age* (with Manuel Castells, Ramon Flecha, Donald Macedo, Henry Giroux, and Paul Willis, 1999).

Toward the end of his life, Freire published two books that combine autobiographical reflections with theoretical discussions and political analysis and that allow us to access the main ideas of his last years. The first was *A sombra desta mangueira* [In the shadow of this mango tree[29]], published in Portuguese in 1995 and in English in 1997 as *Pedagogy of the Heart*. In this book Freire revisited his ideas and his work throughout his life, describing the long journey that took him from being a citizen of his backyard (where he learned to read and write) to becoming a citizen of the world. The topics covered in this book range from the particularities of Brazilian politics to universal themes such as human solidarity. *Pedagogy of the Heart* also includes personal reflections on communion, separation, exile, and political and educational reform. Although he addressed issues related to his religious faith, he shared the feeling that he felt more comfortable discussing his political choices and his pedagogical utopias. Freire rejected fatalism (which was prevalent among many progressives in Brazil at that time) and highlighted his faith in the collective struggle for "overcoming an oppressive reality and for building a less ugly society, one that is less evil and more humane" (Freire 1997:104).

The other book was *Pedagogia da Autonomia*, published in Portuguese in 1996 and in English in 1998 as *Pedagogy of Freedom: Ethics, Democracy and Civic Courage*.[30] In this book, Freire returned to some of the themes that occupied his attention in previous publications, but updated the discussion to the neoliberal context of the mid-1990s. He also shared newly gained insights from his recent experience as secretary of education of Sao Paulo, ranging from issues such as the rights of educators and the commitment to teaching to practical dilemmas faced by teachers in their work. Moreover, in this book, Freire took the opportunity to clarify some issues that had remained obscure in previous works, such as the relationship between freedom and authority, the ideological dimension of education, and his take on postmodernism. In *Pedagogy of Freedom* Freire also connected some of his viewpoints with his own biography. For instance, to stress the importance of the role of the teacher in encouraging students, he recalled that when he was a young learner lacking confidence, a teacher had a profound impact on his self-esteem and performance through praise and support.

When he died, Freire left a manuscript in the form of letters that, together with five other unpublished texts, were compiled into a book by his widow Nita. This book, which Nita titled *Pedagogy of Indignation* (released in Portuguese in 2000; English in 2004), inaugurated the posthumous works of Paulo Freire that would be published in the twenty-first century. Addressed mainly to students, parents, and educators, the book is organized in two parts. The first part, "Pedagogical Letters," includes letters dealing with authority and freedom in the family, the right and the duty to change the world, and the murder of an indigenous person in Brazilia by five teenagers who said that they were "just playing." The second part, "Other Writings," includes texts dealing with the so-called discovery of America, illiteracy and poverty, education and technology, television, hope, prophecy, and utopia. Overall, the main theme of *Pedagogy of Indignation* is the role of education in the project to build a more democratic society.

Nita also collected other unpublished materials written by Freire, and compiled them in two books: *Pedagogia dos Sonhos Possíveis* (2001), published in English as *Daring to Dream: Toward a Pedagogy of the Unfinished* (2007), and *Pedagogia da Tolerância* (2006), which has not yet been translated into English. *Pedagogy of the Unfinished* includes a series of writings, not only recent ones but also several early essays in which Freire developed ideas that he later published in *Pedagogy of the Oppressed.* This book permits a deeper exploration into the project of humanization proposed by Freire, a project that focuses on agency and hope insofar as it assumes that humans are unfinished beings who are always in search of a better world. In this book, Freire also addressed the tensions between critical dreams and educational realities. *Pedagogia da Tolerância* is organized in eight chapters and combines Freire's unpublished texts with transcriptions of his seminars, including exchanges with participants. The book contains an essay in which Freire distinguishes between alienated tolerance and genuine tolerance and also a series of texts in which he discusses issues related to indigenous education, the mechanistic reading of the reproductionist theories of the 1970s, science and mythology, language and culture, critical thinking, dreams, faith, ethics, and aesthetics, Altogether, Freire's last five books

(*Pedagogy of Freedom, Pedagogy of the Heart, Pedagogy of Indignation, Pedagogy of the Unfinished, and Pedagogia da Tolerancia*) complete the earlier trilogy that began in the 1960s with *Pedagogy of the Oppressed* and continued with *Pedagogy of Hope* and *Pedagogy of the City*.

Another important contribution of Freire during his later years was his response to the first 15 chapters of the book *Mentoring the Mentor: A Critical Dialogue with Paulo Freire* in which critical comments were raised by a range of North American scholars. In chapter 16, entitled "A response," Freire addressed what in his view were the most important themes and questions raised by his colleagues in the previous chapters. Among them were whether his "methods" work in a North American context; the key aspects of critical dialogue; what he could and could not offer to educators in other contexts; the influence of factors such as race, class, and gender in his analysis of oppression and liberation; and the multiple identities of oppressors and oppressed. In his response, Freire also discussed the particular and universal elements in his conceptual framework, his own growth and change since *Pedagogy of the Oppressed*, the ethical dimensions of education (including the ethical requirements for teachers and the low attention paid to this in teacher education programs), the barriers to ethical dialogue in totalitarian and "democratic" systems, the differences between oral dialogue and written dialogue (with references to the particular context of the *Mentoring the Mentor* book), the role of democratic teachers and strategies for creating change, the role of a mentor in supporting the development of democratic teachers, the re-creation of his proposals in other contexts, and his fight against any attempts to turn him into a guru or an icon. Freire's text in *Mentoring the Mentor* is written in accessible and clear language, and it brings together in a short piece the main criticisms of his work and his responses to those criticisms. As noted in Chapter 1, at the time of his death Freire was working on a book on neoliberalism and another on ecopedagogy.

Taken together, this later set of publications shows a more reflective and mature Freire, willing to revisit critically his previous work, to express reservations about his certainties, and to entertain new ideas. He was particularly prolific in his last decade, perhaps anticipating that he did not have much time left. When reading those texts, it is important to remember the context of the 1990s. In those years, neoliberalism became hegemonic, with market-oriented policies and ideologies that promoted Social Darwinism and attacked redistributive policies, state intervention, and organized labor. In those years, Francis Fukuyama published an influential book called *The End of History and the Last Man*, in which he argued that capitalist democracy is the last form of government. In Latin America, many formerly progressive politicians and intellectuals started to support neoliberal policies. At the same time, it was in those years that popular organizations like the Landless Peasants' Movement opened a new era of political activism and mobilization, and the Workers' Party, which Freire helped to found a decade before, made significant gains in Brazilian politics at the municipal level, paving the road for the election (and reelection) of Lula da Silva as president of the country a few years later, and allowing creative innovations at the local level. Freire's late writings, in which he simultaneously expressed indignation and hope, reflect his reactions to that context. In terms of potential for future development, perhaps the three main themes that emerge from the texts of the 1990s are the democratization of the school system, the conceptualization of a "pedagogy of hope" that complements (and sometimes corrects) the original "pedagogy of the oppressed"), and the need for the development of an ecopedagogy that expands the anthropocentrism of critical pedagogy.

Recapitulating: seven dimensions and three tensions in Freire's work

In the previous pages, I presented the main works of Paulo Freire in a roughly chronological sequence in order to examine the evolution of his ideas in a biographical context. In this section, I attempt to provide a summary of the main dimensions of his work and discuss some tensions that arise from it. Freire was a prolific writer who drew from different disciplines and traditions. His educational approach combined ideas from a variety of sources and ideological orientations. He claimed to have tried to be systematically coherent in the development of his practice and in his reflections upon that practice, but pointed out that because he also attempted to be creative and critical, he was always ready to learn and to change. He quoted from scores of philosophers, psychologists, sociologists, political scientists, educators, revolutionaries, and theologians, and drew insights from different disciplines and traditions, from Socratic maieutics and Hegelian idealism to Christian and Marxist humanism. In his writings, alongside Marx and the Bible we find Sartre and Husserl, Mounier and Buber, Fanon and Memmi, Mao and Guevara, Althusser and Fromm, Hegel and Unamuno, Kosik and Febvre, Freinet and Claparéde, Dewey and Furter, Chardin and Maritain, Arendt and Heller, Lukacs and Weil, Descartes and Rousseau, Marcuse and Merleau-Ponty, and Cabral and Gramsci. Even though Freire was influenced by these and by other authors, his particular ability was to combine their ideas into an original perspective. Indeed, one of his main contributions was to bring together a range of social theories in order to address the political dimensions of education (in particular, the relationship between education and social change) and to connect the resultant theoretical discussions to concrete pedagogical strategies. In doing so, Freire was able to recognize not only structural constraints but also the role of human agency in changing those structures and the role of educational and cultural action in bringing about transformation. Building on Flecha (2004) and Nuñez (2007), I identify seven dimensions in his proposals: philosophical, ethical, epistemological, sociological, psychological, political, and pedagogical.

(1) Philosophical

Human beings are incomplete and have an ontological vocation to become fully human. This is the project of humanization. Teachers and students, as well as poor and rich people, are unfinished beings that have much to learn from each other.

(2) Ethical

A liberating education is premised on an ethical option for the poor and a commitment to expand life and justice, not to create a world in which the oppressed become the new oppressors, but one in which there is no longer oppression.

(3) Epistemological

Subjectivity and objectivity are joined in a dialectical unity. Learners are active subjects who can produce knowledge and not just passively consume knowledge created by others. Hence, education must combine the act of interpreting existing knowledge with the act of creating new knowledge. Learners can examine long-held assumptions and develop a critical reading of reality. The creation and distribution of knowledge occur in social and historical contexts.

(4) Sociological

Educational policies and practices cannot be isolated from larger social structures characterized by inequalities in the access to economic, political, and cultural resources. Education often reproduces and even reinforces societal inequalities, but it can also contribute to the process of social transformation. Education alone cannot transform society, but society cannot be transformed without it.

(5) Psychological

For many oppressed peoples, the fear of the oppressor and the internalization of the dominant worldview prevent them from recognizing their own culture and from struggling, but they can free themselves from alienating dynamics through a process of liberation that begins with the decolonization of their minds and continues with the development of individual and collective agency.

(6) Political

Education is a political act, and cannot ignore issues of power. The development of a critical consciousness is an important step toward transformative collective actions. In coordination with progressive social movements (united in their diversity), educators can make an important contribution to social transformation, to nurture a more just and peaceful world. This process requires hope, political efficacy, and democratic institutions and practices.

(7) Pedagogical

Unlike banking education, which treats learners as blank slates and reproduces authoritarian relations, liberating education treats learners as subjects who have experience. This approach recognizes the directive role of teachers, but promotes dialogical relationships and participatory research. Its curriculum begins with the reality of the learners, and encourages the problematization of that reality. Education is praxis, reflection, and action of women and men upon the world in order to transform it.

In Freire's work it is also possible to identify three tensions. The first is between his foundational eclecticism and his theoretical coherence. The second is between his Catholic socialization and his Marxist analytical framework. The third is the tension between democracy and authority in his pedagogical approach.

(a) On eclecticism and coherence

The work of Freire draws from many different sources, and it is not easy to identify him with a definitive label or categorize his work within a specific school of thought. As we shall see in Chapter 3, for some commentators such eclecticism suggests lack of academic rigor, a contradictory theoretical framework, and poor scholarship. For others, it shows that he was a true intellectual and an original thinker, unconstrained by disciplinary or theoretical boundaries and coherent in his ethical and political commitments. Linda Bimbi, for instance, observed in the introduction to the Italian edition of *Pedagogy of the Oppressed* that the impossibility of classifying him comes from his absolute incompatibility with inflexible schemes and argued that, for this reason, he was an authentic intellectual (quoted in Gadotti 1994). Although Freire's approach could be regarded as eclectic, it did not consist of a random combination of elements from any theory under the sun. His approach was rather selective and guided by his main concerns and assumptions. Looking carefully at his work, it is possible to note that he was closer to some traditions than to others. Here it is pertinent to consider the two theses proposed by Elias (1994). The first is that Freire's thought is best understood as that of an educational practitioner and theorist. Elias acknowledged Freire's excursions into several disciplines such as philosophy, social theory, political theory, linguistics, and anthropology (and I would add psychoanalysis, communications, and history), but argued that those expeditions were often controlled by Freire's educational interests. The second thesis is that Freire, due to his eclecticism, can be interpreted from different perspectives, but the most fruitful comes from understanding him as a Catholic thinker. Elias claimed that Freire's religious and theological views about people, the world, society, and political change shape many elements of his thought.

There is little to debate in the first thesis. Most of Freire's texts were about sharing and interpreting his own educational practices and approaches, and almost everything he wrote has a connection to education. As Elias notes in a chapter suggestively entitled "Freire's Eclecticism: Drinking from Many Wells," "the various philosophies he draws on—liberalism, existentialism, phenomenology and Marxism—are in the service of understanding the social context of education, the nature of the person to be educated, the process of education, the relationship between students and teachers, the relationship between education and politics, the nature of knowledge, the method of education, and the role of language in education" (Elias 1994:44). In relation to the second thesis, there is little disagreement on the fact that Freire's ideas were infused by the symbols and the language of Catholicism, with recurrent references to vocation, humility, love, trust, communion, prophecy, death and resurrection, and the like. However, Elias pushed the argument one step further and argued that "for Freire all education is religious since it deals with the immanent and transcendent dimensions of human life and activity" (p. 45). A statement of this sort is not only too general but also debatable. Given the significance of other (secular) approaches in Freire's worldview, it would be too constraining to reduce Freirean thought to just one category. Elias himself recognized this fact when he accepted that "Freire defies classification according to our traditional categories," but nonetheless made an attempt to classify him, creating a blended category of three traditions: "The best that I can come up with is a Christian-existentialist-Marxist educator" (p. 44). Although other descriptors may be equally valid, this proposition captures the main idea that Freire was preeminently an educator (and hence this is the noun), and the adjectives referring to philosophical or political orientations could be treated as subject to slight variation. The other interesting aspect of Elias's categorization is that it calls attention to two apparently contradictory sources influencing Freire's work: Christianity and Marxism. This is the topic of the next section.

(b) On being a Christian and a Marxist

Freire was raised as a Catholic in a context in which religion was sometimes used to justify inequality and abject poverty. He recalled those early years in the following terms: "If God is responsible, humans can do nothing. As a child, I knew many priests who went out to the peasants, saying: 'be patient. This is God's will. And anyway, it will earn heaven for you'... this sort of theology is a very passive one ... How can we make God responsible for this calamity?" (Freire 1972b:8). During his youth, Freire found inspiration in the French tradition of Christian humanism, including the writings of Teilhard de Chardain (a philosopher and Jesuit priest who adhered to Husserl's phenomenology), Emmanuel Mounier (a philosopher who founded the personalist movement and influenced the Catholic Worker movement), and Jacques Maritain (a Catholic philosopher who proposed the notion of Integral Humanism and participated in the drafting of the Universal Declaration of Human Rights). In the works of Freire, particularly his discussions on consciousness, critical reflection, human development, community, and human agency, it is possible to see the footprints of these three French philosophers. As a Christian humanist, Freire espoused the intrinsic worth of human beings and believed that they had an "ontological vocation" to make the most of themselves, to become fully human, not as isolated individuals but in communion with others. Likewise, Freire identified injustice, exploitation, and oppression as impediments that prevented people from progressing toward full humanization and hence constituted a distortion of their ontological vocation (Freire, 1972b:20).

Through his involvement with the youth Catholic Action movement, Freire became familiar with the incipient liberation theology movement that endorsed the principle that Christians have a moral obligation to reject exploitation (Gadotti 1994). He was particularly inspired by the ideas, commitment, and pastoral work of Helder Camara, known as the "red bishop" because of his struggle for social justice and human rights during the military regime. It is not surprising, then, that when working with workers and peasants, Freire started to ask questions about the roots of exploitation and to explore answers through Marxist theory. He was prompted to do so not only by the reality of oppression, but also by people's magical religious perspective that understood their misery as a test imposed by God. In conversation with Horton, he recalled: "I began to read Marx and to read about Marx, and the more I did the more I became convinced that we really would have to change the structures of reality, that we should become absolutely committed to a global process of transformation" (Horton and Freire 1990:246). Indeed, in many works, particularly from *Pedagogy of the Oppressed* on, Freire used some of the analytical tools of Marxism. This nevertheless did not make him abandon his Christian humanist philosophy: "God led me to the people, and the people led me to Marx . . . But when I met Marx, I continued to meet Christ on the corners of the streets—by meeting the people" (Freire 1974, cited in Walker 1980:126). Freire admitted that Marxism and Christianity could be regarded by some as contradictory frameworks, but reported he was able to manage that tension: "I always spoke to both of them [Christ and Marx] in a very loving way. You see, I feel comfortable in this position. Sometimes people say to me that I am contradictory. My answer is that I have the right to be contradictory, and secondly, I don't consider myself contradictory in this . . . if you ask me, then, if I am a religious man, I say no . . . I would say that I am a man of faith . . . I feel myself very comfortable with this" (Horton and Freire 1990:247). In sum, it can be argued that it is precisely in this dialogue between Christian humanism and Marxist humanism where we can find the foundation of Freire's philosophical approach and core concepts of his political-educational theory such as humanization, agency, love, freedom, praxis, and hope.

(c) On dialogical education and directiveness

Freire did not identify himself as part of the nondirective education movement that flourished in the 1970s. However, given his emphasis on democratic and dialogical education, his work with culture circles, and his critique of the banking approach, it was not evident whether he defended the directive character of education. In his efforts to distinguish himself from the nondirective movement, Freire stated that he did not advocate either a laissez faire approach or an authoritarian approach but something he called a "directive liberating approach." As observed in our discussion of *Pedagogy of the Oppressed*, Freire used the "banking" metaphor to criticize the traditional teacher-centered educational model and to contrast it to the learner-centered, problem-posing model that he proposed. The "banking" image refers to teachers depositing prescribed knowledge into the "empty minds" of learners, who are considered passive objects of the educational act and whose experience and knowledge is unrecognized. In the banking model, the role of teachers is to transmit information (usually through lectures), and the role of students is to remember that information and retrieve it in test situations. In the banking model, the teacher fills the students' minds with deposits of information of what is considered true knowledge, and students are expected to retrieve that information whenever required by the teacher:

> Education thus becomes an act of depositing, in which the students are the depositories and the teacher is the depositor. Instead of communicating, the teacher issues communiqués and makes deposits that the students patiently receive, memorize, and repeat. This is the "banking" concept of education, in which the scope of action allowed to the students extends only as far as receiving, filing, and storing the deposits. (Freire 1970b:72)

In Freire's "banking" analogy, teachers are characterized as subjects, depositors, prescribers, knowledge purveyors, and domesticators, whereas learners are characterized as objects, containers to be filled, ignorant (empty), and obedient. Moreover, Freire argues that banking education is not only oppressive in itself but also used to indoctrinate students into accepting, justifying, and eventually adapting to oppressive social relations (Laverty 2008). As an alternative to the banking education model, Freire proposed what in different texts he called an emancipatory, problem-posing, liberatory, humanistic, or dialogical model. In terms of the teacher-learner relationship, this model is characterized by an active engagement of the learner in the act of learning, and by dialogue, which Freire conceptualizes as an encounter among people who engage in an act of creation that unites reflection and social transformation.

Freire's juxtaposition of banking and liberatory education has led to at least two confusions among readers of his work. One of them has to do with equating banking education with lectures and the corollary that lectures have no place in a progressive education approach. To dispel any misinterpretation, Freire stated that lectures that are engaging and challenge students to think more deeply about a particular topic certainly have a place in teaching/learning processes, especially if they are combined with questions and dialogues. He claimed that when he criticized "banking education," he was not referring to the expository lesson, because for him the real evil was not the lecture format itself but the type of teacher/student relationship that relied exclusively on information transfer, regarded students as recipients, and negated the possibility of dialogue and critical thinking. Indeed, for Freire, the central issue is not "lecture or no lecture" but the content and dynamism of the lecture, and the extent to which the lecture precludes or nurtures discussion and critical thinking (Freire 1987:40; Freire and Guimaraes 1984).

The second confusion relates to the exact meaning of "dialogical education." Does this mean that the teacher is just one more member of the group and that teachers and learners have similar roles and responsibilities? To a large extent, this confusion, which brings us back to the tensions between directiveness and nondirectiveness, can be attributed to certain ambiguous passages in Freire's texts. Consider, for instance, this paragraph in chapter 3 of *Pedagogy of the Oppressed*:

> Through dialogue, the teacher-of-the-students and the students-of-the-teacher cease to exist and a new term emerges: teacher-student with students-teachers. The teacher is no longer merely the-one-who-teaches, but one who is himself taught in dialogue with the

students, who in turn while being taught also teach. They become responsible for a process in which all grow . . . Here, no one teaches another, nor is anyone self-taught. People teach each other, mediated by the world. (Freire 1970b:80)

The literary style of Freire in this paragraph can lead to misunderstandings. Expressions such as "the-teacher-of-the-students cease to exist" to ensure that "no one teaches another" and "people teach each other, mediated by the world" may be powerful images, but they do not necessarily convey a clear description of the specific role of the teacher in the liberatory education model. It is not surprising, then, that some commentators have included Freire in the nondirective education movement. Freire was asked time and again about this, and he emphasized on several occasions that teachers and students have different roles in the educational process, and that his main concern was about authoritarianism and disrespect:

I have never said that the educator is the same as the pupil. Quite the contrary . . . The educator is different from the pupil. But this difference . . . must not be antagonistic. The difference becomes antagonistic when the authority of the educator, different from the freedom of the pupil, is transformed in authoritarianism. (Freire et al. 1988:76)

Revisiting the issue in *Pedagogy of Hope*, Freire illustrates this concept with an example from a culture circle in Chile in the 1960s. After the peasants in the circle told Freire that he knew things whereas they were ignorant, Freire challenged them to a "knowledge game." Freire asked them: "What is the Socratic maieutic?" Nobody could answer, and Freire scored one point. Then he invited them to ask him a question, and a peasant said: "What is a contour curve?" The game was tied at one-one. They continued playing the game with questions on Hegel, intransitive verbs, and epistemology on one side and questions on soil liming, green fertilizers, and erosion on the other until they got to ten to ten. For Freire, this is a key aspect of the teaching/learning process: when learners recognize themselves not as ignorant objects but as cognizant subjects. For him, teaching and learning are moments in the larger process of knowing—that is, cognizing, which also implies re-recognizing (Freire 1994b:46–7).

Freire argued that respecting students does not mean leaving them to their own fate. This, he argued, would equate with laissez faire—that is, the refusal of teachers to accept their responsibility to education. He also expressed concern about the potential for manipulation that exists in nondirective approaches. He argued that when teachers call themselves facilitators, they distort reality because they create the illusion that the "teacher turned facilitator" has no institutional power. The reality is that although they may conceal their power, they can exercise it any time they want. In navigating these power asymmetries, progressive educators must live with the tension between authority and freedom. The challenge, then, is to find an appropriate balance between directiveness and democracy, avoiding the risks of both laissez faire and domestication. Freire's suggestion is to accept the directive nature of education without manipulating students and, at the same time, accept the democratic nature of education without leaving students to themselves (Shor and Freire 1987:157, Freire and Macedo 1996:201).

This raises a related issue that also led to misunderstandings. If we accept the directive nature of education, should teachers reveal their ideological and political positions to students, or should they hide them? Freire's position on this conundrum could be summed up as "disclosing, but not imposing." In his own words: "the issue is how to teach without imposing on students our own knowledge, and our political and ideological options, but also without omitting them. I don't hide my options from the students. But I also respect their choices" (Freire 1984c:520). Or, as he said on another occasion, "we must say to the students what we think and why. My role is not to be silent. I have to convince students of my dreams but not conquer them for my own plans (Shor and Freire 1987:157). Freire's argument is that when teachers do not reveal their positions to the students openly and explicitly, they do so covertly and implicitly, and this can easily lead to deceiving and manipulating students under auspices of neutrality. Insofar as Freire argues that education cannot be neutral, it follows that it is as unethical for teachers to hide their positions from their students as it is to impose their ideas on them. The challenge for teachers, then, is to be honest and open in revealing their thoughts and values and, at the same time, to respect students who have different opinions: "There is no more ethical or truly democratic road than one in which we reveal to learners how we think, why we think the way we do, our dreams, the dreams for which we will fight, while giving them concrete proof that we respect their opinions, even when they are opposed to our own" (Freire 1998b:40).

Summary and conclusions

Throughout his lifetime, Paulo Freire was involved in different capacities in a variety of educational and political projects around the world. He also produced an extensive literature that addressed a diversity of issues. For perhaps two reasons, these arguments are not necessarily organized in a closed and coherent theoretical corpus. The first is the eclectic nature of Freire's framework: his works were inspired by several traditions (especially Christian humanism, Marxist humanism, existentialism, and the progressive school movement) that were sometimes nicely reconciled in a consistent unit and sometimes were not. The second reason is that, in his texts, Freire did not always present his arguments and concepts in a clear, rigorous, and systematic fashion: sometimes he resorted to a language that was more literary than academic and to a writing style that was more flowery, metaphorical, and verbose than the usual scholarly language. This could be seen as a weakness but also a strength in terms of communication with readers, especially considering that Freire did not write for academic audiences. To recapitulate, the gist of Freire's argument can be summarized in ten main points:

1. Unlike other animals, humans are conscious beings who exist in a dialectical relationship between the determination of limits and their own freedom.[31] Humans and society are not predetermined but unfinished and thus represent a continuous work in progress. Humans have an ontological vocation to be subjects who act to transform the world and who seek to become fully human. Freire refers to this as the struggle for humanization, and emphasizes the role of human agency in this struggle. The unfinished character of human beings and society has ethical and pedagogical implications. The transformational character of reality requires education as a permanent activity.

2. Oppression occurs along lines of class, gender, race, ethnicity, and other factors. All these forms of domination and discrimination should be challenged in a liberatory education model. According to the specificity of each type of oppression, identity politics and the isolation of struggles tend to erode the building of a more powerful movement, to emphasize the differences among oppressed people rather than their shared humanity, and to limit the effectiveness of collective struggle against oppression. The goal of this collective struggle is not to invert the oppressed/oppressor social positions so that the former oppressed become the new oppressors, but to build together a more human and democratic society without exploitation and exclusions.

3. Education is always political, and cannot be neutral. It sides either with the interests of the oppressed or with the interests of the oppressor. Education can be used not only to reinforce and reproduce unequal social structures but also to transform them. Education, then, is a site of conflict that reflects broader societal struggles between forces of reproduction and forces of transformation.

4. Banking education, an oppressive structure based on domination and cultural invasion, creates a "culture of silence" and negates people's ontological vocation to be more fully human. Banking education treats students as objects and is based on a model of unidirectional transmission of information. As a result of banking education and many years of domination and alienation, the oppressed have internalized oppressive structures as natural, and because they "house" the oppressor inside themselves, they fear freedom. This results in general feelings of fatalism and helplessness.

5. Conversely, problem-posing (or liberatory) education draws from a long tradition of progressive education theories and practices and affirms learners as subjects and as active beings in the process of becoming. This type of education brings together the act of knowing existing knowledge and the act of creating new knowledge. Liberatory education is based on dialogue and on active learning in a constant cycle of reflection and action to transform the world. A central element of this cycle of praxis is

the process of conscientization (awareness raising), which implies transit from a magical or semi-intransitive consciousness (e.g., "we are poor because it is God's will") to a critical consciousness characterized by a deeper understanding of social, economic, and political contradictions as an alternative explanatory framework to explain oppressive realities. Liberatory education includes recognition not only of larger structures of domination and oppression but also that those structures are historical and hence can be changed by human action. Liberatory education, then, involves both the denunciation of oppressive structures and the annunciation of a less oppressive world and hence is prophetic and hopeful. Liberatory education also implies the construction of popular power through democratic organizations and coalitions.

6. In terms of political strategies for social change, the first operating principle should be "unity in diversity" and not "identity politics." People are oppressed along different lines such as class, sex, race, ethnicity, and sexual orientation, and the most effective strategy to struggle against oppression is to form alliances and coalitions that respect internal differences. The second operating principle is a permanent effort to widen and deepen democracy. Widening democracy relates to the expansion of rights not only in terms of legislation but also in terms of effective policies and practices that ensure the fulfillment of those rights. Deepening democracy relates to spaces of dialogue and participation in deliberation and decision making—that is, participatory democracy.

7. The political nature of education does not mean that the more practical, instrumental side of education should be neglected. Indeed, as shown in the literacy circles, it is possible to combine "the reading of the word with the reading of the world" and "the reading of the text and the reading of the context." A clear example of this combination is the literacy program based on generative words, which was very successful in the "reading of the word" (learners became literate in 6 weeks to 2 months) and also in the "reading of the world" (adults became politically literate, which was why the military sent Freire to jail and to exile). The choice of generative words was based on a social rationale (relevance to participants) and a technical rationale (linguistic criteria).

8. Education is directive. Teachers have a role different from students and should exercise their authority without being authoritarian, in a democratic and respectful manner. Democracy, however, does not mean a laissez faire model in which students are left alone in their learning. Teachers are expected to recognize the knowledge and experience of their students and to be guided by an ethic of love. Teachers are also expected to have control over their subject matter, not their students. They should not only help students to critically apprehend knowledge but also awaken their curiosity and act as role models and support. They should not hide their stance on issues but should respect students who think differently, "disclosing but not imposing." The main challenge is to find an appropriate balance of directiveness and democracy.

9. Liberatory education can occur in any educational space, not only in adult literacy classes but also in schools, colleges, and universities. Unlike the deschooling movement, Freire believed that it was possible to democratize the formal education system by creating inclusive structures of participation, deliberation, and decision making that involved teachers, parents, students, administrators, staff, and community members. A democratic education system requires schools to be not only more democratic but also more effective and enjoyable. Educators who are seeking a more just, democratic, and human world should reject both determinism (the idea that the only possible role of education is to reproduce the dominant ideology and has no significant role in social change) and voluntarism (the idea that education has the power to change everything). Moreover, they should have an ethical commitment to side with the oppressed and to encourage liberatory education efforts.

10. More democratic, effective, and enjoyable schools require teachers who are generous, committed, democratic, and knowledgeable and who do not dichotomize cognition and emotion. Teachers are critical cultural workers, and as such, they should recognize the dominant values that are present in society, in themselves, and in their students. Teachers should be not only critical but also competent, because professional incompetence destroys

the legitimate authority of the teacher. Teaching is a profession that should be treated with dignity, and teachers deserve respect from society and support from the government. Teachers should be well paid, well trained, and in constant development. Professional development opportunities should be organized around collective exercises of reflection on practice that are complemented by technical advice from mentors attached to specialized government agencies.

This summary is obviously not comprehensive but hopefully provides a useful recapitulation of Freire's ideas and proposals discussed in this chapter. It is true that some of Freire's arguments were not necessarily original, but he recognized the sources from which he drew them, and he used them as scaffolding for his overall theory, combining them in novel and imaginative ways. In retrospect, probably the most important contribution that Freire made to education was to establish explicit connections between education, power, and politics; to situate this discussion within an ethical and philosophical framework that emphasized human agency, justice, and freedom; and to complement this with concrete methodological suggestions emanating from practice together with a message of hope and possibility.

As noted before, in his interviews, lectures, and publications, Freire addressed a great variety of topics, and the emphasis that he paid to those topics at different times of his life can be related to the particular context in which they attracted his attention. In this regard, when we look at the topics that dominated Freire's writings, we can distinguish two main periods. In his first works, during the 1960s and 1970s, Freire dealt mainly with issues related to development, colonialism, culture, communion, adult literacy, rural extension, teacher/student relationship, oppression, cultural invasion, liberation, revolution, and language. This choice of topics is understandable if we consider his activities in those decades: engagement with the Catholic Action movement, literacy work with peasants and workers in northeast Brazil, exile in Chile as a result of military coup, encounter with Marxism, work in rural development, collaboration in literacy campaigns of new revolutionary governments in Latin America and in African multilingual states, and so forth. It is also understandable if we take into account the political and ideological context of that period, characterized by an ascendance of counterculture and revolutionary movements that believed in the desirability and the feasibility of radical social transformation.

Freire's later works during the 1980s and 1990s were influenced by his scholarly activities and his responsibilities as secretary of education. He began to address other theoretical issues (such as postmodernism and interlocking oppressions), to revisit critically his earlier work, to engage in autobiographical exercises, to examine new political and economic realities (e.g., globalization and neoliberal policies), and to position himself in relation to those developments, calling for both denunciation and annunciation, that is, a pedagogy of indignation and a pedagogy of hope. In this period, he also dealt with topics related to educational policy, educational administration, and school reform, including curriculum, teacher education, professional development, school autonomy, mentorship, school councils, decentralization, and leadership. Again, these choices of topics cannot be isolated from Freire's particular location and the general context of that period. As to what he was doing, he was, among other things, a university professor and a government official. As to where he was living, he was in a Brazil that was in transition to democracy after many years of dictatorship but that, at the same time, was part and parcel of economic globalization trends promoting market-oriented policies.

It is important to caution, then, that the different arguments and ideas discussed by Paulo Freire in his works should not be frozen and regarded out of the historical context in which they were produced. Moreover, Freire's work evolved over time, and his ideas changed, sometimes significantly. His methodological contributions should not be regarded as recipes to be transported and implemented anywhere, but as proposals to be adapted and contextualized. His ideas should not be considered as dogmas, but as inputs for discussion and for adaptation to different realities. Last but not least, his methodologies cannot be divorced from the larger philosophical, epistemological, and political framework that guided his thought and practice. For him, the first priority for an educator was to address questions about human beings and about the world, and the issue of methods should be considered later.

Notes

1 Of interest, Freire also wrote poetry. For instance, in 1971 in Geneva he wrote the poem "Obvious Song," in which he talks about waiting, arrivals, and action.

2 I agree with this statement, but we should recall that Freire often praised his English translators for the fine job they were doing with his books.

3 Freire wanted to make sure that his books were accessible to the public, and convinced the publisher of his last book to publish 30,000 copies and to sell it at three reales (three US dollars) so that teachers could readily buy it without budgetary constraints.

4 In colonial Brazil, the term *mocambo* (or *quilombo*) referred to small communities organized by fugitive slaves located in inaccessible areas. In Freire's time, the term referred to huts, simple structures built with local materials in the coastal region of northeast Brazil (Freire 1996:207).

5 Although in this early work Freire focused mainly on adult education, he would eventually adapt these ideas to the formal education system.

6 For Gerhardt (1993:442), the committee's decision was not surprising considering the criticisms to Brazilian universities advanced in the thesis.

7 "Perdí a cátedra e ganhei a vida"; cited in Rosas 2001.

8 ISEB lasted less than a decade. It was created in 1955 as a think thank to design and legitimize the model of economic development of Kubitschek's government, and was forced to close after the 1964 coup d'etat. For a discussion of ISEB's influence in Freire's ideas on development and education, see Paiva 1980.

9 This innovation opened the path for participatory research, which became popular in Latin America during the late 1970s, after a conference organized in Colombia by Orlando Fals Borda.

10 For instance, letters that are silent in Portuguese and Spanish, like h or u in between "g" and "e" (e.g., "guitarra," "guerra," "hospital," "ahora") were avoided in the initial sessions to avoid unnecessary complications. Likewise, less commonly used letters like x, q, z, and k were introduced later.

11 Brown (1974:22) lists the generative words used in four different contexts. In three of them, the first words are tijolo (brick) and voto (vote). As we will see in Chapter 3, this has raised questions about the role of Freire's team in the construction of the lists (see Gerhardt 1989, Taylor 1993).

12 For Freire, total intransitivity is not a form of consciousness at all.

13 On page 157, Freire describes a situation in which a group in a New York ghetto was presented a coded situation showing a pile of garbage on a street corner. Participants thought that the image reflected a street in Africa or Latin America, "because we are in the United States and that can't happen here," without recognizing that the picture corresponded to

the same street where the group was meeting. Freire argued that participants "were retreating from a reality so offensive to them that even to acknowledge that reality was threatening."

14 The transformation experienced by learners in their path toward critical consciousness, particularly regarding the examination of their own assumptions, would be later explored by theories of transformative learning.

15 The English version would be published several years later, together with another essay ("Extension or Communication") under the title *Education for Critical Consciousness*. In reviewing Freire's work during this period, it is important to remember that he wrote *Pedagogy of the Oppressed* after *Education for Critical Consciousness*, but in English they were published in reverse order. Hence, those interested in tracing Freire's evolution may benefit from reading *Education for Critical Consciousness* before *Pedagogy of the Oppressed*.

16 Freire didn't want to contribute to the myth that a critical awareness of the world was the magic wand that would transform complex social realities, and for this reason he refrained from using the word conscientization for many years (Gerhardt 1993).

17 Here it is possible to observe the influence of social psychologist and humanistic philosopher Erich Fromm, particularly through *Fear of Freedom* (1941) and *The Heart of Man* (1964).

18 Jean Paul Sartre (1947).

19 Freire was inspired by the insights of the "prophetic Church," known as church of the oppressed, which had a preferential option for the poor, was committed to radical social change, and had links to liberation theology.

20 For his reflections on those experiences, see Vieira Pinto (1982).

21 For Jaspers, limit situations (*Grenzsituationen*) are moments of implosion associated with negative experiences such as death, guilt, suffering, or acute anxiety, in which the human mind confronts the restrictions and of its existing forms and enters into a different consciousness. In these moments, humans reach a higher and more unified level of reflection (Tornhill 2002:91).

22 In *Pedagogy of the Oppressed*, Freire uses the term "communion" (following the Christian notion of the communion between people and God) to refer to the fusion between leaders and people, an encounter characterized by love, trust, cooperation, genuine dialogue, and solidarity.

23 Fromm observed that the educational practices proposed in *Pedagogy of the Oppressed* constituted a kind of historicocultural, political psychoanalysis.

24 As noted in chapter 2 of *Pedagogy of the Oppressed*, Freire's model of conscientization drew insights from French philosophers André Nicolai and Lucien Goldmann. Nicolai (1960) developed the notions of "perceived practicable solutions" and "unperceived practicable solutions." The notion

of "unperceived practicable solutions" inspired Freire to develop the concept of "inédito viable," or untested feasibility. Goldmann (1966) distinguished between "real consciousness" and "potential consciousness," and argued that people could move from the stage of "real consciousness" to the stage of "potential consciousness" through "testing actions."

25　Despite becoming internationally famous, Freire did not lose his humility. When asked why his books were quickly becoming bestsellers, Freire (1975a) noted jokingly that he was just a "pilgrim of the obvious," in the sense that all he was doing was "saying obvious things, which a lot of people have inside them, but which they have not been able to express."

26　For a discussion of IDAC's initiatives during the late 1970s, see Freire et al. 1983.

27　Weiler (1996:359) mistakenly stated that Freire advocated the use of Portuguese as the language for literacy instruction.

28　Clientelism, or patronage, refers to the use of state resources to reward individuals and groups (usually from low-income communities) with jobs, infrastructure, money, or other benefits in exchange for political support.

29　The title refers to the tree under which Freire learned to read when he was a child. Freire uses the metaphor of the mango tree to discuss the main themes of the book.

30　For a discussion on the logic of this translation, see Clarke 1998.

31　This argument is a slight reformulation of Marx's famous distinction between animals and humans in the opening pages of chapter 7 (Vol. 1) of *The Capital*, in which he compares the labor processes of humans and bees.

Chapter 3

The Reception and Influence of Freire's Work

Introduction: "The million Paulo Freires"

In an article aptly entitled "The Million Paulo Freires," Rosa María Torres (1999) noted that Freire's ideas and positions generated strong sentiments, passionate adherents and rejecters, and very different interpretations, sometimes diametrically opposed. She observed that for some Freire was a romantic and idealist ideologue without a clear political base and whose proposal for social transformation was vague and lacked scientific rigor, while for others he was a revolutionary who suffered persecution and developed a complex and advanced educational philosophy, theory, and praxis.

Indeed, the first thing that could be said about the reception and influence of Freire's work is that it has not been ignored. This is not trivial: to the best of my knowledge, no other educational thinker from the global south had attracted such a wide international attention to his or her ideas. Moreover, Freire's books were read with interest by many people located in different theoretical disciplines and fields of practice, something unusual for texts dealing with educational issues. His ideas were seldom impassively analyzed. On the contrary, they often generated intense debates and passionate reactions, ranging from profound admiration to harsh criticism. Throughout his life, Freire responded to most of those criticisms. Sometimes he agreed with them, in which case he accepted them as valid, reconsidered his original assumptions, and modified his proposals accordingly. Sometimes he did not agree with the critiques, in which case he often engaged in vigorous but respectful debate with those with whom he disagreed. Many of his proposals have inspired individuals, groups, and organizations all around the world to carry out a great variety of pedagogical initiatives during the last three decades. He did not believe in disciples that would spread his ideas like a gospel. As per his request, after his death his ideas are being "reinvented," and this includes not only theoretical discussions and debates, but also practical issues related to the implementation of a variety of projects and programs all over the world.

The public recognition of his work has taken different forms. The first significant official acknowledgment arguably took place in the early 1960s when President Goulart, recognizing Freire's pioneering work with the circles of culture and literacy circles in northeast Brazil, appointed him as president of the National Commission on Popular Culture and invited him to implement a national literacy campaign. The second significant recognition of his career came in the early 1970s, when he was invited first to teach at Harvard and then to act as special educational advisor to the World Congress of Churches, and *Pedagogy of the Oppressed* turned into a major influence in the pedagogical revolution of the second half of the twentieth century, comparable to the contributions made by John Dewey during the first half (C. A. Torres 1998b). This was one of the very few education books to become an instant best seller and, eventually, a classic, translated into many languages and reprinted numerous times. During the 1970s, he was invited to collaborate with educational campaigns, especially in Africa and Latin America, and was recognized as an inspirational figure by popular education movements around the world. Some authoritarian governments, recognizing the emancipatory implications of Freire's educational theories and initiatives with their potential for furthering democracy and nurturing social change, censored his work and banished him. The Brazilian military regime promptly jailed Freire and sent him into exile for 15 years. In the early 1970, Chilean dictator Augusto Pinochet declared Freire "persona non grata,"[1] and the apartheid regime of South Africa as well as the authoritarian governments of Spain and Portugal censored his books. In 1976, the Argentinean military junta collected his publications from bookstores and public libraries and burned them.[2] But by the late 1980s, Freire's work received an important positive recognition in his native land when he was invited to put his ideas into practice as secretary of education of the largest Brazilian city.

Freire also received dozens of honorary doctoral degrees from universities around the world and won several prizes, including the

Reza Pahlevi United Nations Educational, Scientific and Cultural Organization (UNESCO) award for literacy (Persepolis 1975), the King Balduin Prize for International Development (Belgium 1980), the UNESCO Peace Prize (Paris 1987), the Comenius Medal (Czech Republic 1994), and the Paulo Freire Award of the International Consortium Learning (Washington, D.C. 1994). He also received, together with his wife Elza, the prize of outstanding Christian educators, awarded to them by the Association of Christian Educators of the United States in 1985. The UNESCO award for literacy provides a good illustration of both the international reception and the influence of Freire's ideas. Only 5 years after the first English edition of *Pedagogy of the Oppressed,* Freire was invited to make a presentation at the International Symposium for Literacy that took place in Persepolis in 1975. The final document of this symposium (*The Persepolis Declaration*), was so influential in adult education circles that it was called "a turning point for literacy" (Bataille 1976). In turn, the declaration was clearly influenced by Freire's approach to adult literacy. Consider, for instance, the following three passages of the declaration and compare them to the language used by Freire in his first publications:

> Literacy creates the conditions for the acquisition of a critical consciousness of the contradictions of society . . . it also stimulates initiative and participation in the creation of projects capable of acting upon the world, of transforming it, and of defining the aims of an authentic human development.

> Literacy, like education in general, is not the driving force of historical change. It is not the only means of liberation, but it is an essential instrument for all social change.

> Literacy work, like education in general, is a political act. It is not neutral, for the act of revealing social reality in order to transform it, or of concealing it in order to preserve it, is political.

By the early 1990s, Paul Taylor, who otherwise had criticized Freire's approach on several counts, recognized that "Freire has occupied a pivotal place in the formulation of education campaigns around the Third World, and his influence on other European and North American educators has been considerable" (Taylor 1993:149). The following year, John Elias (1994) noted that "Freire is probably the best known educator in the world today: no other educator in recent history has had his books read by as many persons in as many places of the world."

Immediately after his death in May 1997, the Paulo Freire Institute of Sao Paulo received more than 600 messages of condolence from all over the world, including professors from some 150 universities. Later that year, *Taboo: The Journal of Culture and Education* devoted a special issue to Freire that included articles and tributes from many countries. In May 1998, the *New Zealand Journal of Adult Learning* published a special issue on his contributions, and the journal *Convergence* (a publication of the International Council for Adult Education) produced a double issue entitled *A Tribute to Paulo Freire*.[3] In 2001, the Spanish edition of the "biobliography" was published (Gadotti and Torres 1997). Since then, a plethora of books, articles, and theses have been published and many conferences and seminars organized around his lifetime contributions. There are so many that it would be almost impossible to cite them all. Moreover, in the last two decades, many people who I barely knew revealed to me, unprompted, that the work of Freire had been tremendously influential in their educational ideas and practices, and called my attention to community projects inspired by Freire's approach that are often unknown outside of their immediate milieu. Recently, for instance, a woman from El Salvador mentioned her involvement in Freirean-inspired projects in her home country and in North America; a woman from the Philippines recalled her involvement—with a group of teachers inspired by *Pedagogy of the Oppressed*—in a community-based preschool and popular education project in the mid-1980s that was welcomed by the community despite its fear of the Marcos dictatorship; and a young woman from Chile told me how her generation has rediscovered Freire and is using his ideas in community development projects in rural areas.

Currently, over a decade after Freire's death, most of his books are still in print, and web-based searches put Freire among the most frequently cited authors in the field of education. Writing at the time of Freire's death, Coben (1998) said that there were very few adult educators anywhere in the world who had not heard of Paulo Freire, even if they had not read his writings. His international influence is also evident in the way that his name is used to identify institutes, research centers, schools, and community organizations in over 45 countries (Fischman 2009). Freire's impact is also evident in the numerous debates that his intellectual and practical contributions have generated, and in the lively exchanges between those who agree with him and those who critically (sometimes vehemently) argue against him. Indeed, the bibliography of Freire's work amounts to thousands of references and is constantly increasing. As I write these lines, my office is overcrowded with hundreds of books, theses, articles, interviews, and videos that engage directly with Paulo Freire, and I have difficulty catching up with the pace of new publications released every month in different languages and formats (printed and electronic).

Another growing body of literature consists of comparative analyses between Freire's ideas and the ideas of other thinkers, not only from education but also from other disciplines as well. As we shall see in Chapter 4, there is no shortage of comparative studies. Furthermore, for four decades, Freire's work has been examined in thousands of theses around the world.[4] The topics of these theses cover a variety of theoretical and practical issues, including the potential and limits of conscientization (Martin 1975, Schipani 1981, Sloop 1987, Waldow 1992, Slaner 2004), faith education and liberation theology (Beveridge 1984, O'Meara 1988, Organ 2002, Bower 2003, L. F. Smith 2005), educational reform in Sao Paulo (Lindquist 1994, O'Cadiz 1996), the teaching of mathematics and physics in high schools (Ahmadifar 2000, Basu 2006, Brantlinger 2007), literacy in Africa (Harasim 1983), health (Peach 1975, O'Neill, M. 1986, Wallerstein 1988, Ramos 1999, Payne 2001), theater (Evenson 1995, Houden 1997, Byam 1996, Jung 2008), school bullying (Rhone 2008), the role of conscientization in social work (Pinkus 1994), community building in an alcoholics anonymous group (Reed-Jones 1993), transformative adult education (Mayo 1994), prison education (Craig 1981, Stern 1994, Tilley 1998, Crouse 2000, Brazil 2007), peace building (Durnan 2005, Klein 2007), and the influence of Freire's ideas in different countries (Rafi 2003, Nuryatno 2006). Freire's work has also been influential in several aspects of theory and practice, particularly popular education, critical pedagogy, postcolonial studies, urban education, and popular theater. Of most significance perhaps,

Freire's influence is to be found in thousands of past and present educational projects (both in schools and in communities, many of them undocumented) that have drawn on his ideas and proposals so as to make a positive difference in the lives of thousands of people. Many of these efforts still remain undocumented.

This chapter is organized in six sections. To provide some context, I first advance several considerations about the reception of Freire's work. Then, I raise some tentative hypotheses to explain the influence of Freire's ideas. In the third section, I briefly discuss the first reactions to Freire's work, particularly after the release of *Education as Practice of Freedom* and *Pedagogy of the Oppressed*. In the fourth section, I present the main criticisms of Freire's works and ideas. In the fifth section, I include some responses to those criticisms. In the final section, I provide a summary and conclusions.

The reception of Freire's work: preliminary considerations

Before discussing the reception and influence of Paulo Freire's work, I would like to advance four considerations. The first is that Freire's publications encompassed four decades and many publications. This is important, because most of the literature on Freire (both pro and con) tends to focus on the first period—particularly on *Pedagogy of the Oppressed*—without recognizing the changes of his ideas over time. This is something that frustrated Freire, who was often asked to clarify the same issues.[5] He explained that each one of his books represents a particular moment in his evolution and reveals points of development in his thinking (Freire 1985a:180). As R. M. Torres (1999:245) commented: "apologists and critics denied him in the end the right to err and to rectify, to advance and to perfect, to continue developing his thoughts, as must be allowed to any person and as is required by any serious and honest intellectual." Along the same lines, Roberts (2000) lamented the decontextualized, fragmented, and distorted character of many commentators of Freire's work, both among those who considered themselves "Freireans" and among those who were his detractors. If we examine Freire's lifetime publications, we can identify at least two distinct periods. His first writings, during the 1960s and 1970s, dealt with issues of development, colonialism, culture circles, adult literacy, rural extension, teacher/student relationship, oppression, power, revolution, and language, with a focus on the global south. In the second period, during the 1980s and 1990s, Freire did not abandon completely those topics, but incorporated issues of educational policy, school reform, curriculum, teacher education, and educational administration—both in developing and developed countries. In these last two decades, he also favored dialogue books, with interlocutors from both developing and developed countries. More significantly, in his later publications he acknowledged some of the points made by his critics, corrected several of his original formulations, and developed new contributions and insights.

A second issue is the tendency to elevate Freire into a myth, a guru, a radical hero, or an academic god.[6] This has two modes of expression. The first is to believe that almost all the concepts and formulations used by Freire in his books were completely original. Some admirers have gone so far as to credit him with ideas that may have inspired him but obviously preceded him, such as respect for learners and their knowledge, the acknowledgement of learners' reality as the starting point for the educational process, the importance of dialogue as a pedagogical tool, and even terms like praxis and conscientization[7] (R. M. Torres 1999). Although Freire never claimed to have invented these terms or ideas and several times made clear that he hadn't, some people still attribute to him certain ideas and concepts that have a longer history. The second expression of this tendency is the expectation that the "guru" will have answers to all the calamities afflicting the planet. Furter (1985) cautioned about the dangers of this attitude, arguing that when people become myths in their lifetime, as did Freire, the more they publish and the more comments their works generate, the more difficult it becomes to distinguish the one from the other. Freire felt particularly uncomfortable being regarded as a guru by followers who were applying his proposals uncritically and dogmatically without making any effort to adapt them to their own context. With the difficulty of distinguishing between Freire as a person and Freire as a myth, observed Furter, we cannot tell whether the ideas we associate with him are to be counted among his intentions, practical achievements, and successes and failures, or whether they are simply what he has come to represent in the minds of his contemporaries. This is a crucial point, which led Furter to conclude that Freire was being asked to provide a universal panacea to all the educational ills of our time, and was regarded as a guru who offers solutions to problems of which he was not even aware. The problems associated with turning Freire into a fetish had also negative consequences for debates on his ideas, because it limits the scope for disagreements and critical challenges (Coben 1998). It should be noted that Freire himself expressed frustration over this situation. Gerhardt (1993) reported that Freire was worried about becoming the "guru" of an international community of followers who saw in his work the new evangelism of liberation. On the contrary, he was happy to engage in honest and stimulating intellectual debates, especially within progressive circles (Gadotti 1994, Roberts 2000). Along the same lines, Kincheloe (1997:viii) revealed that in his personal interactions with Freire, "he was genuinely thrilled by the frank critiques of those who shared his democratic and pedagogical passions."

The third issue is the demonization of Freire's work in some circles. If the fetishization of Freire consists in asking him to be all things to all people and to have appropriate responses to all problems, his demonization consists in accusing him of contributing to many of the world's problems (e.g., colonialism, cultural invasion, or alleged declines in student achievement), in denying him of any originality, or in indicting him for problematic aspects in the implementation of programs inspired by his ideas. The fourth consideration relates to the reduction of Freire's theories to a simple pedagogical method (Araujo Freire and Macedo 1998). This has led to a process in which his ideas are "watered down," co-opted and subjected to domestication. By "taming" Freire's radical proposals, his overall theoretical analysis and political/pedagogical approach are reduced to a set of group dynamics and student-led projects (Aronowitz 1993, Findsen 1998, Glass 2001, Borg and Mayo 2002, Fischman 2009). As Roberts (2000:13) pointed out, "this has led to a proliferation of supposedly Freirean courses and programs where teachers, often with the best of intentions, have assumed that modifications in teacher-student roles and changes in subject matter suffice as examples of liberating education." Indeed, it has been argued that Freire's works have been stripped of their politics and appropriated by a wide range of actors, including social democratic governments in

Europe, authoritarian socialist movements in Africa and Latin America, reformist poverty programs in North America, and more recently neoliberal governments in different parts of the world (Gibson, 1994:11; CCD 2001; Nkomo 1999).

Why did *Pedagogy of the Oppressed* become an instant best seller?

The introduction to this chapter provided clear evidence of the influence of Freire's work around the world. Particularly puzzling is that *Pedagogy of the Oppressed,* a book written in the late 1960s in Chile by a Brazilian educator, became an instant best seller worldwide, and has remained popular ever since. Why was this book so influential? This is a pertinent question, especially considering that some of his ideas were not particularly original and that Freire explicitly rejected the idea of having "disciples" that would be in charge of "spreading the word."[8] I have six tentative explanations—not mutually exclusive—to address this question.

One possible explanation is that Freire's almost instant success with *Pedagogy of the Oppressed* rests not only on its own merits (which are many), but also in the historical context at the time of its publication whereby it was able to overcome the paralyzing effects of both the excessive optimism of the 1960s and the unwarranted pessimism of the 1970s (Gadotti 1994). On the one hand, the *pedagogism* of the 1960s expected, somehow naïvely, that schools would solve all social troubles, and such misplaced optimism resulted in feelings of impotence and frustration among many educators. On the other hand, the *reproductionist* theories of the 1970s conceptualized the "educational apparatus" as a tool of domination for reproducing unequal social relations, and this led many educators concerned with social justice and democracy to surrender to despair and abandon educational activities, or to advocate for the deschooling of society. In this context, Freire was able to offer not only a critique but also an alternative. Indeed, his approach recognized both the possibilities and limits of education, going beyond voluntarism ("education can do everything") and paralysis ("education can do nothing").

A second explanation, which complements the first and puts the publication of *Pedagogy of the Oppressed* in historical context, is that Freire emphasized the role of education in social transformation at a time characterized by intense social conflicts, military coups, revolutionary activity, anticolonial resistance, radical proposals, and the ascendance of a variety of social and counterculture movements that included liberation theology and antiracist, feminist, radical humanist, environmentalist, peace, and deschoooling movements. At the same time, some influential writings of that era portrayed the system as all-powerful (e.g., Althusser's structural analysis, Marcuse's *One Dimensional Man,* and Illich's *Deschooling Society*) and presented a rather pessimistic view about the possibilities of social change. Moreover, at that time, most educational publications and debates were isolated from these political and social upheavals and were still centered almost exclusively on issues related to content, objectives, methodologies, evaluation, and other curriculum-related topics. In that context, Freire's call for hope, his vision of utopia, and his faith in human agency represented a much more welcome and inspirational message more in tune with what was needed at the time. With his writings, he ignited the imagination of many by keeping a vision of utopia, not in the sense of idealistic, impossible and impractical vision but in the sense of dreaming possible and attainable dreams and acting upon them (Araujo Freire 2006, Gadotti 1994, Gadotti and Torres 1997, R. M. Torres 1999, Roberts 2000).[9] His concept of "untested feasibility" captured well the notion of grounded hope, recognizing structural limits but at the same time placing an emphasis on human agency. Moreover, the idea that education could play a key role in social change by nurturing, through dialogue, a critical consciousness and a transformative collective praxis was certainly appealing to an entire generation of radical thinkers, activists, and educators. Finally, his argument that education could challenge oppression and nurture liberation appealed to many who understood education to be not only a technical activity guided by curricular content and methods but also a pedagogical and political project guided by an ethical commitment to full humanization and social justice.

A third explanation can be found in the universal and transdisciplinary nature of Freire's ideas advanced in *Pedagogy of the Oppressed.* Although his universal claims have generated criticism from some quarters, it also helps to explain why his message resonated with readers from different countries, who interpreted the dichotomy between oppressors and oppressed in terms of their own contexts and their own struggles. At the same time, his transdisciplinarity helps to explain why his interpretations were so attractive to a wide range of people coming from different ideological and epistemological traditions (humanists, Marxists, Christians, existentialists, phenomenologists, progressive educators, etc.) and disciplinary backgrounds (education, psychology, sociology, philosophy, anthropology, social work, theology, etc.).

A fourth explanation is that the ideas that Freire presented in *Pedagogy of the Oppressed* were not regarded by readers just as abstractions coming from nowhere. Those ideas were granted a high degree of credibility—especially by educators and community organizers—because they were not generated at a university desk but emerged from concrete experience with real people in marginalized communities. The fact that Freire's proposals were not a mere intellectual exercise but a reflection of his practice, coupled with the fact that his practice was considered highly successful in strict pedagogical terms (as reported, for instance, in Cynthia Brown's booklet *Literacy in 30 Hours*) explains why many educators took him seriously.

A fifth explanation for the positive reception of *Pedagogy of the Oppressed* can be found in its pedagogical message, which came at a time in which many educators and students were dissatisfied with traditional pedagogies. In that context, such concepts as "banking education" and "problem-posing education" were appealing because they challenged basic assumptions and taken-for-granted educational practices, and gave educators a new language to review their theories and to implement new approaches. As we noted before, many of Freire's ideas on traditional and alternative pedagogies were not necessarily new (think Rousseau, Dewey, Claparede, Montessori, Milani, Piaget, and Sartre, among others), but he managed to convey them in a novel and clear form that was easy to grasp. Perhaps the reason why Freire was able to convey these concepts in a clear and explicit way stems from his claim that he was "a pilgrim of the obvious" and was saying things that people already knew but were unable to express. In particular, *Pedagogy of the Oppressed* struck a chord with many young progressive educators who felt that they had the intuition but not the language to make the connections between education and politics. The words of Joe Kincheloe (1998:viii) reflect this sentiment: "As an aspiring teacher in my early twenties, I had an inarticulated, immature vision of a proto-critical pedagogy. For me, reading *Pedagogy of the Oppressed* was not merely a lesson in politics and pedagogy but a personal affirmation that I was not alone with my intuitions and passions." Likewise, David Diamond, director of Headlines Theatre, in a special issue on Freire organized by the Journal Taboo in Fall 1997, remembered that when he read *Pedagogy of the Oppressed* he was stunned because Freire had articulated what he knew and felt but did not have the words for.

Last but not least, the impact of *Pedagogy of the Oppressed* can also be explained by Freire's capacity to make not only an intellectual connection with his readers but also an emotional connection, especially with practitioners. As Rosa Maria Torres (1999:245) suggested, the wide appeal of *Pedagogy of the Oppressed* can be attributed to Freire's capacity to communicate, to establish a connection with his readers, and to see the role of education in a different light:

> Maybe the greatest contribution of Paulo Freire is having been able to communicate and connect with so many people—a Babel of ages, races, religious beliefs, economic positions, ideologies, educational backgrounds and professions—and to help them see that there is something called education and something called poverty and oppression, that there is a relationship between the two, and that this can be one of liberation or one of further oppression.

Indeed, the testimonies of several generations of educators indicate that, beyond the validity of criticisms of particular arguments, theoretical assumptions, and methodological approaches presented in *Pedagogy of the Oppressed* and beyond the appropriateness of Freire's responses to his critics, the book has played, and still plays, an inspirational role at the level of educational practice. In the words of Fischman (2009:232):

> Celebrated and attacked with equivalent passion by religious and secular intellectuals, Marxists, feminists, postmodernists, and critical scholars, Freire has been endlessly quoted and misquoted, and yet, his

ideas seem to symbolize and retain a unique appeal, that almost
guarantees that somewhere at this very moment, an educator in a
classroom, in a school playground, or university hall will say, proudly,
that she/he is implementing a Freirean project inspired by the reading
of *Pedagogy of the Oppressed.*

First reactions to *Pedagogy of the Oppressed*

Freire's work attracted national and international attention ever since
his involvement in adult education and community development in
Brazil. As mentioned before, as early as 1962, Ivan Illich extended a trip
to Rio de Janeiro to visit Freire in Recife so that he could learn more
about his circles of culture.[10] In the midst of one of their conversations,
Illich made a prescient comment: "One day you might be better known
than you are today. I think within 10 years your ideas will have entered
a number of places in the world" (cited in Gadotti 1994:113). A few
months later, Paulo confided to his wife Elza that if he continued with
that line of work, in 1 or 2 years he would either attract UNESCO's
interest in his project or end up in prison. Little did he know at that
time that both things were going to happen. Several years later, Illich's
prophecy was fulfilled when *Pedagogy of the Oppressed* became an almost
instant best seller worldwide. Although the book consisted of a theoretical reflection about an adult education project in Brazil, its appeal
was broad and its readership extensive. In universities, *Pedagogy of the
Oppressed* has been used in education courses—such as philosophy of
education, educational administration, or adult education—and in other
disciplines, including theology, sociology, philosophy, social work, and
communications. Moreover, many university professors reported that
Pedagogy of the Oppressed had a profound impact on their thinking about
the world and in some cases changed their lives or their professional
trajectories (e.g., Kincheloe 1997, Murrell 1997, Martin 1998, Mayo
2004). In countries where the book used to be forbidden, people managed to read photocopies in their homes or in study groups organized by
youth, workers, adult educators, teachers, and others. This happened in
several Latin American countries, but similar situations—albeit with
contextual variations—took place in other parts of the world. Consider,

for instance, Siddartha's reminiscences (1999:2) about the circulation of *Pedagogy of the Oppressed* in Asia in the mid-1970s:

> My involvement with the man and his ideas began 25 years ago when a small group of university students called the Free University, of which I was a part, worked till the early hours of the morning to type onto stencils what was a pirated edition of Paulo Freire's classic *Pedagogy of the Oppressed*. By the end of the next day the first hundred copies of the book had rolled off the cyclostyling machine and were made available to discerning Indian readers. We had got hold of the pirated book from the Philippines, a good many years before the Penguin volume was to appear in our bookstores. At the time, Freire's ideas on transformative education and political change made for heady reading, particularly to those who were young, angry and idealistic.

Pedagogy of the Oppressed had a profound impact on the educational activities of the Black Consciousness Movement in South Africa during the antiapartheid struggles, and particularly on Steve Biko who read it in the early 1970s and used to say that the most potent weapon in the hands of the oppressor is the mind of the oppressed (Collins 1974, Nekhwevha 2002). Although *Pedagogy of the Oppressed* discussed educational ideas in the context of adult literacy programs, its early impact also inspired teachers in the formal school system. For instance, Wallace (2008) recalls that in her first years as a teacher in apartheid South Africa she encountered Freire's writings and tried to embody his philosophy of education by pursuing four main goals: the development of learners' ownership of their learning through the investigation of relevant problems and a deepening understanding of social life, the development of dialogue and mutual respect in the interaction between learners and teachers, the development of learners' self-confidence and autonomy in decision making, and the nurturing of their awareness of their own powers of reflective participation in their affairs.

The impact of *Pedagogy of the Oppressed* was not only felt in countries of the global south. In North America, for instance, only 8 years after its first English edition, *Pedagogy of the Oppressed* was already considered one of the "classic texts" of socialist pedagogy, and its second chapter was included in an anthology published by Monthly Review Press (Mills and Ollman 1978). The book inspired grassroots groups in the North American literacy movement, in the English as a Second Language (ESL) community, in labor education circles, and in welfare rights organizations that applied Freirean principles to materials production and to teaching/learning activities (Barndt 1998, Pruyn 1996, Martin 1998, Campfens 1999). In teacher-training programs in US universities, *Pedagogy of the Oppressed* has achieved near-iconic status since its first edition in 1970 (Stern 2009). In Europe, the influence of Freire's work could be traced to the early 1970s, when a pedagogical and political movement inspired by Freire's ideas emerged (Schachtner 1999:124), and a marble sculpture of Freire was installed in a public square of Stockholm in 1972, together with six other personalities who performed exceptional work in the struggle for peace and solidarity (Gadotti 1994). One of the first references to Freire's work could be found in an interview that Ivan Illich did with the German weekly *Der Spiegel* in February 1970. In Spain, Freire's influence was felt even earlier, when a group of young adult educators, in the midst of Franco's dictatorship, managed to access a Portuguese edition of *Education as a Practice of Freedom*. Ramón Flecha, who was part of that group, reported that as a result of those readings they shifted their main pedagogical approach (based on popular theater) to the simultaneous reading of the word and the world. For the next decade, Freire became the main reference for popular movements undertaking cultural literacy projects, and his texts were discussed—often in clandestinity—by Christian communities, progressive education movements, leftist organizations, and libertarian cultural groups. In 1978, inspired by Freire's dialogical approach to education, Flecha founded the Centro La Verneda-Sant Martí, a democratic learning community that still operates in a working-class neighborhood of Barcelona.

In Italy, one of the earliest influences of Freire's ideas on educational practices could be noticed in the pedagogical and methodological approach used by the labor movement in the famous "150 hours" of paid educational leave. This was an entitlement won by workers during contract renewal in 1973 after a trade union survey revealed that approximately 70 percent of Italian workers had not completed basic secondary school. Although the inspiration of the 150 hours labor education movement came from different sources, we should recall that *Pedagogy of the Oppressed* had been published in Italy in 1971 and circulated broadly among progressive educators. Freire's influence can be observed both in the purpose and methods of the 150 hours system. With regard to purpose, the 150 hours system was different from traditional training and retraining because it was not connected to job improvement or individual advancement. It was conceived as a pedagogical-political project to offer basic educational opportunities to workers together with the nurturing of critical awareness and social action. With regard to methodology, the 150 hours used generative themes and an interdisciplinary curriculum. There were no "lessons" taught by teachers through lectures, but instead facilitated study circles. The topics were chosen by common consent. The starting point for the discussion of those topics was the experience and knowledge of circle participants, who would then embark on group projects and research on problems chosen by the collective (De Sanctis 1977).

Also in 1973, a "Paulo Freire Working Group" was created in Hamburg to demand that topics in adult education courses should not be selected arbitrarily by teachers, but derived from the thematic universe of the learners and oriented toward the transformation of consciousness and the collective solution of practical problems. Around that time, an organization called INODEP (Ecumenical Institute for the Development of Peoples) was established in Paris. This organization, inspired by the theory and methodology of Freire's generative themes, developed a methodology called *enquête conscientizante* (conscientizing research). In 1975, a working group called "Conscientizaçao" (and later renamed "Paulo Freire Society") was created with participants from Belgium, France, Switzerland, Italy, Holland, and Germany (Schachtner 1999, Schroeder 2001). In 1978, the School of Continuing Education of the University of Nottingham (UK) started to offer programs in adult education that, based on Freirean principles, attempted to develop them further. That program ran continuously for almost two decades, until it was terminated in 1996 (Allman 1988). In Sweden, Freire's pedagogical ideas were introduced in the early 1970s by progressive religious groups, and his texts were intensely discussed in church study-circles and in international development missions (Selander 1990). These are just a few examples of Freire's early influence outside of Latin America, where his impact since the 1960s has been extensive and has inspired educational initiatives in almost all countries of the region.

The introduction of Paulo Freire's thought to US circles in the late 1960s and early 1970s led to an explosion of interest among educators, anthropologists, sociologists, philosophers, "multiculturalists," political scientists, personnel service administrators, and the public at large (Collins 1998:115).[11] First reactions to the English version of *Pedagogy of the Oppressed* came swiftly. Almost immediately after its publication, a myriad of articles, books, seminars, theses, videotapes, and conferences on Paulo Freire came into being, adding to the incipient literature that had emerged in the late 1960s. John Ohliger and Anne Hartung (1972) compiled the first annotated bibliography on Freire, and although it included only materials published up to 1971, it already had 184 entries. Even at that time, the existing bibliography on Freire was definitely larger, partly because Ohliger and Hartung's list was far from complete and partly because some of the 184 items were not isolated publications but collections of several articles and documents. This annotated bibliography included several categories, including Freire's approach to literacy education, educational philosophers' views on Freire, negative criticisms, and the worldwide impact of his approach.

Early reviews of *Pedagogy of the Oppressed* ranged from laudatory commentaries to harsh criticisms. For Ivan Illich it was a "truly revolutionary pedagogy"; Jonathan Kozol (1972) called it one of the most intelligent and inspired writings on the subject of reading; and Shaull (1970) reported experiencing a feeling of excitement from its humanizing proposals, from its reflections of an educational process carried out in the midst of a struggle to create a new social order, and for combining theory and practice. Other early critiques were less positive. Friedenberg (1971) did not mince words: he called *Pedagogy of the Oppressed* "a truly bad book" and complained, among other things, about its pedantic style and the consistent understatement of the opposition. Another early criticism came from Epstein (1972), who argued that Freire's approach amounted to cultural invasion because it imposed a worldview from without and because it was initiated by Freire's coordinators (who became the subjects) and not by the peasants (who were considered the objects). Epstein also contended that Freire's method was oppressive and that its universal claims threatened the cultural diversity of groups. Likewise, Knudson (1971:1261) contended that the serious, urgent tone of *Pedagogy of the Oppressed* "reveals a crusader who, after the good fight, stands ready to generalize his theories and strategies to all oppressed," and Harman (1971) argued that the text was not "truly revolutionary pedagogy" but a pedagogy for revolution, and objected that Freire's insistence on revolution as the only solution to the oppressed tended to obscure some of the more salient ideas pertaining to education and pedagogy.[12] From an opposite perspective, in the early 1970s, orthodox Marxists and Maoists challenged *Pedagogy of the Oppressed* for its "naïve idealism" in assuming that people could change the world through conscientization and for proposing dialogical principles of political organizing instead of "vanguardist" models of revolutionary change. Over time, as Freire's work grew and became more well known, the body of literature on his texts also expanded. This is the topic of the next two sections.

Seven criticisms of Freire's work

Critiques on Freire's work can be classified in three main groups. On one extreme are those who regard Freire as a guru and render his work a dogma. On the other extreme are those who reject the totality of his work due to prejudice or to ideological and political differences. In between them are those who express agreement and disagreement on specific issues, and those who may sympathize with his ideas but experience difficulties implementing them. Criticisms range from the uninformed and hostile to the insightful and respectful. Critics come from different persuasions, including conservatives, orthodox Marxists, feminists, postmodernists, poststructuralists, and neoliberals (Gadotti 1994, R. M. Torres 1999, Kane 2001, Apple 2008, Au 2009). Some critics focus on issues of style and language; others point to theoretical weaknesses. Some argue that his proposals have little relevance for the "developed" world; some accuse him of imposing Western culture on traditional societies; and others criticize his overreliance on utopias, the normative overtones of his theory of liberation, his failure to address adequately questions of race and gender, and the metaphysical argument of humanization as an ontological vocation. Last but not least, some take issue with problems in the implementation of programs inspired by his approach (Ellsworth 1989, Aronowitz 1993, Ladson-Billings 1997, McLaren 2000a, Glass 2001, Torres and Reyes 2008, Bowers 2007). For the sake of exposition, I have organized the critiques into seven categories: (1) language; (2) lack of originality; (3) contradictions; (4) universal categories and dichotomies; (5) antidialogue, manipulation, and authoritarianism; (6) conscientization as cultural invasion; and (7) implementation and outcomes.

(1) Language

Most of the criticisms of Freire's writing style are directed at *Pedagogy of the Oppressed*, a text that, paradoxically, has also been commended for its inspirational tone. As noted before, in an early review of the book Knudson (1971) complained about the vagueness of Freire's language and about the excess of redundancies; tautologies; and boring, endless repetitions, while Friedenberg (1971) criticized its pedantic style and Freire's peculiar avoidance of his own extensive experience to illustrate his ideas. Another criticism, raised mainly by North American feminists, relates to the sexist language used by Freire who, in his first publications, instead of employing a gender-inclusive language, used, for example, the term "man" as a universal category to indicate "humankind." Other commentators argued that Freire's style is obscure, verbose, convoluted, unclear, and metaphysical, and that his language is often illogical, over-emotional, unclear, inconsistent, and replete with dense jargon, academic abstractions, complicated prose, and an excessive display of theoretical erudition and newly coined expressions. Moreover, they claimed that his ideas not only are elusive and difficult to follow because of his flowery writing style but also tend to be disconnected from reality and overly intellectualized (Foy 1971:91, Boston 1972, Leach 1982, Rafferty 1983, Fetterman 1986, Ayers 1987, Taylor 1993:2, Collins 1977 and 1998, Coben 1998, McLaren 2000a). Along the same lines, Kohl (1990) acknowledged that Freire's language could seem inaccessible, abstract, and excessively intellectual, but added the caveat that this applied mainly to readers unfamiliar with dialectical argumentation or theological debates. Similarly, Balke (1986) observed that Freire's texts probably lose some readers who are unable to invest the time and effort to navigate his philosophical-linguistic discourse and that some of his texts may be accessible exclusively to leftist readers who are comfortable with the language of liberation. Having said that, there is a general consensus that Freire's later books (particularly the "dialogue books") have a much more readable, direct, and accessible style than the earlier ones, allowing Freire's geniality, compassion, wisdom, and humanism to emerge more openly (Collins 1998:117).

(2) Lack of originality

Freire has been identified as the eclectic thinker par excellence (Coben 1998). Eclecticism, per se, is not necessarily a problem, but in the case of Freire it has been argued that the excessive borrowing of ideas from different sources has deprived his approach of originality and has led to internal contradictions in his theoretical framework (an issue that I will address next). Regarding the lack of originality, Taylor (1993:34) argued that calling Freire's thinking "eclectic" underestimates the degree to which he borrowed directly from other sources. Using a more direct language, Egerton (1973) stated that "there is no originality in what Freire says. It's the same old rap." Likewise, Leach (1982) pointed out that Freire has been perceived as a quaint, rather unoriginal, and eclectic philosopher and that he rightly deserves the accusation that he has borrowed concepts that cannot be torn from the particular material and economic contexts in which they are embedded. More specifically, it has been claimed that the main argument of *Pedagogy of the Oppressed* borrows extensively from Hegel's master-slave dichotomy (Peters 1999, Roberts 2000:110) and from Kosik's *Dialectic of the Concrete* (Taylor 1993). Others have noted that in *Pedagogy of the Oppressed* it is also possible to find echoes of Sartre (the notion of "digestive education"), of Buber (some of the principles of dialogical education), and of Fanon and Memmi (the idea of the colonizer inside the mind of the colonized), among others. It has also been argued that Freire's model of conscientization was an elaboration of Febvre's categorization of consciousness. According to Taylor (1993:35), it was Lucien Fevbre (1878–1956), a

French historian with strong connections to Brazil, who provided Freire, through his disciple Fernand Braudel, with the notion that consciousness was stratified but capable of accelerated or retarded evolution.

Moreover, it has been noted that Freire's arguments have many parallels to those advanced by John Dewey, Ivan Illich, and Carl Rogers. Like Dewey, Freire regarded education as a process of personal growth and social-self realization, rejected the nutritionist model of education (which Dewey calls "pouring in" and Freire "banking education"), and adhered to a learner-centered model in which the activity of the learner is a basic principle of the learning process. Moreover, Freire adopted from Dewey the notion that the democratization of education (promoting cooperative work and democratic practices in the classroom, the school, and the educational system) constitutes an important contribution to the larger project of society's democratization. It is also argued that Freire borrowed from Dewey—and from the progressive school movement in general—the importance of connecting the curriculum to the study of the local natural and social environment. Some parallels were also found with Illich: both criticized the traditional school for its bureaucratic structures and practices, agreed that the educational system produced student alienation, concurred that educational projects should promote creativity and autonomy, and were ardent humanists who put a high value on freedom. Similarities can also be found with Roger's philosophical foundations and educational principles, including his emphasis on dialogue to facilitate the rehumanization process of alienated people, his belief in the innate self-actualizing tendency for growth that exists in each person (Freire's "ontological vocation toward full humanization"), his faith in the potential of human beings, his confidence in their competency to analyze and solve their problems, and his call for a learner-centered and holistic education in which the responsibility for the educational process lies with the learner (Rogers 1969, Gadotti 1994, O'Hara 1989). The parallels between Roger's *Freedom to Learn* and Freire's *Pedagogy of the Oppressed* were so significant that Rogers (1977:106) recalled: "The principles he has come up with to build his framework are so completely similar to the principles of *Freedom to Learn* that I found myself open mouthed with astonishment."

(3) Contradictions

A related claim is that Freire's eclecticism has led to insurmountable contradictions. A common contention raised by those who connect Freire's eclecticism to the use of contradictory analytical frameworks is that his attempt to marry Marxism and Christian theology has not been successful. This charge has been raised decade after decade since the first critiques to Freire's work in the early 1970s. For instance, Nasaw (1972) stated that on first reading, Freire's eclecticism is refreshing but when considered more carefully "it's a disaster," and pointed out that Freire failed in his attempt to combine his Christian ethical categories with his Marxist concept of historicity. In the 1980s, Plunkett (1986) claimed that Freire was unable to reconcile his structuralist Marxism, his humanistic commitment to personal values, his enquiry into the epistemology of power relationships at the micro-level, and his suggestions about the potential of a prophetic church. Likewise, Berthoff (1986:28) observed: "Freire is difficult to read because he is both a Christian and a Marxist, and those lexicons are sometimes at odds with another." More recently, Gibson (2007 and 2008) argued that Freire's attempt to be a devout Catholic Marxist was bound for failure from the start because it was a flatly impossible contradiction, as it is not possible to address material inequalities with abstract and idealistic ethical religious propositions.

Ironically, Freire has been criticized by some Christians for his Marxist approach and by some Marxists for his lack of Marxist interpretation. Vicente Scherer, the cardinal of Porto Alegre (Brazil), criticized Freire because he "accepts Hegelian dialectics and the Marxist interpretation of history" and contradicts the principles of Christian doctrine (cited in Gadotti 1994:127). Some Marxists, however, characterized Freire as an "idealist Hegelian" (Pérez Cruz 2009); they argued that he did not pay enough attention to the state and to economic relations of exploitation, and that he often reduced social class—a material category—to a moral and religious category, equivocating constantly between idealism and materialism, sometimes recognizing the primacy of the material base, and sometimes ignoring it. Marxists also criticized Freire's notion of class struggle for being too abstract and mechanistic, determined mainly by a generic consciousness of oppression and not by concrete power relations (Isaacs 1972, Bugbee 1975, Walker 1980:136–8, Gibson 1994, Coben 1998:92, Youngman 2000).

Furthermore, at the beginning of the 1980s, when Freire went to Cuba on a study visit, his work was either ignored or harshly criticized by Marxist educators (R. M. Torres 1999, Perez-Cruz 2009, Betto 2010). At that time, in a work that circulated widely in Latin America's progressive intellectual circles, Vanilda Paiva (1980) argued that Freire's work in Brazil in the 1960s was part of the project of national development and modernization promoted by the governments of Kubitschek (1956–61) and Goulart (1961–64). Paiva contended that, at that historical moment, Freire's understanding of conscientization was not a matter of class consciousness but a type of consciousness that would allow people to evolve from a traditional and authoritarian society to a modern and democratic one. For Paiva, Freire's model of social change at that time was premised not on class struggle but on social reform promoted by consensus among different social groups and classes, and his pedagogical model aimed at nurturing democratic individuals that could fit well in the transition that Brazilian society was experiencing. Given this analysis, Paiva concluded that, in the Freirean model, there was an essential contradiction between a nondirective pedagogical model based on democratic and dialogical principles and a directive ideological model based on historical, social, religious, and cultural proposals.

(4) Universal categories and dichotomies

Another criticism of Freire, especially of his earlier work, has to do with his tendency to use a universal language and binary oppositions to describe reality. Those critics complain that his prose is full of abstract generalizations (e.g., "oppression," "revolution," "liberation") that are seldom explained in detail, and of polar antagonisms, such as oppressor-oppressed, reactionaries-progressives, humans-animals, passive-active, humanization-dehumanization, liberation-oppression, denunciation-annunciation, or banking-liberating education. Although this mode of presenting ideas in opposing categories may have some appeal as a pedagogical device, may shed light on certain issues, and can help to distinguish more clearly between different realities under study, it runs the risk of oversimplifying those ideas and realities; of overemphasizing dichotomies; and of ignoring the contradictions, subtleties, and shades of grey that characterize the real world. Two concepts in particular have raised complaints of universalism and dichotomization: oppression and banking education.

The concept of oppression attracted considerable discussion over the years. This is not surprising considering that oppression is a central category in Freire's framework. Critics on the left and the right have challenged Freire's conceptualization of oppression for being too abstract and general, for having universal pretensions, and for expressing oppressive relations in a simplistic and dichotomist way. Although early critics acknowledged that Freire made an attempt to define "oppression" ("any situation in which A objectively exploits B"), they found such a definition vague and unhelpful in orienting educators and practitioners on the ground. They also argued that Freire's categories of oppressor and oppressed were presented in a vacuum (rather than being rooted in a social or economic context), and this made it difficult for those who did not live in northeast Brazil to find it useful (Knudson 1971, Epstein 1972, Bugbee 1973). In trying to relate Freire's categories to a North American context, Woock (1972) asked whether teachers in public schools are oppressors or part of the oppressed and, more generally, who exactly are the oppressors and the oppressed in North America. Urban (1972) raised a similar criticism, observing that *Pedagogy of the Oppressed* did not help in understanding either revolution or education, and complained about the absurdity of attempts to apply Freire's analysis to young middle-class students in North America. In addition to concerns about the ambiguity and generality of Freire's analysis of oppression, critics have challenged him for lack of clarity about the specific meaning of the words "oppressor" and "oppressed." Sol Stern, a conservative commentator who criticizes Freire for his "pernicious ideas," contends that his conceptualization of the oppressor is vague and imprecise:

Seldom does Freire ground his description of the clash between oppressors and oppressed in any particular society or historical period, so it's hard for the reader to judge whether what he is saying makes any sense. We don't know if the oppressors he condemns are North American bankers, Latin American land barons, or, for that matter, run-of-the-mill, authoritarian education bureaucrats. His language is so metaphysical and vague that he might just as well be describing a board game with two contesting sides, the oppressors and the oppressed. (Stern 2009:2)

More sympathetic commentators have also criticized Freire for his imprecision in defining who exactly are the oppressed. They lamented that Freire failed to provide a clear definition, especially because "the oppressed" appear so extensively in his work as the historical subjects of social change. Along these lines, Taylor (1993:133) pointed out that in reading Freire's texts, it is unclear whether the concept of "oppressed" refers to the working classes, the nonliterate, the socially deprived, or those who (for whatever reasons) perceive themselves to be oppressed. Ellsworth (1991:453), addressing the issue from a different perspective, contended that Freire's appeal to universal propositions such as *oppressors* and *oppressed* has contributed to the oppression of those who are in the margins and that the rationalist ideals espoused by Freire—liberation, humanization, and the like—are nothing but "repressive myths." Ellsworth's main argument is that Freire's theory, by essentializing oppression, is inadequate for confronting the specifics of oppression for particular groups. A few years later, Coben (1998) made a similar charge when she contended that, in Freire's formulation, the oppressed remain a "generic other" and concluded that such a universal concept as oppression cannot account for oppression in a particular social category. Moreover, Coben argued that Freire's model of oppression lacks an understanding of power, and for this reason, it is "just too simple and indiscriminate to accommodate the multifaceted and contradictory nature of power relationships in terms of gender, class, or any other social category" (p. 97).

Summing up, Freire's model of oppression has been challenged on at least three grounds. First, it has been criticized because it attempted to establish master narratives and universal prescriptions based on particular historical and cultural assumptions that do not account for contextual differences. Second, it has been claimed that Freire dealt with relations of oppression without providing clear definitions, analytical rigor, or an examination of material conflicts, instead using vague and abstract language and a social-psychological and cultural analysis of oppressor-oppressed situations that fail to explain how oppressive relations operate in real historical situations. Such failure was attributed to a simplistic understanding of social change that was anchored in the assumption that a critical consciousness automatically leads to structural transformation. Third, it has been claimed that the oppressor-oppressed dichotomous conceptualization constituted an oversimplification that failed to address the multiple and contradictory dimensions of oppression at different societal levels (Fischer 1980, Elias & Merriam 1980, Schipani 1984, Ellsworth 1989 and 1993, Giroux 1993, Weiler 1993 and 1996, Scapp 1997, Coben 1998, Joldersma 2001, Glass 2001, Laverty 2008).

The third issue (failure to address the multiple and contradictory dimensions of oppression) generated criticism about Freire's lack of attention to nonclass-based oppressions, especially (but not only) along racial and gender lines. Furthermore, it has been argued that in Freire's "binary model," a conceptual equivalence exists between "oppressed" and "poor," implying that only the poor are oppressed and all others are oppressors (Elias 1976). By applying such class reductionism, Freire failed to recognize the existence of other forms of oppression and ignored the various forms of domination and social struggle addressed by feminists, minorities, ecologists, and other social activists (Brady 1994). Thus, it has been claimed that Freire did not deal adequately with issues of race and gender and that these constituted blind spots in his work (hooks 1993, Ellsworth 1989, Weiler 1996, Ladson-Billings 1997, McLaren 2000a, Haymes 2002, Leonardo 2005). Although Freire discussed gender and race issues in later publications, it has been noted that his pronouncements on the subject are superficial (Coben 1998:93) and that none of his talking books involved a sustained conversation between Freire and either a woman or a person of color (Mayo 2009:18).

Moreover, it has been observed that by overemphasizing class oppression, Freire did not pay sufficient attention to the subjectivity of individual experience and neglected the existence of overlapping forms of oppression in which the same person is simultaneously oppressor and oppressed, depending on different social locations. For instance, as Ellsworth (1989:453) indicates, a peasant male may be oppressed by a landowner at work but, at the same time, oppress his wife at home, and

Freire said little that could help explain the interchangeability of roles between oppressors and oppressed and the implications for the process of conscientization and liberation. Along the same lines, Mayo (2000:276) asks whether the concept of "class suicide" discussed by Freire in *Pedagogy of the Oppressed*[13] can be applied to race, gender, or sexual orientation (as in situations where whites teach blacks, men teach women, or heterosexuals teach homosexuals) and contends that there is little in Freire that deals with this issue.

The other concept that generated criticism is the "banking education" metaphor. Freire's tendency to use binaries creates the impression that he asked educators to advocate for one side only and totally reject the other side. One of the main confusions that arose from this basic formulation was the tendency to interpret banking education as synonymous with traditional education, and liberatory education with nondirective education. Laverty (2008) argued that one of the problems with the banking metaphor (which is one of the most powerful in contemporary education) is its simultaneous overestimation and underestimation of traditional education. On the one hand, the banking metaphor overestimates the real power of the teacher vis-à-vis the students. On the other hand, it underestimates the value of good lectures and other positive elements of traditional education. She contends that by equating banking education with traditional education, Freire made it extremely difficult to defend traditional education. At the same time, the other side of the equation (liberatory, dialogical, or problem-posing education) also created confusion. Because of such expressions as "teacher/student" and "student/teacher," many readers assumed that Freire was proposing a nondirective education in which teachers and learners play similar roles and in which good teaching relies on skillful facilitation regardless of the teachers' competence in their disciplines. As discussed in Chapter 2, Freire had to invest much time and energy to clarify these confusions.

(5) Anti-dialogue, manipulation, and authoritarianism

Some critics have argued that the pedagogical model of Paulo Freire is nothing other than banking education in disguise. They argue that, contrary to what Freire's claims, the model is not really dialogical but antidialogical and there is little that can be called "liberatory" or "emancipatory." They charge that educators control the agenda from beginning to end and (based on their own ideological biases or political agendas) make unilateral decisions about the content to be learned and impose that content in direct or subtle ways. One of the early criticisms along these lines came from Griffith (1972), who contended that Freire left no doubt of his concern to control and restrict the freedom of those who could not see the superiority of his system and the superiority of the new ruling group, a small cadre of revolutionaries that had passed some undefined loyalty test. Similarly, Epstein (1972) found Freire's model to be contradictory insofar as the peasants were asked to rely on themselves for overcoming their ignorance while, at the same time, they were to be made aware by others of their state of oppression. Epstein claimed that Freire had failed to provide a satisfactory resolution to this contradiction.

Likewise, Walker (1980:143) claimed that Freire's model was not only antidialogical but also elitist. It was antidialogical because genuine dialogue should be based on real political equality between participants (and not just an abstract commitment to equality in spirit or in principle), but in Freire's model the dialogue was initiated by the leaders (and not by the oppressed) through a process in which an enlightened vanguard reached out to the unenlightened. It was elitist because it was based on the assumption that "the people" are incapable of learning, that "they are stupid." Along the same lines, Margonis (2007) claimed that because his dialogue was already framed by a revolutionary narrative, Freire was unlikely to respect the knowledge of the students, ("many of whom would have never considered revolution before the Freirean literacy program began") thereby preempting the possibility of subaltern knowledge to be developed (p. 66). The charge of elitism goes hand in hand with a related criticism: that conscientization is patronizing. Zachariah (1986) stated that it is patronizing because oppressed people do not need to be conscientized by middle-class do-gooders to recognize that they live desperate lives marked by exploitation, poverty, hunger, and disease. What they require instead, said Zachariah, are allies willing to struggle with them against those who oppress them rather than those who offer them hope through conscientization, which is worse than deceitful.

An associated criticism of conscientization is that it is a tool that can be easily subjected to manipulation, indoctrination, and brainwashing, albeit disguised as a coinvestigation in which learners and educators participate through free dialogue as equals. The argument usually goes as follows: given that the content, the steps, and the end goals of the conscientization process are largely defined by outside agents who have a clear political and ideological agenda and given that, in this teaching/learning process, educators have more power than learners in defining "the truth," educators can readily impose their agendas in more or less subtle ways. As Foy (1971:92) caustically remarked in an early criticism: "One suspects that in Freirean pedagogy, as in Socratic dialogues and Maoist cadre training, the more informed and disciplined mind of the teacher is still in control." From this viewpoint, Freirean educators are likely to be perceived as outside agitators or party activists that use manipulative tactics to indoctrinate and who can quickly create a new domination in the name of liberation (O'Meara 1973, Fisher 1980, Walker 1980, Zachariah 1986, Fetterman 1986, Gerhardt 1989, Knowles 1989, Stotsky 1990, Caulfield 1991, Paulston 1992, Taylor 1991, Elias 1994, Jay and Graff 1995).

Among those who have advanced the "manipulation argument," there have been some who have explored the specifics of Freire's literacy program. One of them was Paul Taylor (1993), who contended that, despite Freire's claims of dialogical and negotiated learning, the hidden or personal agenda of the educators had a controlling influence on the program (pp. 76–8). The main evidence offered by Taylor to build his case is that some of the key generative words were imposed by Freire's team rather than collected from the everyday language of people in their communities. Otherwise, he claims, it is difficult to explain why three clearly different groups—one in a city slum, one in a coastal town, and one in an agricultural colony—should all select *brick* and *vote* as their first generative words.[14] This led Taylor to argue that the literacy circles were not dialogical but directive, without any learning partnership or a dialogue among equals (p. 129). More poignantly, Taylor concluded that although Freire's literacy model was theoretically an alternative to banking education, in practice it was more a form of "enlightened banking education" (p. 77), later referring to this contradiction as the dialectical relationship between "the power of literacy" and "the literacy of power" (p. 147).

For Freire's critics, the issue of power in the conscientization process is problematic for two reasons. The first is that the educators tend to impose their ideological views and political agendas on the learners, sometimes overtly (Gerhardt 1989:541) and sometimes in a covert and hidden way disguised as "correct thinking" (Taylor 1983:88, Jay and Graff 1995:203; Coben 1998:82). Stotsky (1990) argued that the more advanced reading materials used by Freire clearly illustrate the nature of their political content, suggest little possibility for the development of critical thinking, and reveal that the philosophy underlying *Pedagogy of the Oppressed* seems less a theory of liberatory education than a theory of literacy as an instrument of social control. Even more sympathetic commentators are aware of this problem. Giroux (1993), for instance, called our attention to some contradictions raised in Freire's work, and warned against the risk of imposing ideas that follow the dictates of authority instead of helping learners develop their own, even if those dictates are perceived as correct and part of a radical project. He wondered what would happen if the language, politics, and rationality of the educator are not the same as those of the oppressed, and then asked: "how can the task of validating certain forms of 'correct' thinking be reconciled with the pedagogical task of helping students to avoid authoritarian dictates, regardless of how radical they are?" (Giroux 1993:181). Addressing the same issue from a different perspective, Saviani (1983) argued that the main problem with Freire's pedagogical approach is the conflation of educational and political practice. According to Saviani, this is problematic because education is about a relationship between nonantagonists in which the teacher acts in the interest of the learner, whereas politics is about a relationship between antagonists with contradictory interests. For Saviani, taking a cue from a particular reading of Gramsci similar to that of Entwistle (1989), the political role of education in promoting justice and democracy consists of redistributing knowledge and imparting a quality education to the oppressed classes.[15]

The second problematic issue raised by critics is that Freire advocated a grassroots approach from a hierarchical position in the government.

These critics point to the contradiction that the emancipatory political agendas pursued by Freire in his educational work have often been connected to a state bureaucracy. They observed that most of Freire's educational work, from the literacy circles in Brazil to the extension programs in Chile, and from the literacy campaigns in Africa and Nicaragua to his position as secretary of education in Sao Paulo, occurred within the boundaries of government programs. They argue that this had an impact not only on the curricular content of the programs but also on the limits of social change that could be generated through his "emancipatory" education. As for the content of the programs, Coben (1998), for instance, examined the content proposed for the post-literacy programs in Brazil in the 1960s and noted that they dealt with the act of studying, with national reconstruction, and with topics related to work and transformation and that these topics were reflected in the key words used in the notebooks such as "unity," "discipline," "work," and "vigilance." Coben suspects that most of these words derived from the government rather than from the people, as Freire insisted they should. Regarding the limits of social change, critics found it ironic that in most of his books Freire advocated community-based programs oriented toward social change whereas in most of his work he was connected to programs initiated by government offices. From their perspective, to promote bottom-up strategies through top-down interventions was contradictory and a nonstarter. More importantly, these critics claimed that Freirean conscientization programs could not subvert the system if such educational programs were financed, supported, and/or protected by government institutions, precisely because the role of these institutions is to perpetuate a particular system (MacEoin 1972,[16] Mathew 1980, Coben 1998).

The issue of Freire's involvement in government programs was also raised in relation to the Guinea-Bissau literacy campaign: although Freire and his team were in favor of using local languages, the government imposed the use of Portuguese. Another aspect of this issue relates to instances in which Freire was not only supported by governments in his work but was in office himself. Was Freire able to practice what he preached and adopt a democratic model of management and leadership? For the most part, it seems that Freire did not abuse his authority, but there have been instances in which he exercised power in an authoritarian way. In Freire's administration as secretary of education in the municipality of Sao Paulo, C. A. Torres (1994) reports that Freire was accused of authoritarianism and nepotism for including four books (two authored by him, one by his older daughter, and another by his collaborator Moacir Gadotti) in the bibliography for an examination given to teachers seeking positions in the Secretary of Education. Because of this, others accused Freire of being an ideologue for forcing people to read his works and of trying to make a profit by making his books compulsory reading for the entrance exam.

(6) Cultural invasion

This criticism constitutes a serious indictment because it is not just about a particular aspect of Freire's work (which could be advanced in the context of a general appreciation of his lifetime contributions) but because it implies an overall rejection of his approach. His critics argue that his work, contrary to what he claimed, does not help the oppressed to liberate themselves, but oppresses them even more. The crux of the argument, which may sound perplexing to many Freireans, is that his conscientization model is a colonialist and imperialist project of cultural invasion that contributes to the ecological crisis. One of the first commentators to advance the argument that conscientization amounts to cultural invasion was Erwin Epstein (1972), who argued that Freire's projects imposed a worldview from without and were initiated by Freire's coordinators (the subjects) who were expected to arouse the peasants (the objects). In an argument that would be taken up by others in the following decades, Epstein also contended that Freire's method was oppressive and that its universal claims threatened the cultural diversity of groups. A couple of years later, Peter Berger (1974) argued that Freire's conscientization was elitist and paternalistic because it was based on the assumption that a certain group of people, dehumanized and unable to recognized their situation, required the help of others to rescue them. Berger, who was a sociologist and a Lutheran theologian, claimed that Freire's approach to consciousness raising was little different from the evangelical missions of the past because it was conceived as an act of conversion in which one group imposes its truth on others in order to save them. Ivan Illich (1982), a former Catholic priest who had known Freire for many years and who otherwise celebrated his work, made a similar accusation. He contended that conscientization was not only a kind of political self-help adult education organized mostly by clergymen to help the poor discover they were "human" but also a professionally planned and administered ritual to ensure the internalization of a religious or secular ideology combined with the standardization of vernacular probity through a "catholic" set of institutional rules.

Along similar lines, C. A. ("Chet") Bowers, a professor of environmental studies at the University of Oregon, contends that conscientization is just a new expression of the old process of colonization. In several works that originated in the early 1980s (e.g., Bowers 1983, 2003, 2005, 2007, 2008), he argues that Freirean interventions are essentially practices of cultural invasion that assume that Western theorists possess the answers to how other cultures should live and aim at replacing traditional views with a modernist and anthropocentric worldview. Bowers is vehement in his critique of Freire and does not mince words. For instance, he uses provocative titles such as *The Constructivism of John Dewey and Paulo Freire: A Trojan Horse of Western Imperialism?* or *How the Ideas of Paulo Freire Contribute to the Cultural Roots of the Ecological Crisis*, and accusatory statements like "the imperialistic nature of the Freirean cannon" (2005:viii). Bowers claims that Freire, by using a language that makes constant reference to liberation, social transformation, revolution, progress, critical reflection, and praxis takes for granted Western assumptions about the progressive nature of change and the importance of literacy and critical reflection. In relation to the progressive nature of change, Bowers charges that Freire fails to recognize the importance of tradition in functions such as food security, healing practices, creative arts, and values of moral reciprocity among humans and between humans and the environment. In relation to Freire's focus on literacy and critical thinking, Bowers criticizes Freire for failing to realize "that literacy itself is a colonizing process that reinforces a modern sense of individualism, privileges sight over other senses, and fosters abstract thinking that is integral to critical reflection" (2005:3). Among others who share the claim that Freirean pedagogy is grounded in Enlightenment philosophy and individualism are some collaborators of

Bowers (e.g., Rasmussen 2005, Robinson 2005, Vasquez 2005, and Esteva et al. 2005).

(7) Implementation and outcomes

Last but not least, some criticisms do not necessarily aim at the writings of Paulo Freire but at the outcomes of programs in which he was directly involved or were inspired by those writings. With regard to programs in which Freire was directly involved (albeit in different roles and with different degrees of responsibility), some commentators have pointed out that his projects in Brazil in the early 1960s were pilot experiments too small to test fully the applicability of his theories; that his efforts in Chile in the late 1960s did not significantly reduce the literacy rate; and that the Guinea-Bissau literacy program in the late 1970s failed because of defects in his approach, the use of Portuguese, inadequate provision of materials, and poorly prepared facilitators (Harasim 1983, Facundo 1984, Zacharakis-Jutz 1986)[17]. Likewise, it has been charged that the famous literacy campaign carried out by the Sandinistas in Nicaragua in 1980 was flawed with problems. For instance, it has been claimed that the quality of the pedagogical interventions was uneven, that genuine dialogical approaches were seldom employed, and that the efforts were not sustained over time, making the success ephemeral. Moreover, it has been reported that his pedagogical reforms as secretary of education of Sao Paulo during the late 1980s and early 1990s generated resistance among many teachers and administrators and produced mixed results (C. A. Torres 1994, Stromquist 1997, O'Cadiz et al. 1998, Weiner 2003, Mayo 2010).

Regarding issues related to the application of Freirean-inspired programs, Rosiska Darcy de Oliveira and Pierre Dominice had already sounded the alert in the early 1970s about a growing gap between the success of Freire's writings and the practical application of his thinking. They attributed this gap to problems of historical agents incapable of putting into practice real radical alternatives and the difficulty of determining the times and the places when struggle leads to real social change (Oliveira and Dominice 1974). One study found that most consciousness-raising programs, alone or in combination with skill development programs, have not achieved expected social changes (Gottlieb and La Belle 1990). Another study on Freire-inspired programs in rural Zaire found that while Freire's approach may be effective as an educational strategy, its revolutionary potential appeared to be somewhat limited in rural Africa (Ewert 1977). The evidence that led Ewert to this conclusion was that people in rural communities did not perceive themselves as an oppressed class in an unequal social structure, and hence they were more likely to exploit their connections with the elite than to unite in a struggle against the oppressors. Blanca Facundo (1984) also addresses the problems of transferability. After evaluating several Freire-inspired programs in the United States and in Puerto Rico, she concluded that the theories of Paulo Freire were not transferable from the context of northeast Brazil to the "inner Third World" of the United States. A few years later, in a paper suggestively entitled "Why Doesn't This Feel Empowering?" Elizabeth Ellsworth (1989) reported that her attempt to introduce a Freirean approach in a university course on media and antiracist pedagogies not only failed to achieve the expected positive impact on empowerment but actually produced unhelpful results that exacerbated the very conditions she was trying to address, such as Eurocentrism, racism, sexism, classism, and banking education. Likewise, Taber et al. (2006) reported that dialogical approaches could bring to the surface ingrained prejudices, hatred, and anger that educators might not be prepared to handle, particularly when working in unfamiliar contexts. Also in relation to the implementation of Freirean approaches in higher education, Lather (1991) and Filax (1997) have warned about the mistake of attributing resistance to critical pedagogy to the false consciousness of students.

Responses to the criticisms

According to Gadotti (1994), Freire acknowledged the criticisms of his work and the challenges to his theories when he was made aware of them, but usually he preferred not to respond to them directly. His approach, Gadotti reports, was an attempt to formulate a better explanation of his ideas and his positions without entering into sterile and destructive arguments, especially with those who tried deliberately to attack his proposals in order to make them nonviable as institutional practices (p. 129). Freire himself declared that he welcomed criticism, but complained about those who criticized him without reading his books. In *Pedagogy of Hope*, he recounted a story about a meeting of leading Brazilian intellectuals in which one participant said that Freire's works were no longer relevant to the national debates on education. When another participant asked what books written by Freire the person had studied, the answer was "None, but I've read about him" (Freire 1994b:64). In that sense, Freire's books have acquired an iconic status, signifying that it has become permissible to condemn them without reading them.[18] For Freire, in order to criticize other people's ideas, people should first make a serious effort to familiarize themselves with those ideas. In this section, I will address responses to the criticisms here discussed. Some of these responses come from Freire himself; others were advanced by a variety of authors.

(1) Language

In response to these criticisms, Freire acknowledged that he had a tendency to use academic terms (be they sociological, psychological, philosophical, or theological) that could be perceived as "difficult" or inaccessible by some readers. His position on this issue, expressed in *Pedagogy of Hope*, was to challenge readers to engage actively with "difficult" words by examining their etymologies, their meaning, and the different ways in which they have been used in scholarly literature. He questioned the legitimacy of the complaint when it came from readers who tended to close any book, not just *Pedagogy of the Oppressed*, and declared it to be "unreadable" when they did not understand the meaning of a sentence and had made no effort to do so (62–3). Freire also lamented that some readers think they are wasting their time when they have to pause in the reading of a text to find the meaning of a word or the context of a concept by consulting such basic sources of information as dictionaries (including those of philosophy or sociology), encyclopedias, and the like. Freire argued that, on the contrary, this exercise was not wasted but study time. He noted that some people just "keep on reading," hoping that, magically, on the next page, the indecipherable word might come up again in a context in which they will see what it means. But for him, reading a text is not just a careless exercise; it is an active task in which the reader's role is that of a determined, critical, and humble subject of learning (64).

Addressing the criticism about his recurrent use of metaphor in his texts, Freire observed that he was inspired by the wealth of symbolism in the speech of urban and rural workers with whom he worked and that he had been exposed to the sonority of popular speech since his adolescence in the village of Jaboatão. He also pointed to studies of metaphors by linguists and philosophers and to the use of metaphorical language in literature and science (56). In discussing why many North American educators find Freire's prose elusive and irritating, D'Arcy Martin (1998:121) argued that the problem was not that he wrote badly (after all, he was a specialist in language) but rather that he thought differently:

> Most readers in North America find Paulo's style bewildering, not because he uses jargon or rhetoric, but because his thought patterns are different from their own. Their efforts to "explain" his writing, then, reflect a refusal to adjust their own intellectual process to accommodate a thinker who sees the world relationally rather than factually. Hence it turns out to be more fruitful to assume that Paulo knows what he is doing in his choice of words than to assume that he does not. Pulling fragments out of his writing, and criticizing them in isolation, accomplishes little. A critical stance on Paulo's theoretical work needs to start from his dialectical coherence among assumptions, values, methodology and language.

In response to criticisms about the overemotional tone of the language that he uses in his books, Freire (1997a) questioned the logic that insists on the abstract compartmentalization of *feeling* from *knowing* and claimed that he *knows* with his entire body: with feelings, with passion, and with reason: "I refuse to accept a certain type of scientistic criticism that insinuates that I lack rigor in the way I deal with these issues or the overaffective language I use in the process. The passion with which I know, I speak, or I write does not, in any way, diminish the commitment with which I announce or denounce. I am a totality and not a dichotomy" (Freire 1997a:30).

As to the use of sexist language in Freire's first books, Paula Allman (2010) observed that she found far too many feminist writers and activists dismissing outright the writings of Freire (and other progressive authors) on the grounds of the male bias in their language. Although Allman acknowledged that some feminists like bell hooks (1993) handled this situation with wisdom and understanding, putting the sexist language in historical context, she contended that it is better not to be distracted by what in the end is "an extremely counterproductive and self-defeating position when it comes to the eradication of all forms of human oppression" (p. 9). In fairness, Freire himself recognized the problematic nature of his early texts and expressed his gratitude and his debt to the many North American women who wrote to him in the early 1970s after publication of the English version of *Pedagogy of the Oppressed*. In those letters, the women spoke about the contradiction between the general progressive and emancipatory content of the book and its sexist and discriminatory language, which assumed that the concept "men" included all humanity. In *Pedagogy of Hope*, Freire recalled that when he was reading the first letters of criticism, his initial reaction was to recall what he had been taught since his childhood: that when people talk about "men," they are including women as well. We should, of course, remember that Freire was born in 1921 and that the masculinist language was the norm when he wrote *Pedagogy of the Oppressed*. *The* gender-inclusive language movement became prominent only in the third part of the twentieth century.

However, after further consideration, Freire (1994b:67) noted that the letters made him realize "how much ideology resides in language." In those reflections, Freire was also eager to point out that he considered language to be an important issue. Addressing those who claimed that this was just a small grammatical concern distracting from the real struggles against oppression and colonialism, he asserted that this was not just a grammatical issue but also an ideological one that precisely reflected the larger dynamics of oppression:

And let it not be said that this is a minor problem. It is a major problem. Let it not be said that, since the basic thing is to change a wicked world, recreating it in terms of making it less perverse, the debate over sexist language is therefore of minor importance, especially since women do not constitute a social class. Discrimination against women, expressed and committed by sexist discourse, and enfleshed in concrete practices, is a colonial way of treating them, and therefore incompatible with any progressive position." (Freire 1994b:55)

Freire did not limit himself to responding to criticisms of language but took action. In relation to sexist language in his publications, he started referring to "women and men" or "human beings" in all his books ("I would rather write an unattractive line sometimes than omit to express my rejection of sexist language"), and he requested of his publishers that all subsequent editions of his previous books have nonsexist, gender-inclusive language. As to the accessibility of his texts, although he defended his right to use academic terms, in his later publications (particularly in the dialogue books) it is evident that Freire made an effort to be "simple but not simplistic," making his arguments easier to follow and ensuring that his language did not interfere with communication with his readers. Indeed, in the second part of his works (those published in the last two decades of his life), there is significant reduction of unnecessary jargon and less reliance on prior philosophical and theological knowledge on the part of the reader.

(2) Lack of originality

As discussed in the section on criticisms, it has been argued that Freire's excessive borrowing led to a scarcity of originality. First of all, it is worth noting that Freire never denied that he found inspiration from authors who preceded him. For instance, in *Pedagogy of the Oppressed* he explicitly recognized that the idea of banking education derived from Sartre's notion of digestive education, and he explained many times that the concept of conscientization was not his own invention but a formulation of Instituto Social de Estudos Brasileiros (ISEB) colleagues. In footnote 24 of *Education for Critical Consciousness*, Freire (1973:51), to illustrate the point that he lacked originality, pointed out that in the campaigns carried against him, it was said that he was not "the inventor of dialogue," as if he had ever made such a preposterous claim. In response to those accusations, Freire argued that on the subject of originality he always agreed with Dewey (1916:187), who stated that originality does not lie in the "extraordinary and fanciful," but "in putting everyday things to uses which had not occurred to others." If we use Dewey's conceptualization as our guideline, it is clear that Freire was original. Whereas it is true that he participated in the import of European doctrines and ideas into Brazil, he adapted them to the local socioeconomic context and, as Gerhardt (1993:11) pointed out, he expanded and refocused them in a thought-provoking way, even for scholars and practitioners in developed countries. Likewise, Preiswerk (1995) argued that Freire's originality consisted of articulating a transformative educational practice with a philosophical synthesis of different ideological families.

Moreover, although some similarities can be found with Dewey, Illich, and Rogers, it is also possible to identify important differences. Freire differs from Dewey in at least four aspects. First, from a philosophical perspective, Dewey's theory is grounded in a naturalism that relies on a scientific, evolutionary, and developmental approach, whereas Freire's conception is rooted in a humanist view that relies on cultural, social, and historical understandings of freedom. This multidimensional analysis of culture and society proposed by Freire, together with the introduction of anthropological elements in the analysis of local reality, would become an important dimension of the culture circles and the literacy-teaching process (Gadotti 1994, Glass 2001). Second, whereas Freire adopted several postulates proposed by Dewey and the progressive school, he adapted them to the particular contexts of marginalized adult learners in developing countries. Although Dewey never argued that his pedagogical proposals should be restricted to children's education, in his analytical focus and in his practice (e.g., the laboratory school) adult learners were at the periphery.[19] Conversely, Freire's educational theory and practice had adult learners at the center for most of his life. In so doing, Freire broadened the scope of the progressive education movement, taking it beyond school walls. Third, and probably the most notable difference, is Freire's explicit emphasis on the impossibility of the neutrality of education and, hence, on the recognition of its political nature, and particularly, on the connection between educational activities and collective, emancipatory projects of social transformation. Freire appreciated the important methodological contributions made by Dewey and the progressive school movement. He shared the critique of the traditional relationship between teachers and learners and of the fragmentation of knowledge, but noted that his own criticism also extended to the capitalist mode of production (Gadotti 1994, R. M. Torres 1999).

Regarding Illich, Freire was more optimistic about the possibilities of transforming schools into more democratic, inclusive, and engaging institutions, and identified two problems with Illich's deschooling proposal. The first related to the prerequisites to engage in the learning webs. In order to study a subject, read data on a computer or find a learning mate, or establish communications with a specialist, learners were expected to have access to a computer and have some basic level of education, including an acceptable command of the 3 R's. In Illich's model, the solution to this problem was assumed as given, but it was not clear which social institution would be responsible for the giving. Perhaps Illich could argue that families could provide the computers and teach basic numeracy and literacy to their children, but this argument fails to take account of the different levels of cultural and economic capital existing in society. This connects to the second problem: the actual operation of the learning webs. Freire argued that by abandoning universal public education and leaving educational endeavors to informal social interactions, his proposal had a bias in favor of middle- and upper-class groups, which have much easier access to social, cultural, and economic opportunities and thereby could take more advantage of the learning webs than lower-income groups. Whereas Freire acknowledged the problems with schools described by Illich and was aware of the role played by the educational system in reproducing social inequalities, he argued that schools were still one of the few social equalizers, that is, one of the few avenues of upward mobility for the poor. Unlike Illich, who perceived schools as monolithic, bureaucratic, and unredeemable institutions, Freire considered them as historical and social institutions where class conflicts take place and where change can occur (Gadotti 1994). For Freire, then, the task of progressive reformers was not to eliminate schools altogether but to make them more democratic, inclusive, relevant, and joyful. Toward the end of his life, he would be able to test these ideas when he had the opportunity to work in the educational bureaucracy.

In relation to Rogers, it is possible identify at least two major differences. The first has to do with the general orientation of their work. Rogers had a psychological perspective (with a focus on therapy and self-fulfillment) and Freire a sociopolitical one, more concerned about the connections between education, power, and democracy. Whereas Rogers was interested in individual healing, self-actualization, and group dynamics, Freire was interested in the development of critical consciousness and social transformation. This can be explained by their different contexts: Rogers worked in the developed countries mainly with middle-class participants who felt alienated from the mainstream, whereas Freire worked in developing countries with illiterate peasants and workers in contexts of extreme inequality and oppressive structures. The second difference, which sometimes was not sufficiently recognized, has to do with their pedagogical approach. Rogers advocated nondirectiveness and argued that educators should act as facilitators who should refrain from teaching, guiding, or directing the process because group members were expected to choose, collectively and individually, their own path toward their own goals. Freire, instead, argued that education is always directive because the educator comes to the group with goals and with a program to achieve those goals.

Moreover, unlike Rogers, Freire did not see the educator as a facilitator. For him, the term "facilitator" suggests an abdication of the role of educator and the endorsement of a laissez faire approach to education in which anything goes. For Freire, the main role of a teacher is to teach, and facilitation is just part of teaching. In his own words: "I consider myself a teacher and always a teacher. What I want to make clear also is in being a teacher, I always teach to facilitate. I cannot accept the notion of a facilitator who facilitates as not to teach" (Freire and Macedo 1995:378). For Freire, the educator is not equal to the students and has a different responsibility in the teaching/learning process, and argued that educators should not be forced to choose between a laissez faire approach and an authoritarian approach, because it is possible to be directive without being authoritarian and to be democratic without abandoning students. In his approach, directiveness should not imply authoritarianism in the same way that freedom should not imply chaos. Unlike Rogers, Freire contended that being a directive educator does not mean domesticating students or imposing an agenda on them, and distinguished between the "directive liberating" and the "directive dominating" educator. Whereas the dominating directive educator domesticates, manipulates, and monopolizes the objectives and the content of the education process, the liberating educator encourages classroom comradery and, rather than seeking to control the students, engages with them as cognitive subjects (Shor and Freire 1987). As for the parallels between *Freedom to Learn* and *Pedagogy of the Oppressed*, Freire and Rogers were writing their books at the same time in different parts of the world, and there is no evidence that they had any knowledge of each other's works at the time (Gadotti 1994).

In sum, it could be argued that Freire made four original contributions. First, he made an original contribution to the understanding of the connections between education and politics that expanded the original insights of the progressive school movement and of the theories of reproduction. Second, he made original contributions to the then-nascent movement of participatory action research. Third, he generated a Copernican revolution in the field of adult literacy, providing an original and effective alternative to the traditional adult literacy approaches of the past. The originality of his literacy approach does not reside only in the efficacy of his innovative literacy methods, but, above all else, in the originality of his philosophical, political, and methodological approach designed to develop a critical consciousness as part of a humanizing pedagogy (Bimbi 1971, Araujo Freire and Macedo 1998). Fourth, he made an original contribution to school democratization by adapting popular education principles to the context of the formal education system.

(3) Contradictions

An issue recurrently raised by Freire's critics is that his eclecticism was unable to combine successfully Marxist philosophy and Christian theology. In Chapter 2, I already discussed the tensions between eclecticism and coherence in the work of Freire and between some alleged contradictions such as dialogue-directivity and being simultaneously a Christian and a Marxist. In that section, I referred to a conversation with Myles Horton in which Freire defended his right to be contradictory,[20] although he immediately added that he saw no contradiction between his Catholic faith and his Marxist ideology, because these approaches are complementary (Freire 1973 and 1990:247). Cooper (1995) agrees, arguing that Freire successfully reconciled Christianity and Marxism, but his combination was misunderstood because Marxist educators missed his theology and Christian educators downplayed his Marxism. In examining Freire's contradictions resulting from his eclecticism, Walker (1980) believed that the sources of Freire's approach could be found in two places: in the theory and practice of national liberation movements and the doctrine of socialism; and in a form of existential Christianity. For Walker, the second is the more fundamental influence on Freire, who stands clearly in the broad Catholic tradition of syncretism, which consists of synthesizing Christianity with various other theoretical and practical elements (159). Mackie (1980:107), however, writing in the same book as Walker, identifies Freire as a former liberal democrat who became a revolutionary socialist and who adopted Marxist analysis. In general terms, this transition is accurate because Freire initiated his literacy work in Brazil under the auspices of a populist government and shifted to a more radical political stance after the 1964 coup d'état and his exile in Chile. At the same time, this is not the same as claiming that Freire managed to use adequately the tools of Marxist analysis. As previously discussed, some have argued that although Freire borrowed categories from Marxism, he failed to undertake a serious Marxist analysis because he lacked detailed understanding of class and power.

Some commentators who discuss this issue align themselves with Walker and contend that Freire's limitations to undertake a serious and rigorous sociological and economic Marxist analysis can be explained by the fact that he was not a traditional Marxist scholar. As noted in the previous chapter, Elias (1994:44) argues that Freire's thought is best understood as that of an educational practitioner and theorist, and that his eclectic work is best interpreted if we consider him primarily a Catholic thinker. Paul Taylor (1993:6) concurs, observing that in Freire the language of the Christian faith is more than metaphors and language devices: "it is actually the skeleton or underpinning of his philosophical and social analysis." Likewise, Cheryl Bridges-Johns (1993) argues that Freire's pedagogical enterprise is centrally founded in his Christian faith, and Diana Coben (1998:88) points out that Freire is best understood as a radical Catholic whose inspirational and prophetic optimism sprang from the milieu that produced liberation theology.

Other commentators (Au 2007, Allman 2010) side with Mackie, arguing that the philosophical basis of Freire, all throughout his work, should be interpreted as Marxist. Some of them, like Youngman (2000) identify two distinct Marxist influences in Freire's work, which correspond to different periods. In the 1970s, according to this analysis, Freire's ideas were strongly influenced by humanist Marxism—particularly the culturalist tradition—expressed through his concerns with alienation, consciousness, dialectics, and praxis, and also in his opposition to existing capitalist society, on the one hand, and to the dogmatism, vanguardism, and sectarianism of certain sectors of the left, on the other. During the 1980s, Freire incorporated concerns about the structural determinants of education and utilized Marxist economic concepts such as the mode of production, material conditions, social relations of production, and so on. For Youngman, although Freire rejected economic reductionism, he did not reject a materialist stance. Moreover, the strength of his political economy approach lies in his analysis of processes of social domination, ideology, and hegemony in adult education and of its linkage to liberating education and oppositional social movements.

It should be noted here that Freire himself acknowledged the criticism, based mainly on his first writings, that he focused excessively on individual freedom and autonomy instead of on socioeconomic structures. In a lecture that he gave in Argentina in 1985, he said that at the time of his first publications, he was too idealistic because he assumed that a critical perception of reality necessarily implied its transformation. In that speech, Freire (1985c) attributed such an implication to the influence of psychologism and subjectivism on his ideas at that period of his life, but he pointed out that he had overcome that phase since at least 1972 and lamented that some commentators were still criticizing his first books without paying attention to his self-criticism. In sum, there is general agreement in the literature that Freire's approach was eclectic. The term "eclecticism" can be used in a pejorative or in a laudatory way. Some attach a negative connotation to the term, implying that the "mix-and-match" efforts often lead to internal incoherence and unsuccessful results. Others prefer the term interdisciplinarity, and argue that the crossing of boundaries of academic fields and schools of thought and the careful selection of theories can complement and combine ideas in a novel way so as to illuminate a particular issue and eventually produce a new and useful synthesis. The open question is to what extent did Freire borrow excessively, chaotically, and contradictorily (as some critics claim) and to what extent was he able to develop, from the different elements, an original formulation that was something other than the sum of the parts (as some Freireans claim). Gadotti (2001:72), for instance, argues that Freire was able to integrate the core elements of different currents of thought without repeating them mechanically, and Franco observed that, on reading Freire, one may have the impression of listening to familiar sounds while at the same time, experiencing an overall harmony that is new. More recently, Dale and Hyslop-Margison (2010:77) argued that the beauty and collective integrity of Freire's philosophical synthesis overrides some potential dissonance.

(4) Universal categories and dichotomies

Freire has been criticized for talking about "the oppressed" in abstract, universal, and generic terms without providing a straightforward answer to the question: "Who are the oppressed?" One possible response is that this question can only be answered in each specific context. Another response can be found in Taylor (1993:133), who observed that only the nonoppressed would pose such a question because, in the real world, the oppressed know who they are. For them, the question has mere academic interest, and a more relevant question would be: "Who are the oppressors?" Regarding Woock's argument that Freire failed to help us understand who exactly are the oppressors and the oppressed in North America, two comments can be made. The first is that demanding Freire to tell us who exactly are the oppressors and the oppressed in the North American context or on which side of this equation North American teachers are to be found is not only unrealistic but also unfair. In *Pedagogy of the Oppressed*, Freire reflected on his experience in northeast Brazil. How should readers expect Freire to explain relations of oppression everywhere on Earth? The second problem with Woocks's argument is an internal contradiction. On the one hand, he acknowledges that *Pedagogy of the Oppressed* is useful in explaining relations of oppression in northeast Brazil, and on the other hand, he complains that because the book is not rooted in a social or economic context, relations of oppression are left in a vacuum and cannot be grasped. If the two propositions are true, as he seems to claim, his argument does not hold. A related criticism, which came especially from Marxist quarters, was that Freire's universal conceptualization of the oppressed did not connect explicitly to the concept of class. In response to such charges, Freire argued that his critics had not paid enough attention because, in *Pedagogy of the Oppressed*, there were 35 references to social class (cited in Gadotti 1994;128–9).

Ironically, at the same time as he was criticized for his lack of attention to social class, Freire was also challenged for focusing too much on class. These critics claimed that Freire limited his conceptualization of oppression to an understanding of economic oppression within an authoritarian political structure while ignoring other forms of oppression and domination, especially those based on race and gender. In a dialogue with Macedo, Freire acknowledged that this criticism was pertinent, especially in his earlier work: "When I wrote *Pedagogy of the Oppressed*, I tried to understand and analyze the phenomenon of oppression with respect to its social, existential, and individual tendencies. In doing so, I did not focus specifically on oppression marked by specificities such as color, gender, race, and so forth. I was more preoccupied then with the oppressed as a social class" (Freire and Macedo 1996:223). He added, however, that he always struggled against all forms of oppression, and in *Pedagogy of Hope* he expanded his conception of oppression by recognizing the interconnected relationships of racial, gender, and class discrimination: "Sex does not explain everything. Nor does race. Nor does class. Racial discrimination is by no manner of means reducible to a problem of class. Neither is sexism" (Freire 1994b:156). Nevertheless, in his conceptualization of interlocking oppressions, Freire gave preeminence to class exploitation as the dominant form of discrimination: "Without a reference to the division between the classes, however, I, for one, fail to understand either phenomenon—racial or sexual discrimination—in its totality" (p. 156). Freire lamented that those who had emphasized the identity politics of antiracist and antisexist movements had neglected to integrate the concept of social class within their analyses of discrimination, and called for "unity in diversity" to bring together different social movements in order to act together for social transformation while mutually respecting particular differences. To avoid misunderstandings of this issue, Freire asserted several times that he firmly believed that all discrimination was immoral. In *Pedagogy of Freedom*, for instance, he stated that all discriminatory practices, be they along class, sex, or racial lines, "offend the essence of human dignity and constitute a radical negation of democracy" (Freire 1998b:41). At the same time, he made clear that the analysis of oppression should not look at these dimensions in isolation from each other: "We cannot reduce the analysis of racism to social class, but then again, we cannot understand racism fully without class analysis" (Freire and Macedo 1987:226–7). In this regard, Gibson (1994) argued that Freire's grasp of the reciprocal interactions of class, race, sex, and nationality as simultaneously pivotal to conscious action for change predated both feminism and postmodernism.

Another criticism was that the binary approach used by Freire was simplistic because it presented the complexities of the real world in terms of false dichotomies. To some extent, Freire's proclivity for oppositions can be explained by the particular contexts in which he lived and worked, characterized by severe inequalities and intense social conflicts. At that time, slogans that appealed to dichotomies were commonplace and demanded people to choose between irreconcilable options (e.g., liberation or dependency, reform or revolution, tyranny or freedom, dictatorship or democracy) that were aligned with particular political projects, social movements, and political parties. Having said that, Freire often claimed that his conceptual strategy was precisely to analyze, in a dynamic and historical manner and using a dialectical approach, the tensions resulting from existing contradictions. He also employed a dialectical perspective to understand everyday situations, and noted that when he was secretary of education, his dialectical approach helped him to consider simultaneously the possibilities and limits of the educational system, and that a less dialectical person may have resigned in desperation (Torres 1994:106). Influenced by Hegel, Marx, Kosik, and others, Freire argued that a dialectical examination of reality was necessary in order to move forward both in the deeper analysis of that reality and in practical interventions aimed at change. Several commentators (e.g., C. A. Torres 1976, Gadotti 1994, Roberts 2003, Allman 2010) asserted that Freire was able to overcome false dichotomies through a dialectical analysis of reality. For Au (2007), this is a very important aspect to consider in reading Freire, because without a firm understanding of the dialectical materialist foundation of Freire's approach, critical misunderstandings are likely to manifest. He makes the case that Freire's approach was rooted in Marxist dialectical materialism since his earliest writings and remained consistent throughout the corpus of his work.[21] Taylor, however, argued that Freire's method could never realize its objective of praxis as a process of active reflection and reflective action: "The nominalist discerning of the word cannot turn to action because, by definition, it can never go beyond the passivity of a 'reading' of a word" (p. 80). Although Taylor's criticism is well taken, it is possible to identify two problems with his argument. First, it is not self-evident that reading words is a passive act (even if the words have been selected by an external team) because the very pursuit of connecting phonemes and graphemes is an active endeavor. Second, Taylor does not discuss another dimension of Freire's literacy method: "reading the world" through moderated group discussions about social reality. This is arguably an active process with significant potential to transform reflection into action (see Roberts 2000). Moreover, Freire clarified several times that a critical awareness of the world was not the magic wand that would transform complex social realities (Gerhardt 1993).

The other frequently criticized dichotomy in Freire's framework is his use of "banking" and "liberatory" education. In Chapter 2, I discussed some of Freire's responses to the confusion that arose with the perception that they were antinomic terms. Here I would add that Freire was also accused of suggesting that teachers' expertise was unimportant, even an impediment, because it might promote banking education. In fact, the opposite is true. Freire strongly argued that teachers should be competent and knowledgeable about the content of their discipline, be it physics, history, or language: In an interview with Dillon (1985:19), Freire was quite explicit: "If I don't know, I cannot be a teacher," and added that, as teachers, "we must become prepared, competent, capable; we should not frustrate those students who come to us hoping for answers to their expectations, to their doubts, to their desire to know."

Years later, in *Pedagogy of Hope*, he returned to this by stating that teachers and students are not identical for countless reasons. He asserted that "dialogue between teachers and students does not place them on the same footing professionally," and added that "dialogue is meaningful precisely because the dialogical subjects, the agents in the dialogue, not only retain their identity, but actively defend it, and thus grow together" (Freire 1994b:101).

(5) Antidialogue, manipulation, and authoritarianism

In the discussions on dialogical education, directiveness, and Rogers, I addressed some of the issues raised by Freire's critics on the topic of antidialogue, manipulation, and authoritarianism together with some of Freire's responses. To avoid unnecessary repetition, here I would just add that Freire's approach has been criticized as "antidialogical" due to the limited participation of learners in the selection of the generative words. One response to this criticism can be found in Roberts (2000), who admits that some elements of Freire's literacy work were nondialogical but argues that they were not necessarily "antidialogical." Roberts observes that Freire's model fostered dialogue, not a type of dialogue in which anything goes, but a dialogue that took place within given parameters. Moreover, Freire's choice of generative words was based on a balance between the need to find words that, on the one hand, were intimately connected to the participants' lives and, on the other hand, fulfilled technical requirements such as linguistic criteria.

Regarding the charge that his pedagogical approach ran the risk of manipulation, Freire observed that any educational practice (including a nondirective one) ran such a risk. As to criticisms of directiveness and authoritarianism, Freire (1994b:66) claimed that educational practice was always directive whether it was authoritarian or democratic, and argued that whenever the directivity of the educator interfered with the creative and investigative capacity of the student, the necessary directivity became manipulation or authoritarianism. In this context, the ethical duty of teachers is to express their respect for differences in ideas and positions, even those diametrically opposed to theirs. A related critique has to do with Freire's understanding of conscientization as a linear and

static progression through stages, from magical to critical consciousness. While it is true that, in his first publications, Freire used this
evolutionary model, in his later work he conceptualized conscientization more as a dynamic and ever-evolving process (Roberts 1996). For
several years, Freire refrained from using the term conscientization
because he believed that it created too many, unnecessary misunderstandings. Toward the end of his life, he started to use it again because
he believed that it was a rich and dynamic concept that indicated movement and the preparation for action (Araujo Freire, cited in Borg and
Mayo 2000). Finally, the criticisms of nepotism and authoritarianism
related to the required books during his mandate as secretary of education were undeserved, because the decision to include those texts in the
bibliography was not taken by Freire: the selection of books, as well as
the preparation, implementation, and evaluation of the examinations,
was made by a prestigious private foundation (C. A. Torres 1994,
O'Cadiz et al. 1998).

(6) Cultural invasion

The argument that Freire's approach promotes and justifies cultural
invasion was first advanced by authors such as Epstein, Berger, Illich,
and Walker, and more prominently by Bowers, who has become one of
Freire's most relentless critics. Bowers claims that Freire thought he
knew better than the oppressed about their difficulties because he
believed that they had a lower level of consciousness and he was better
placed to organize their struggles against oppression. Therefore, concludes Bowers, Freire felt justified in imposing on them his own set of
cultural beliefs. Such an attitude, Bowers says, was not only arrogant
and elitist but also amounted to cultural invasion. Along the same lines,
Bowers charges that Freire did not respect local traditions, perpetuated
colonialism and Western imperialism, and contributed to the environmental crisis.

Freire was aware of Bowers' criticisms, and they exchanged their
differences in public at least once in a debate that took place at the
University of Oregon in July 1987. Freire was surprised and unhappy
when he learned that some people accused him of being arrogant, elitist,

and a "cultural invader" because those were traits that he personally criticized and combated. He claimed that those charges were based on a distorted understanding of his work and a naïve view of educational practice as a neutral activity in which the role of the teacher is simply to transfer knowledge to the students. Indeed, it is curious, and to some extent ironic, that Freire is accused of promoting cultural invasion if we consider that, in *Pedagogy of the Oppressed* (published originally in 1968), he had already criticized extensively practices of cultural invasion, with over a dozen (negative) references to cultural invasion and with an entire section of chapter 4 devoted to this concept. In that section, Freire (1970b:152) argued that cultural invasion occurs when the invaders "penetrate the cultural context of another group, in disrespect of the latter's potentialities," and then "impose their own view of the world upon those they invade and inhibit the creativity of the invaded by curbing their expression." They do so, Freire noted, because invaders believe in their own "superiority" and in the "inferiority" of the invaded. As if this was not clear enough on where he stood regarding practices of cultural invasion, he added:

> cultural invasion is thus always an act of violence against the persons of the invaded culture, who lose their originality or face the threat of losing it. In cultural invasion (as in all the modalities of antidialogical action) the invaders are the authors of, and actors in, the process; those they invaded are the objects. The invaders mold; those they invade are molded. The invaders choose; those they invade follow that choice—or are expected to follow it. The invaders act; those they invade have only the illusion of acting, through the action of the invaders. (Freire 1970b:152)

Already in that early stage of his trajectory, Freire was aware that cultural invasion could be carried out not only by the dominant elite but also by well-intentioned professionals. Freire was referring to educators, social workers, agronomists, sociologists, economists, engineers, doctors, nurses, priests and pastors, and sometimes those who were part of the revolution and were expected to act in the interest of the oppressed. Freire considered this type of cultural invasion particularly appalling, and attributed it to the reactivation in the new society of elements of the old society, including bureaucratization and paternalism. Freire contrasted cultural invasion with cultural synthesis in which the external actors do not go to the communities to teach, transmit, or give anything, but rather to learn together with the people about the people's world:

> In cultural invasion the actors (who need not even go personally to the invaded culture; increasingly, their action is carried out by technological instruments) superimpose themselves on the people who are assigned the role of spectators, of objects. In cultural synthesis, the actors become integrated with the people, who are co-authors of the action that both perform upon the world. (Freire 1970b:180)

Having said that, it is also true that in the first chapters of *Pedagogy of the Oppressed*, Freire made reference to the need to assist the oppressed in their transit from a magic and traditional consciousness to a critical one, and this is precisely the type of "evidence" used by Chet Bowers and his collaborators to argue that Freire advocates imposing a different worldview and that this is nothing less than cultural invasion. I suggest that if we examine objectively not only *Pedagogy of the Oppressed* but also the entire corpus of Freire's production, it will be possible to find some sentences here and there that support Bower's argument, but the overall conclusion will be that Freire did not endorse practices of cultural invasion but explicitly condemned them.

Since Freire's death in 1997, Bowers's most recent waves of criticism (e.g., Bowers 2003, 2005, 2007, 2008) have generated numerous responses from Freirean and non-Freirean scholars alike, and some of them have engaged directly with Bowers in public debate. For instance, Peter McLaren and Bowers engaged in a vibrant exchange in the journal *Capitalism Nature Socialism* (Bowers 2007, McLaren 2007). In his appraisal of Bowers's arguments against Freire, McLaren (2007:101) charged that "Bowers' intellectual rendezvous with Freire has resulted in a hypertrophied critique that is more public display than systematic analysis" and that "when it comes to evaluating Freire's work, Bowers acts like a mulching machine, thinning out the overstock of Freire's ideas on the pedagogy of the oppressed and leaving few seeds of promise to be harvested." Besides this public exchange, we can find in the literature other texts that address Bowers's criticisms. Among them are Roberts (2000 and 2010), McLaren and Houston (2004), Kahn (2005), and Au (2007 and 2009). These publications contend, first and foremost, that Bowers's accusations are based on a nonhistorical and nonholistic reading of Freire that focuses on his early writings, particularly *Pedagogy of the Oppressed*. They also argue that Bowers creates an arbitrary dichotomy between "Western" and "non-Western" cultures, homogenizes a diversity of Western ideas and practices, and romanticizes "non-Western" cultures. Furthermore, they claim that Bowers misreads Freire in assuming that because he (Freire) rejects banking education (the "depositing" of knowledge in the minds of the students), he also rejects cultural transmission from generation to generation (Kahn 2005, Roberts 2000, McLaren 2007).

Another issue of contention is Bowers's attack on Freire for his alleged lack of environmental concerns. Bowers and his collaborators articulated this criticism in the book *Rethinking Freire: Globalization and the Environmental Crisis,* published in 2005. One of the problems with this argument is that the main evidence used by Bowers and his colleagues to show that Freire had not ecological concerns consists of references to his early works, particularly *Pedagogy of the Oppressed*. Some of the contributors to the book are even explicit about this strategy. One of them, for instance, said: "I am aware that the later Paulo Freire has made clarifications and modifications of his ideas, but I have chosen to remain with the Freire of *Pedagogy of the Oppressed,* his most influential book" (Siddhartha 2005:93). It is Siddhartha's prerogative to select the sample for his analysis, and if this is the case, it is difficult to refute the argument that *Pedagogy of the Oppressed,* written in the 1960s as a reflection on the dynamics of domination and liberation in the context of workers and peasant communities in Brazil and Chile, is largely silent on the topic of the environmental crisis. However, it is unfair to generalize from this and claim that Freire had no ecological preoccupations. While it is true to say that Freire was not an environmental educator, in several texts and interviews he recognized the relevance of ecological issues and, according to his colleague Moacir Gadotti, toward the end of his life he was writing a book on ecopedagogy. Moreover, the Paulo Freire Institute of Brazil was deeply involved in the collective drafting of the Earth Charter (2000), a process that started a few months before Freire's death. Furthermore, in his last book, *Pedagogy of Indignation* (2004:47), Freire observed that ecology had gained tremendous importance and recommended that it should be present in any educational practice of a radical, critical, and liberating nature. Besides, ecological themes featured prominently in the thematic complexes tackled in the popular public schools (O'Cadiz et al. 1998).

Bowers also argues that Freire's pedagogy advances the colonial project (associated with Western rationalism and the European Enlightenment) and undermines traditional cultures because it promotes individualism. However, as discussed in detail by Freire himself (Freire 1973, 1982b, Freire and Macedo 1995) and by other authors (Au and Apple, 2007, McLaren 2007, Au 2009), his theory of transformation is not individual but social and based on human collectives, and he recognizes a fluid, dialectical relationship between the individual and world. In the words of McLaren (2007:104–5), Bowers's specious claim that Freire's pedagogy supplies "the form of individualism needed by the industrial culture is in contradistinction to Freire's actual work and undercuts and subverts Freire's emphasis on collectivity in both thought and action." An additional argument advanced by Bowers and his colleagues that Freire promotes colonialism is that the Guinea-Bissau literacy campaign in which Freire acted as international advisor used the colonial Portuguese language. However, it is pertinent to remember that Freire opted for Creole as the main language of instruction, but the government rejected his advice (Freire and Macedo 1987, Freire and Faundez 1989, Mayo 2004, McLaren 2007).

Nevertheless, Freire agreed with some of the arguments advanced by Bowers and other thinkers influenced by postmodernist ideas, especially challenges to the arrogant and dogmatic certainties of modernism and to the totalizing Eurocentric and androcentric logic of the modernist project. At the same time, he distinguished between a conservative and a progressive postmodernism. For Freire, the former portrayed the obstacles to social change as inevitable and insurmountable, while the latter was radical, democratic, and utopian. The former perceived the current period as one in which social class, ideologies, left-and-right projects, and dreams were no longer relevant, whereas the latter emphasized the reinvention of power and the struggle for progressive social change from an attitude of humility, openness, and respect for plurality (Freire 1993a, 1994b, 1997a). Although Freire accepted, and even endorsed, some of the premises of postmodernism, it can be argued that he remained entrenched in a "critical modernist" position, one that advocated a universal human ethic challenging the inequalities of capitalism and calling for an emancipatory educational project that nurtured democracy and humanization.

(7) Implementation and outcomes

Regarding the implementation of his ideas, Freire has been criticized, among other things, for the meager results of the literacy campaign in Guinea-Bissau in the late 1970s, for the low-quality pedagogical interventions in the Nicaraguan literacy campaign in the early 1980s, for several aspects of his work as secretary of education of Sao Paulo in the early 1990s, and for the problems that arose in some of the projects inspired by his ideas and carried out by people around the world. In relation to the Guinea-Bissau's literacy campaign, I have already indicated that Freire attempted to persuade the leadership of that country to use Creole as the main medium of instruction. He was concerned with the language issue from the beginning: "On our third visit to Guinea-Bissau, I began to see the difficulties in learning the Portuguese language being encountered by the popular groups— difficulties that contradicted the initial information they had given us in response to our anxiety about the language issue" (Freire and Faundez 1989:107). Freire and his Instituto de Açao Cultural (IDAC) colleagues tried to raise the issue, but at that time this was a delicate subject, one that generated intense internal debate in the government, and one on which public discussion was discouraged. Then, Freire soon discovered that his recommendation was out of the political boundaries imposed in his work, and he had to accept Portuguese as the language of instruction, even if his method was not designed for second-language acquisition (C. A. Torres 1993:135). Although Freire acknowledged the relevance of Portuguese for Guinea-Bissau's needs as a newly independent country, he called for the development of a cultural policy that encouraged the different ethnic groups to express themselves in their own language, that introduced written Creole, and that had Portuguese as a key foreign language:

> I admitted, obviously, what it would mean in terms of effort, knowledge, investment and struggle for Creole to take on the role of the national language . . . The issue under discussion was not that of totally denying the importance of the Portuguese language—that would have been naïve—but of not conferring on it the role of being the teaching medium of the people over a long period of time. The moment would have to arrive when Portuguese would be studied as a privileged foreign language. (Freire and Faundez 1989:108)

However, the political leadership of Guinea Bissau opted for Portuguese as the main language of instruction. Freire argued that the key issue to be discussed in examining the failure of the Guinea-Bissau literacy campaign was not his literacy method but the appropriateness and feasibility of conducting the campaign in the colonizer's language:

> With or without Paulo Freire it was impossible in Guinea-Bissau to conduct a literacy campaign in a language that was not part of the people. My method did not fail, as has been claimed . . . The issue should be analyzed in terms of whether it is linguistically viable to conduct literacy campaigns in Portuguese in any of these countries. My method is secondary to this analysis. If it is not viable to do so, my method or any other method will certainly fail." (Freire and Macedo 1987:112–13)

In relation to the 1980 Nicaraguan literacy campaign, it is true that in many cases the literacy *brigadistas* used a traditional banking approach instead of a Freirean dialogical approach. Four comments could be made in response to this. The first is that the literacy campaign was carried out in a context of a national emergency, with a country just emerging from the chaos and destruction caused by a powerful earthquake and a war and a new government with no previous governing experience. In this context, to expect a perfect implementation of a massive pedagogical intervention would be unrealistic. The second is that although the workshops attended by the literacy workers emphasized dialogical approaches, once these young and inexperienced volunteers (most of them secondary school students) were in teaching roles in real classrooms, they tended to revert to the only pedagogical approach that they were familiar with through their own schooling experience, which was a banking model. The third comment is that, despite the methodological shortcomings, the campaign was successful in reducing illiteracy rates from 50 percent to 12.5 percent. Last but not least, it is not clear to what extent the pedagogical limitations of the campaign should be squarely placed on Freire, as he was only one of many domestic and international advisors who had to accept the possibilities and limits of a particular social reality.

Regarding Freire's tenure as secretary of education, when he approved school lunches for poor students, he was accused of promoting "assistentialism" (a position highly criticized in his writings) and hence of contradicting his theory with his practice. Freire himself clarified that his practice did not contradict his theory because he always rejected assistentialism as being a patronizing, charitylike strategy that created dependency without addressing the roots of inequality, but he defended assistance to those in need as a precondition for learning. He was also criticized for being authoritarian, but as Freire noted several times during his time as secretary of education, he made a concerted effort to democratize the administrative apparatus and to transfer power to the schools:

> We started by making an administrative reform so that the Secretariat could work in a different way. With administrative structures that only made authoritarian power viable, it was impossible to develop a democratic administration that was in favor of school autonomy. (Freire, cited in O'Cadiz et al. 1998:249)

It is also important to remember that if some of the objectives of the programs undertaken by the secretary of education of Sao Paulo were not achieved, it was not only due to the quality of the programs themselves but also to broader and deeply rooted structural and cultural dynamics and socioeconomic inequalities (Stromquist 1997).

As for criticisms linking Freire to problems that arose in Freirean-inspired projects or from ideas he formulated in his different publications, in many cases it is unfair to blame him for those texts or actions.

As Freire (1994b:88) stated, "I cannot accept responsibility for what is said or done in my name contrary to what I do and say." A case in point is—again—the book *Rethinking Freire,* edited by C.A. Bowers and Apffel-Marglin, in which several contributors describe the trials and tribulations of pedagogical interventions that took place in the 1960s and 1970s and were inspired by Freire's theories. However, as Kahn (2005) observed, most of the interventions described in the book were only loosely connected to Freire through a handful of sentences taken from *Pedagogy of the Oppressed,* and there is no evidence that the activism depicted as "oppressive technocracy" was the result of Freire's theories and propositions. Likewise, it is unfair to blame Freire for the tendency to reduce his complex notion of culture circles to a simple rearrangement of chairs or for failures in adapting his proposals to a particular context (Facundo 1984, Hussey 1999). In this regard, Kane (2001) distinguishes two kinds of "pseudo-Freirean" projects: those that use some of Freire's methods but devoid them of their political orientation,[22] and those that are aligned with his political orientation but experience methodological difficulties. The question here is to what extent this can be attributed to Freire's failure to articulate pedagogical interventions in a clear manner, or to other factors such as co-optation or the inability of the educators to apply Freire's ideas creatively. This question can only be answered project by project.

Summary and conclusions

Since the mid-1960s, Paulo Freire's ideas on education have had a significant impact, first in Brazil, and then in Latin America and internationally, especially after the publication of *Pedagogy of the Oppressed* in English in 1970. The book became an instant success, partly due to its own merits and partly to the historical context at the time of its publication. Over time, the book became both a blessing and a curse for Freire: a blessing precisely because of its success, expressed not only in its wide readership and multiple translations but also in its contribution to the understanding of the relations between education and politics; a curse because, for almost four decades, both sympathetic readers and critics tended to focus on *Pedagogy of the Oppressed,* without paying enough attention to his many other books, especially to those written in his later phase (Roberts 2000). Freire himself was frustrated with this because, like many other intellectuals who are self-reflective and take the critiques of their work seriously, he revised many of his ideas throughout his life. As Mayo (2004) noted, Freire was a "person in process," constantly in search of greater coherence.

Throughout his life and beyond, the work of Paulo Freire has been praised and criticized and has generated intense debate among educators. Within Latin America's popular education movement, Freire has been a standard point of reference: the question is whether to adopt him, to adapt him, or to reject him.[23] In North America and other parts of the world, he has been an inspiring figure in the critical pedagogy movement. His literacy circles and the method of the generative word have been recognized as a significant leap forward from the traditional approach to adult literacy programs. Peter McLaren (2000:141) claimed that "Paulo Freire was one of the first internationally recognized educational thinkers who fully appreciated the relationship among education, politics, imperialism, and liberation" and added that "no one has done more than him to move the struggle forward over the role of education as a vehicle for liberatory praxis."

The influence of Freire's ideas can be found in adult education, higher education, elementary and secondary schooling, and even early childhood education. His philosophical and pedagogical approach has been criticized for different reasons, ranging from idealism, utopianism, mysticism, and irrelevance (Taylor 1993:149) to populism, vanguardism, authoritarianism, and cultural colonialism. For almost three decades, feminists across the United States have fiercely criticized the sexism of his language and his lack of serious gender analysis; Marxist scholars have harshly challenged him for his failure to provide a systematic analysis of class, capitalism, and schooling; and educators, scholars, and organizers of color have criticized him for his emphasis on class rather than race in the struggle for social and economic justice (Darder 2002:43–4). If I had to choose one paragraph that summarized these criticisms, I would select this one from Coben (1998:113):

Freire's rhetoric is seductive, yet his pedagogy of liberation remains a romantic ideal, and like any other romantic ideas it has its dark side.

Ultimately, I do not accept Freire's inconsistent class analysis, his universalistic concept of oppression, his idealism and his bizarre notion of a revolutionary leadership composed of patriarchal, charismatic, indeed messianic, members of the petit bourgeoisie.

Freire was an eclectic thinker who drew from different traditions. For some, this was problematic and confusing, and created insolvable internal contradictions. For others, one of the main merits of Freire was precisely his creative integration of contributions from different disciplines into a framework that had education at its core. In the debates on his eclecticism and the different sources of his ideas, it has been claimed that Freire was more an educator and a philosopher than a social scientist and more a Christian than a Marxist. Others such as Youngman (2000), however, have credited Freire with generating a new and wider awareness of the relevance of applying Marxist theory to the study of adult education and the effort to understand its nature, effects, and potential and have praised him for providing a framework that addressed not only economic dependency but also its cultural dimension. Moreover, in his later books, Freire demonstrated that he acknowledged some of the key issues raised by his critics such as a gender-inclusive language, a more thorough and radical analysis of capitalism in the era of neoliberal globalization, and a more explicit recognition of racism and prejudice in his class-based analysis of exploitation and discrimination (Darder 2002). Indeed, in *Pedagogy of Hope* and other books, Freire addressed some of the main criticisms raised in his previous work, including omissions, gaps, and language issues. He apologized deeply for the sexism of his first writings (although the use of the term "man" as a universal concept to indicate "human beings" was common at that time) and credited North American women with making him aware of his mistake, at the same time making a commitment henceforth to use inclusive language in all his publications, including reprints of his prior books.

As we have seen in this chapter, there are a million Paulo Freires. For this reason, in examining the reception and influence of Freire's work, it is useful to distinguish between what Freire did and say, how others have interpreted those words and deeds, and what practices have been implemented in his name, with or without his knowledge. It is also helpful to distinguish between the criticisms that come from those who generally share his analytical premises and his politics of educational and social change, and those who do not. Addressing the latter category of critics, Allman (1999) argued that Freire was a radical thinker and that any other interpretation had to be attributable to the ideological lenses of the reader and not to the ideas themselves. She doubted that any further clarification or deeper analysis on the part of Freire would make any difference to the way in which readers who are unaware of structures of oppression interpret his writings. In any case, Freire is not with us anymore to clarify or expand any ideas that require further elaboration. Now, it is up to us to interpret and reinvent his ideas, particularly those that are most relevant to address the challenges of the twenty-first century. This is the topic of the next chapter.

Notes

1 Peter Mayo (1997) suggests that by doing this, Pinochet paid Freire his supreme compliment.
2 General Albano Harguindeguy, then minister of education, argued that Freire's pedagogical ideas "were contrary to the fundamental values of our Western and Christian civilization" (*Clarín*, October 20, 1978). When Freire learned this, he said to Elza: "this finally convinces me that I am really dangerous" (Freire 1985c:14).
3 See *Taboo: The Journal of Culture and Education* (Fall 1997), *New Zealand Journal of Adult Learning* 26(1), 32–47 (1998), and *Convergence*, Vol. XXXI, No. 1–2, 1998.
4 I identified at least 765 theses (mostly doctoral dissertations) written in English up to 2009. If we add all the doctoral dissertations that I missed, all master's and undergraduate (honors) theses in English, and the hundreds of theses in other languages, and then add all the work produced after 2009, it is reasonable to estimate that thousands of theses have engaged with Freire's work.
5 Among them were the supposedly nondirective nature of his pedagogical approach, the sexist language of his earlier publications, the developmentalist emphasis of his original framework, the relationships between reflection and action, the ontological distinction between humanization and dehumanization, the multidimensionality of oppressive relations, and clarification on concepts like "banking education" or "conscientization."

6 The terms "living myth" and "guru" can be found, among others, in Furter (1985), Gerhardt (1993), and Gadotti (1994). Coben (1998) uses the term "radical hero," and Roberts (2000) called Freire an "academic god." Along the same lines, Aronowitz (1993) noted that by the early 1990s Freire's name had reached near-iconic proportions in the United States, Latin America, and many parts of Europe.

7 As pointed out, contrary to the beliefs of some commentators, Freire did not invent these terms. Praxis is a concept of Greek origins that refers to the unity of theory and practice, and it has been used widely in different traditions. Conscientization was a concept coined by ISEB members in the early 1960s.

8 As Gadotti and Torres (1997) noted, there could be nothing less Freirean than the idea of a disciple, who is a follower of ideas. On the contrary, Freire always challenged others to "reinvent" the world, pursue the truth, refrain from copying ideas, and develop their own dreams.

9 Admittedly, some commentators disagree with this appraisal. Stanley (1972), for instance, argued that utopianism is a significant problem in Freire's thought, because he placed extraordinary emphasis upon education as instrument of liberation.

10 Dom Helder Camara, Freire's mentor, suggested to Illich to visit Freire.

11 One of the problems that generated confusion among some of those who accessed Freire's early work in English was the sequence of translation of his first publications. His first major book, *Education as a Practice of Freedom*, was written in 1967, followed by *Pedagogia do Oprimido* in 1968. However, the English edition of *Pedagogy of the Oppressed* (1970) preceded *Education as a Practice of Freedom*, which was published as part of the book *Education for Critical Consciousness* (1973). This inverted sequence was unfortunate because *Education as a Practice of Freedom* provides a clear introduction to Freire's work and sets the foundations and the context to reach a better understanding of *Pedagogy of the Oppressed* (Collins 1998). Some of the difficulties experienced by English readers in accessing the ideas in *Pedagogy of the Oppressed* may have been avoided if they had had the opportunity to read first *Education as a Practice of Freedom*.

12 Interestingly, David Harman was a professor of education at Harvard at the same time that Freire was a visiting professor, so it is possible that they crossed paths.

13 Freire borrowed the concept of "class suicide" from Amilcar Cabral. It refers to the process by which the progressive members of the elite sacrifice their class position, privileges, and power to struggle with the working masses.

14 Taylor refers to the four lists of generative words presented by Cynthia Brown on page 22 of her booklet *Literacy in 30 Hours* (Brown 1974).

15 For a discussion on Saviani's argument, see Da Silva and McLaren 1993.

16 MacEoin (1972) reports that for years he had been searching for an instance in which peasants have broken out of their oppression, even at a local level, but have found none, and he asked Freire; he admitted that neither had he.

17 The debates on the Guinea-Bissau literacy campaign were addressed in Chapter 2.

18 This definition of iconic books was formulated by Bereiter (cited in Olson 2001:225).

19 Dewey had some connections to adult education, including his involvement with Hull House, a Chicago settlement house and education center founded by social reformer Jane Addams. Still, in comparison with Freire, his interest in adult education was marginal.

20 On a previous occasion, Freire (1979:11) said something along the same lines when he felt frustrated by the accusations of being contradictory: "Many people say I am a contradictory man, and I say I have the right to be contradictory. Let me be in peace with my contradictions."

21 However, in discussing his first books, Freire recognized that back then he did not fully understand the dialectical relationship between theory and practice: "My mistake was not that I recognized the fundamental importance of a knowledge of reality in the process of its change, but rather that I did not take these two different moments—the knowledge of reality and the work of transforming that reality—in their dialectical relationship. It was as if I were saying that to discover reality already meant to transform it" (Freire 1975:15, quoted in Coben 1998:75). In subsequent publications, especially from *Pedagogy of the Oppressed* on, Freire presented a more sophisticated and dialectical analysis of praxis.

22 An example was the Movimento Brasileiro de Alfabetizacao (MOBRAL), created by the Brazilian military dictatorship. MOBRAL used the method of the generative word but removed its critical and political dimensions.

23 Freire was part of the popular education movement for many years. In a two-way street, he made important contributions to the movement, but was also influenced by it (see Gadotti 1994, R. M. Torres 1999).

Chapter 4

The Relevance of Freire Today

Introduction: The contemporary legacy of Paulo Freire

Noted historian Eric Hobsbawm conceptualized "the short 20th century" as the period from the start of World Word I in 1914 to the collapse of the Soviet Union in 1991. Freire's lifetime (1921–97) corresponded closely to Hobsbawm's timeframe. He lived through major events of the twentieth century, including the Great Depression; World War II; and, in the context of Latin America, the populism and developmentalism of the 1950s, the revolutionary movements and military coups of the 1960s and 1970s, the return of democracy in the 1980s, and the neoliberalism of the 1990s. Moreover, as Kirkendall (2010:166) reminds us, Freire's practice as an educator corresponded almost exactly to the Cold War period (1945–91), and his analyses and proposals should be interpreted with that background in mind. Judging by the reception given to his work, the amount of debate generated by his publications, and the number of projects inspired by his approach during his lifetime, it is obvious that Freire's contributions were very relevant for the twentieth century. Less obvious, however, is to what extent those ideas are still significant today. In this final chapter, then, I set out to explore the relevance of Freire's ideas for the twenty-first century. I start by addressing the questions of whether Freire has been ignored and forgotten since he passed away in 1997, and whether revisiting his ideas is merely a nostalgic trip to the past, as some have claimed. After exploring the evidence, I will conclude the first part of the chapter by arguing that Freire's ideas are far from being ignored or forgotten. On the contrary, the opposite trend can be observed. In the second part of the chapter I explore the inspirational role of Freire for twenty-first-century educators and discuss some issues regarding the reinvention of Freire.

Has Freire been forgotten in the twenty-first century?

Two years after Freire's death, Gronholm (1999:161) lamented that Freire's philosophical approach and his contributions to radical adult education "has partly been forgotten in the profit-seeking, market oriented milieu of adult learning in the end of the 1990s." More recently, Stevens (2010) claimed that "Freire's insights into the social, cultural and political dimensions of education have had a huge impact on schooling in the developing world, but less so in the West, with the exception of theorists such as Michael Apple, Henry Giroux and Manuela Guilherme." However, the available evidence shows that today Freire has not been ignored or forgotten, and contrary to Stevens's assertion, the impact of Freire's works on Western educators is significant. First, numerous full-length authored books on Freire have been published in several languages, and at least 15 of them are in English:

Paulo Freire: His Life, Works and Thought (Collins 1977)
The Texts of Paulo Freire (Taylor 1993)
Paulo Freire: Pedagogue of Liberation (Elias 1994)
Reading Paulo Freire (Gadotti 1994)
Education and Democracy: Paulo Freire, Social Movements and Educational Reform in Sao Paulo (O'Cadiz, Lindquist, and Torres 1998)
Education, Literacy and Humanization: Exploring the Work of Paulo Freire (Roberts 2000)
Reinventing Freire: A Pedagogy of Love (Darder 2002)
Liberating Praxis. Paulo Freire's Legacy for Radical Education and Politics (Mayo 2004)
Engaging Paulo Freire's Pedagogy of Possibility: From Blind to Transformative Optimism (Rossatto 2005)
Paulo Freire and the curriculum (Grollios 2009).
Paulo Freire in the 21st Century: Education, Dialogue, and Transformation (Roberts 2010)
Paulo Freire and the Cold War Politics of Literacy (Kirkendall 2010)
Paulo Freire: Teaching for Freedom and Transformation: The Philosophical Influences on the Work of Paulo Freire (Dale and Hyslop-Margison 2010)

Freire, Teaching and Learning: Culture Circles across Contexts (Souto-Manning, 2010)

Paulo Freire's Philosophy of Education: Origins, Developments, Impacts and Legacies (Irwin 2011).

As we can see, over two-thirds of these full-length books were produced after his death, attesting to the currency of his ideas and to his contemporary legacy. In addition, a number of edited books that focus exclusively on Freire have been produced in the twenty-first century in English (e.g., Steiner, Stanley, Krank, McLaren, and Baruth 2000; Slater, Fain, and Rossatto 2002; Bowers and Apffel-Marglin 2005; Torres and Noguera 2008; Shaughnessy, Galligan, and Hurtado 2008; Nieto 2008; Wilson, Park, and Colón-Muñiz 2010) and in other languages (e.g., Bambozzi 2000; Gadotti 2001; C. A. Torres 2001; Araujo Freire 2001; Gadotti, Gómez, and Freire 2003; Monferrer, Aparicio, Murcia Ortiz, and Aparicio 2006; Streck et al. 2008; Ghiggi and De Castro 2009). This bibliography is complemented by the proceedings of the fora organized regularly by the international network of Paulo Freire Institutes, by publications that do not deal exclusively with Freire but engage substantially with his ideas or compare them with those of other authors, and by many recent theses and journal articles in different languages.

Those who claim that Freire has been forgotten may argue that these scholarly publications are only read in small academic circles, with little impact on educational practice. Again, this is not so. For instance, most adult education programs with which I am familiar provide students with the opportunity to study Freire's ideas. Moreover, Freire's books also have a significant presence in many teacher education programs around the world, including North America: Steiner and Rozen (2004) examined the curricula of 16 schools of education in the United States (14 of them top-ranked institutions) and found that *Pedagogy of the Oppressed* was one of the most frequently assigned texts in their philosophy of education courses. In reality, US teachers have been using Freire's ideas in the classroom for some time (Shor 1987, McLaren and Lankshear 1994), but the interest has increased in the last decade. It is true that the possibilities for implementing Freirean approaches in the United States became more limited in the twenty-first century, as educational policies have tended to favor one-size-fits-all approaches with defined learner outcomes and standardized tests (Lindquist 2009). However, despite these pressures, a number of initiatives are being carried out. For instance, Antonia Darder (2002) and Sonia Nieto (2008) included hundreds of pages written by teachers who are attempting to "reinvent" Freire's ideas in the US public education system, and Souto-Manning (2010) discussed the use of Freirean cultural circles in schools and in teacher education. Likewise, aiming at translating Freire's ideas into practice, Murrell (1997) applied Freire's framework to the development of an African American emancipatory pedagogy, Rossatto (2005) developed a proposal for a Freirean curriculum for US classrooms, Macedo and Steinberg (2007) applied Freire's ideas to media literacy, and Carr (2011) advanced 100 proposals that could contribute to democracy through education. Furthermore, Latin American immigrant communities in the United States regularly organize literacy projects, community development, and labor-organizing efforts based on Freire's political and pedagogical approaches (Pruyn 1996, Juma 2008, Nicholls 2010). Freire's ideas have also inspired a variety of school projects. For instance, The Queens High School of Teaching, Liberal Arts and the Sciences, a public high school of 1,200 students in Glen Oaks (New York) has created a Learning Community called "Freire," and the Paulo Freire Freedom School was inaugurated in 2005 in Tucson (Arizona), guided by a vision that emphasizes social justice, environmental sustainability, holistic development, transformative learning, and intercultural education. Through active participation in the democratic structures of this middle school, students develop leadership, conflict resolution, peace-building, deliberative, and decision-making skills. The philosophical approach of the Paulo Freire Freedom School calls for integral development addressing the whole person (body, heart, mind, and soul) and the whole community (the social, cultural, political, and economic structures) both locally and globally.

In the United States, initiatives inspired by Freire go beyond the confines of K–12. In Indiana, the Saint Mary's College Center for Women's Intercultural Leadership (CWIL), a program explicitly based on Freire's philosophical approach, organizes "catalyst trips" to deepen students' understanding of difference and to connect them with community practices in order to develop a democratic and engaged citizenry. The program includes community-building activities and the creation of safe and challenging spaces for collective reflection on delicate issues like white privilege or racism (Bazata et al. 2007). At the College of Educational Studies at Chapman University (California), the Paulo Freire Democratic Project undertakes participatory research and assists schools in their quest for democratic, safe, and violence-free cultures. Also in California, professor Ron Glass coordinates an innovative project in a low-income community that attempts to build a movement linking schools and community transformation. Adapting Freire's methods to twenty-first-century technologies, the team project uses digital stories as the main tool for the "codification" of peoples' experiences, and builds dialogues around these as a way of establishing a learning process that is also a political organizing and mobilization process (Glass 2009). Freire's ideas provide insights and inspiration to many other groups, from museum educators to community development organizations to schoolteachers. For instance, Wendy Woon, the education director of the Museum of Modern Art (MoMa), traveled to Brazil in fall 2010 with other colleagues to research current practices in Brazilian museum education, and particularly to learn about the legacy of Freire's work on current practices of museum education. Concern America, a nonprofit organization based in Santa Ana, California, organizes "Training for Transformation" workshops for adult learners that are based on Freire's educational beliefs and aim at building participatory democracy and civil society rooted in the values of cooperation, justice, trust, mutual respect, and concern for the common good. Another initiative is a collaborative network linking universities, schools, and neighborhoods called CAFÉ (California Association of Freirean Educators), established by the Paulo Freire Institute at the University of California, Los Angeles. The ideas of Freire and Boal have also inspired the creation of Pedagogy and Theater of the Oppressed (PTO) a nonprofit organization aimed at "challenging oppressive systems by promoting critical thinking and social justice" that has organized a well-attended annual conference since 1995 (Boal 1979, Borg and Mayo 2002, Steinberg 2010). Other recent initiatives inspired by Freire include "Photography of the Oppressed" and "Videogames of the Oppressed" (Grace 2009, Frasca 2010).

Freire has not been forgotten in Europe either. Allman (2010) devotes an entire chapter, entitled "Freirean Critical Education in an Unlikely

Context," to discuss the vicissitudes of developing and implementing a course on Freirean pedagogy for 14 years at a British university. In other universities, Freirean approaches are also regarded as foundational in community development courses (Ledwith 2005). In many European countries, Freire-inspired initiatives abound. Two examples are the Adult Learning Project in Scotland (Kirkwood and Kirkwood 2011) and the Universidad Rural Paulo Freire, created in 2006 in Spain to mediate scientific knowledge and popular knowledge, promote sustainable development, and strengthen the social economy.

European groups have also hosted several international conferences. Other examples are the Universitas Paulo Freire (UNIFREIRE), created after the second International Paulo Freire Forum held in Bologna in 2000; the Paulo Freire Institute of Italy, established in Milan a few years ago to update, reinvent, and promote the pedagogical and cultural contributions of Paulo Freire; and the Centro de Pesquisa Paulo Freire (Paulo Freire Research Centre), hosted by the Universidade de Évora in Portugal (Linhares and Trindade 2003). In Canada, the Transformative Learning Centre of the University of Toronto acknowledges Freire as one of its main inspirations, and it has organized several conferences and symposia to discuss his ideas. In one of them, held in October 2003, Joao Pedro Stedile, the leader of the Landless Movement of Brazil, and Sandra Luciana Dalmagro, its pedagogical coordinator, talked about the educational dimension of the movement, and about their adaptation of Freire's ideas to their context. In that conference there were also interesting exchanges between Chet Bowers, one of Freire's staunchest critics, and Moacir Gadotti, the director of the Paulo Freire Institute in Brazil, on issues related to ecopedagogy. More recently, the Transformative Learning Centre hosted the conference "Remembering Freire, Reinventing Freire," held in Toronto on May 2007 on the occasion of the tenth anniversary of Freire's death. The conference attracted a large number of participants, filling to capacity the auditorium of the Ontario Institute for Studies in Education. Also in Toronto, the Catalyst Centre (a popular education worker co-operative) uses Freirean approaches in its projects, sometimes in collaboration with colleagues at York University. Freirean educators can also be found in Quebec (particularly at the Paulo and Nita Freire International Project for Critical Pedagogy in McGill University) and in British Columbia, especially at the University of Victoria and at the University of

British Columbia. In that province, some aboriginal childhood education programs also draw on Freire's philosophy of education.

In Asia, Freire's work is not being forgotten either. In China, several authors have discussed the applicability of a Freirean framework to a variety of fields, including adult literacy, online language courses, health education, comparative and international development, educational theory, social work, participatory research, and political education (Guo 1998, Liu 1998, C. Wang 1996 and 2004, R. Wang 2000, Dong 2002, Cheng 2003, Ku et al. 2005). In Korea, authors have examined the applications of Freire's approaches to the local context in areas ranging from human rights education to language teaching to educational reforms (e.g., Lee 2000, Shin 2005, Kim 2006). In Japan, Freire's perspectives have been applied, inter alia, to inform feminist critical pedagogies, language teaching, and minority youth (Kubota 1998, Maehira 1994, Ohara 2001, Suzuki 2003). In Homidanchi, an impoverished working-class district of Japan affected by layoffs, the Escola Comunitária Paulo Freire provides educational services to Latin American immigrant youth who have abandoned their studies. The school, which also coordinates the Ecological Space Paulo Freire, proposes an education that is concerned with disadvantaged groups, nurtures full human development, and aims at fostering free and conscious citizens who control their own history. In Timor Leste, Freire has been influential in the popular education movement for several decades, and his proposals are used in a variety of grassroots initiatives, ranging from literacy projects to programs aimed at engaging men in solving gender issues (Dos Reis 2004, Durnan 2005). In the Philippines, many popular education groups are still inspired by Freire's ideas, including Education for Life, an organization that coordinates the project "School of the People, School of Life" to promote grassroots leadership formation and community empowerment, and that recognizes Freire's work as one of its main influences. In Bangladesh, BRAC (Building Resources Across Communities), one the largest nongovernmental organizations in the world, uses a revised version of Freire's conscientization model (Rafi 2003). In India, Freirean methods are used to teach literacy (in Bengali and other languages), in some cases fruitfully combining Gandhian and Freirean approaches, and in educational programs aimed at the transformation of Christian communities (Sarkar 2003,

Pramasam 2005, Bhattacharya 2008). Moreover, based on Freire's insights on participatory research and dialogical processes, Singhal et al. (2007) developed a visual approach to participatory communication and applied it successfully to projects in Indian communities. As a testament to the international flows of ideas, Singhal's project in India was inspired by a situation experienced by Freire in a literacy project in Peru decades before.[1]

In Africa, Freire's presence is still felt. In South Africa, for instance, where Freire's ideas influenced social movements during the antiapartheid era, the TASC project (Thinking Actively in a Social Context), inspired by Freirean principles and approaches, has been implemented in a secondary school for 14 years. Likewise, a 1-year course entitled "Training for Transformation: Adapting Paulo Freire's Work to Our Changing Reality," is being taught in Cape Town (organized by The Grail Centre), and a Paulo Freire Institute has been created at the University of Natal. Some South African scholars (e.g., Thomas 2009) have proposed to reexamine Freire's theoretical work in order to develop more participatory, democratic, and bottom-up struggles for social justice in post-apartheid South Africa, and others (e.g., Manyozo 2003) have cautioned about the co-optation and depoliticization of Freire's liberatory education in South Africa's participatory social development advocacy programs. The influence of Freire is also noticeable in other African countries, especially in Portuguese-speaking countries where Freire used to work, such as Angola, Mozambique, Guinea-Bissau, and Cape Verde (Dorvlo 1993, Godonoo 1998, Baatjes and Mathe 2004, Kavaya and Ghiggi 2008).

Not surprisingly, one region of the world in which the work of Paulo Freire is unlikely to be ignored or forgotten is Latin America and the Caribbean. In this region, Freire's impact on adult literacy has been unparalleled, but his influence went well beyond it. Moreover, his work has inspired a variety of movements and initiatives. Just in Brazil we could mention, as examples, the Theatre of the Oppressed movement (Boal 1985), participatory budgeting experiments (including school participatory budgeting), and the Escola Cabana reforms in Belem (Apple 2008), as well as the political and educational efforts of the landless movement and Via Campesina expressed in initiatives like the Latin American Institute of Agro-ecology Paulo Freire and Citizen School projects. Regarding the latter, Peter Mayo (2004) argued that the greatest contribution of Freire's later works lies in the demonstration of his ability to introduce concepts connected with popular education to the school system:

> The democratic, popular public school is very much a community school that is not the exclusive domain of teachers and educational administrators but that is open to many other people with a stake in education, including parents and other guardians, community representatives, students, janitors, cooks and so on." (Mayo 2004:82)

These and other initiatives inspired by Freirean ideas have been adopted and adapted by collectives in other Latin American countries, and some have been compiled in publications. For instance, Moacir Gadotti, Margarita Gomez, and Lutgardes Freire (2003) edited a collection with more than 20 chapters that include descriptions and discussion of Freirean-inspired experiences in Latin America. Freire's inspirational role can be found today in many schools, educational institutions, and community organizations named after him that abound in Latin American countries, especially in Brazil where the people's love for Paulo Freire has also been expressed through art, including the song "Education, a Springboard for Freedom," presented by the Escola de Samba Leandro de Itaquera in the 1999 Rio de Janeiro Carnival. The parade displayed a large sculpture of Freire, and the main song made reference to the main themes of Freire's work.[2] In Nicaragua, the Universidad Paulo Freire is a new institution that has been in operation since 1997 in four cities (Managua, Carazo, Matagalpa, and San Carlos). In Chile, a Freirean approach was used in a project promoting digital literacy, active citizenship, and community economic development with agricultural cooperatives from 2006 to 2010 (Fundación para la Innovación Agraria 2009), and an NGO called Escuela Popular Paulo Freire El Canelo de Nos has been promoting popular and environmental education in low-income communities over 25 years, and is still going strong. In the Bahamas, the three phases of Freire's approach were applied successfully to a remedial writing program that addressed gender issues (Fiore and Elsasser 1987). As noted before, the Latin American popular education movement continues to draw inspiration from Freire and continues to debate vigorously his theories and his proposals for action (Nuñez 2007). Although Freire was not the founder of the popular education movement (in reality, there is no one clear and identifiable founder), he belonged to this movement and made a significant contribution to it, and it is beyond doubt that he is the most prominent name associated with popular education in Latin America (Kane 2001). Even in Cuba, where in the past Freire's ideas were ignored or rejected for ideological reasons, today they are being taken up by a vibrant network of popular educators and academics, mainly through the Centro Martin Luther King and the Cátedra de Estudios Comunitarios Paulo Freire, established in Cienfuegos in 2000 (Pérez Cruz 2004 and 2009, Betto 2010).

Freire's ideas are sometimes being adopted in ways that, at first glance, seem removed from the theories that he advanced in his classic texts. For instance, in some Latin American countries his ideas have spearheaded work in early childhood education programs (M. Freire 1983; Pérez Alarcón, Abiega, Zarco, and Schugurensky 2002). In addition, Freire's theories have been used to explain informal learning processes outside of schools and of nonformal education programs. For instance, Baltodano (2009) applied a Freirean framework to analyze the process of conscientization of the Mothers of the Plaza de Mayo movement in Argentina. Likewise, Butte (2010) used Freire's approach to examine the educational dimension of protest, particularly regarding struggles for inclusiveness carried out by people in the disability movement. Interestingly, famous futurist Alvin Toffler stated that the Paulo Freire method, developed in the 1960s, is still the best approach to teach and learn informatics. He noted that youth spontaneously create "circles of culture" in which all are teachers and learners (Gadotti and Torres 2009). Of special interest because of feminist critiques of his early work, Freire's approaches are also being used in feminist adult education work. For instance, in *Gender in Popular Education: Methods for Empowerment,* Shirley Walters and Linzi Manicom (1996) brought together a group of feminist adult educators from South Africa, India, Canada, the United States, Malaysia, Australia, and the Philippines to discuss issues related to the implementation of Freirean-inspired initiatives in grassroots organizations, development projects, formal institutions, and community education programs. Currently, Walters and Manicom are completing a new edited volume entitled *Feminist Popular Education: Creating Pedagogies of Possibility*, with the accounts of 21 experienced educator/activists from around the world (Walters and Manicom forthcoming 2011). Another movement that has adopted Freire's approaches is peace education. Freire didn't refer to himself as a peace educator and was sometimes critical of peace education programs, but his ideas can be seen in recent writing on this topic (Toh 2004, Durnan 2005, Atack 2009, Kester 2010). Moreover, in a recent article in the *Encyclopedia of Peace Education*, Lesley Bartlett (2008) concluded that, despite his death a decade before, Freire's ideas continue to resound throughout the field of peace education pedagogy.

Perhaps one of the clearest signs that Freire's ideas have not been ignored in the twenty-first century is the vibrant and growing international network of Paulo Freire Institutes that includes people and institutions in many countries throughout the world. As stated in the Valencia Charter (2008), the main impetus for the creation of the Paulo Freire Institutes and allied institutions was a commitment to the reinvention of Paulo Freire's ideas. Today, there are Paulo Freire Institutes in Argentina, Austria, Brazil, Egypt, England, Finland, Germany, Italy, Korea, Malta, Portugal, South Africa, Spain, Taiwan, and the United States. The different institutes the form this international network enjoy autonomy in developing and managing their own independent programs and for contributing to the international network through a variety of initiatives, including research centers and endowed Paulo Freire chairs, the Paulo Freire University online, and the biannual Forum Paulo Freire.[3] In addition to this forum, each institute often organizes local and international conferences on different topics. In addition, United Nations Educational, Scientific and Cultural Organization (UNESCO) organized a two-phase conference (the first part held in Recife in 2002 and the second in Paris in 2003) on the work of Paulo Freire entitled "Education and Social Transformation: Questioning Our Practices; Exchange of Knowledge and Practice in the light of Paulo Freire,"[4] to discuss the relevance of Freire's ideas for contemporary education. There is also a Paulo and Nita Freire International Project for Critical Pedagogy that operates from McGill University (Canada) and a Foro-Red Paulo Freire in Peru. In many other countries there are active popular education networks influenced by Freire's ideas.

The American Educational Research Association, one of the most prominent international professional organizations, has a large and dynamic special interest group dedicated exclusively to discuss Freire's contributions.

These examples suggest that Freire's ideas are still relevant today, and provide meaningful insights for practitioners and academics interested in improving our understanding of the connections between education and democracy, and in implementing transformative educational practices. As Kincheloe (2008) observed, if one accepts the premise that the act of bringing about social, economic, and political change is a pedagogical one, it follows that the task of educators is more central to the radical project than has traditionally been believed and that Freire's contributions provide important insights to illuminate the nature of this task. Along the same lines, Rossatto (2005:21) argued that "Freire's understanding of the world is very current and very accurate," and claimed that the contemporary dynamics of economic globalization and workers' exploitation calls for the development of Freirean-inspired pedagogies of cooperation and solidarity to construct a more just society. Similarly, McLaren (2010) contends that Freire's perspectives can help deepen the debate about the role of the university in contemporary North American culture, and Grollios (2009) suggests that Freire's perspectives can also be useful for curriculum planning, especially for teachers and curriculum specialists who are uncomfortable with the dominant theoretical assumptions and practices of curriculum planning. For Grollios, Freire's popular, radical, and democratic approach remains timely, particularly in the current context of neoliberal and neoconservative educational reforms. We can conclude this section by saying that presently there is a considerable community of scholars and practitioners interested in the critical examination, creative extension, and imaginative application of Freire's ideas. It should be noted, however, that this international "Freirean community," like other communities, is not a homogeneous one. Within it we can find many examples of dialogue, collaboration, and friendship, but we can also find disputes for ideological, political, professional, and personal reasons. Like in other communities, there are internal tribes that often ignore each other, sometimes attack each, and occasionally talk to each other.

Freire and other thinkers: the usefulness of comparative analyses

Another way to assess the relevance of Freire's ideas for the twenty-first century is to explore the extent to which they contribute to the collective development of an emancipatory educational theory and practice in relation to the ideas proposed by other influential thinkers. Exploring the complementarities and differences between Freire's ideas and the ideas of others may clarify some issues that are confusing and help to build a theoretical corpus that draws on the best analyses and proposals of compatible authors. Interest in comparing the ideas of Paulo Freire with the frameworks of other authors can be traced back to the 1970s and 1980s, but it has really taken off in the twenty-first century and, given current trends, is likely to continue in the future. As of today, I found approximately 120 publications that compare Freire with other thinkers. Some of these comparative exercises have been undertaken mainly for analytical purposes and are useful to explore the flow of ideas over time. Others were carried out to extract lessons for theory and practice in order to assist progressive educators in the creation of new syntheses that bring together the most important elements from the different perspectives. The comparative exercises range from Plato, Confucius, and Lao-Tzu to a variety of contemporary authors. Here is a nonexhaustive list, in no particular order:

1. Freire and Plato (Gee 1997, Quinn 2001, Shim 2008)
2. Freire and Confucius (Shim 2008)
3. Freire and Lao Tzu (Fraser 1997, Roberts 2010)
4. Freire and J. J. Rousseau (Arieta Molina 2002; Streck 2002, 2008, 2010)
5. Freire and Friedrich Hegel (Sloop 1992, C. A. Torres 1994)
6. Freire and José Martí (Alvarado 2007)
7. Freire and Simón Rodríguez (Rojas Osorio 2002, Puiggrós 2005)
8. Freire and Nikolaj Grundtvig (Spicder 2000; Bhattacharya 2005, 2010)
9. Freire and Antonio Gramsci (P. Mayo 1988, 1999, 2000; Leonard 1993; Allman 1988 and 1999; Battersby 1999, 2006; Coben 1998; Semeraro 2007; Ainley and Canaan 2005;

Fischman and McLaren 2005; Roberts 2004)

10. Freire and Jürgen Habermas (Pietrykowski 1996, Mezirow 1996, Rojas 1988, Alvarez Larrouri 1997, Provencal 2008, Sherman 2002, Morrow 2002, Morrow and Torres 2002, Block 2004)
11. Freire and John Dewey (Betz 1992, Abdi 2001, Zhang 2001, Bowers 2006, Mcdonough and Portelli 2004, Leary 2005, Feinberg and Torres 2007, Walsh 2008)
12. Freire and Ernst Bloch (Giroux and McLaren 1997; Fischman and McLaren 2000; Van Heertum 2006; Misoczky, Moraes, and Flores 2009)
13. Freire and Mahatma Gandhi (Rodrigues 1984; Zachariah 1986; Narayan 1999; Holst 2001; Mann 1995; Bhattacharya 2005, 2010)
14. Freire and Mathew Lippmann (Accorinti 2002)
15. Freire and Sigmund Freud (Sloop 1992)
16. Freire and Vygotsky (Marsh 1996, Trueba 1999, S. Freire 2000, Vera John-Steiner 1977)
17. Freire and Bertold Brecht (Otty 2000)
18. Freire and Carl Jung (L. R. Alschuler, 1992)
19. Freire and Rabindranath Tagore (Bhattacharya 2005, 2010)
20. Freire and M. M. Pistrak (Gadotti 1994)
21. Freire and Lorenzo Milani (Mayo 2007, 2010)
22. Freire and Celestin Freinet (Watling and Clarke 1995)
23. Freire and Lawrence Kohlberg (Smith 1976, Amorim and Berkenbrock 2007)
24. Freire and Benjamin Bloom (Chew and Jones 2007)
25. Freire and Ernesto Che Guevara (McLaren 2000b)
26. Freire and Saul Alinsky (C. Rogers, Rao, E., Rogers, and Wayangankar 1998)
27. Freire and Maxine Green (Allsup 2003, Blier 2002)
28. Freire and David Kolb (McGlinn 1999)
29. Freire and Jean Piaget (Becker 1983, Fortes 2007)
30. Freire and Theodore Bremeld (Collins 1973)
31. Freire and Peter Drucker (Rodriguez-Talavera 1993)
32. Freire and Myles Horton (Manke 1999, Kirman 2003)
33. Freire and Alfred North Whitehead (Roemer 2006)

34. Freire and Mary Belenky (Schroeder 1996)
35. Freire and Patricia Collins (Allen 2002)
36. Freire and Michel Foucault (Johnston 1994, Cho and Lewis 2005)
37. Freire and Ivan Illich (Allman 1988, Darder et al 2003, Khan and Kelllner 2008 and 2010)
38. Freire and Vincent Tinto (Barbatis 2008)
39. Freire and Mikhail Bakhtin (Bowers 2005, Rule 2009)
40. Freire and Forrest Chisman (Demetrion 1997)
41. Freire and C. A. Bowers (Greenwood 2008)
42. Freire and Reuven Feuerstein (Hirsch 1986, 1993)
43. Freire and Hanna Arendt (Hendricks 2003)
44. Freire and Nel Noddings (Kirman 2003)
45. Freire and Georg Lukacs Lewis, T. E. (2007)
46. Freire and Martin Buber (Armstrong 1983, Menconi 1999, Curzon-Hobson 2002, Shim 2008)
47. Freire and Richard Hoggart (Smith 1999)
48. Freire and Herbert Marcuse (Van Heertum 2006)
49. Freire and Peter Elbow (Yagelski 2006; Perry 1991, 2000)
50. Freire and Gustavo Gutierrez (Druliner 1992, Rivera 2004)
51. Freire and Margaret Wheatley (Bennett 1996)
52. Freire and Malcolm Knowles (Ali 1982, Sawyers 1994)
53. Freire and bell hooks (Boice-Pardee 2002)
54. Freire and Jack Mezirow (Lau 1992, Clare 2000, Morris 2005)
55. Freire and Charles Taylor (Collyer 1996)
56. Freire and Erich Fromm (Dagostino-Kalniz 2008)
57. Freire and Donald Murray (Yagelski 2006)
58. Freire and Jane Loevinger (Darnell 1981)
59. Freire and Marie Augusta Neal (Lamb 1984)
60. Freire and Nannie H. Burroughs (Price Clemetson 1992)
61. Freire and Michel de Montaigne (Solberg 1999)
62. Freire and Lillian Weber (Spielman 1990)
63. Freire and Fritjof Capra (Woelflingseder, M. 1991)
64. Freire and Maria Montessori (Hedeen 2005)
65. Freire and Carl Rogers (O'Hara 1989)
66. Freire and Ettore Gelpi (M. Mayo 1997)
67. Freire and Enrique Pichon Riviere (Ana Quiroga)
68. Freire and Fedor Dostoevsky (Roberts 2005)

69. Freire and Hermann Hesse (Roberts 2007, 2009)
70. Freire and Johann Heinrich Pestalozzi (Da Silva Sousa 2009)
71. Freire and E. D. Hirsch (Miller 1989)
72. Freire and Enrique Dussel (Amorim and Berkenbrock 2007, Mandiola 2010)
73. Freire and Julius Nyerere (Mulenga 2001)
74. Freire and Jacques Ranciere (Lewis 2010)
75. Freire and Augusto Boal (Smith 1999)
76. Freire and Bogdan Suchodolski (Unesco 1992)
77. Freire and David Mamet (Strasburg 2001, 2005)
78. Freire and Emannuel Levinas (Margonis 2007, Gomez 2009)
79. Freire and Hans-Georg Gadamer (Peters and Lankshear 1994)
80. Freire and Janusz Korczak (Fonvieille 1997)
81. Freire and James Banks (Hudalla 2005)
82. Freire and Marx (McLaren and Farahmandpur 2002, Malagón Plata 2010)
83. Freire and Islam (Nuryatno 2006)
84. Freire and feminist pedagogies (Butterwick 1987, Weiler 1993)

It is pertinent to note that not all these comparative analyses are of the same depth. Some of these comparisons are full-length books, others are journal articles or book chapters, and some are papers presented at scholarly conferences. Sometimes, like in the last two cases, Freire's work is compared not with another person but with entire religious or social movements, like Islam or feminism. As we can observe, the five thinkers that have attracted more interest from comparativists are Gramsci, Habermas, Bloch, Dewey, and Gandhi. It would be interesting to know why this is so. During my search, I found some additional comparisons between Freire and other educators, scholars, and community activists (e.g., Eduard Claparéde, Pierre Bovet, Moses Coady, the new European sociologists of education) but because they were only made in passing I did not include them on the list. Overall, I confess that I was surprised at the amount of scholarly comparisons that I found, and I imagine that there are many more comparative works out there that I have been unable to capture. It is beyond the scope of this section to discuss all these comparisons. Such exercise would merit a book in its own right, and hopefully one day somebody will write it. Some may complain that this tendency toward comparing Freire to other authors is going a little too far, becoming almost a comparativist fever. Nonetheless the intention is well meant: to find differences and similarities in order to build a theoretical framework and an agenda for action that brings together the best contributions from different thinkers. In my view, as long as the comparisons make sense and bring new insights to the conversation, this is a worthwhile exercise that should continue.

"Be the change you want to see in the world": Freire as an inspirational figure

The relevance and influence of Paulo Freire around the world today is due both to the clarity and quality of his ideas and to the legacy of his example because, following Gandhi's call for "being the change we want to see in the world," Freire constantly aimed at enacting in practice what he proclaimed in his theories, and personally embodied the idea of praxis that he wrote about (P. Mayo 2004, C. A. Torres 2008). As such, he was a philosopher and an educational theoretician who never separated theory from practice: he was not simply the author of inspiring books, but also a person who whose writing derived from and consisted of reflections on his own courageous engagement in the public sphere in a variety of contexts worldwide. For R. M. Torres, his inspiration emanates from his hope in people and his uncompromising commitment to challenge injustice even in times of adversity:

> Paulo, the great communicator, the great inspirer, helped millions of people discover and bring to the surface the best of themselves: their human, generous, compassionate side, the inner drive to become a volunteer, an inventor, a hero, a revolutionary. In a world where both wealth and poverty grow uncontrollably, where individualism annihilates common sense and the most basic human solidarity, where not only the end of ideologies but the end of work is proclaimed, Freire continued to speak, to the very last minute, about hope, liberation and utopia, terms that many have archived as antiquated and obsolete. (R. M. Torres 1999:249)

Others emphasize his humility, which Freire never lost despite being internationally famous. As mentioned in Chapter 2, when he was asked why his books were quickly becoming best sellers, Freire replied, somehow apologetically, that he was just a "pilgrim of the obvious," which a lot of people know but which they may be unable to express. He also engaged in fierce self-criticism, a notable feature of honest intellectuals. Since the publication in the 1960s of his first two books (*Education as a Practice of Freedom* and *Pedagogy of the Oppressed*) Freire never stopped listening attentively to his critics, reformulating his thought, or disclosing publicly his mistakes. In sum, as Gadotti and Torres (1997) have pointed out, Freire's life "taught us the meaning of honesty, decency, creativity and struggle." These and other civic virtues embodied by Freire could be seen through a number of anecdotes throughout his life.

As an illustration, I will provide an example from the late 1980s when Freire was back in Brazil after 15 years of exile. At that time, he could have easily confined himself to his comfortable position as a university professor, writing books and articles, and giving lectures, speeches, and interviews around the world. At that time, already in his late sixties and after a long trajectory of political and social engagement that included prison and exile, nobody would have called into question his stature as a committed intellectual (Mayo 2004). However, Freire made the choice of a civic life over books and took a considerable risk by accepting the challenging task of working as secretary of education of Sao Paulo. This was indeed risky because undertaking an educational reform in such a large, complicated, and economically polarized city with limited funds while managing a complex bureaucracy could end in serious problems at the level of implementation, and carried with it the possibility that the imperatives of reality might force him to contradict in practice some of his theories. Freire's choice was clear: civic and political engagement was more important than academic security or the satisfaction of publishing another book.

Freire's decision to accept this appointment spells out at least four related messages for twenty-first-century educators. The first is about the importance of actively engaging in public affairs. As Mayo (2004:120) noted, "Paulo Freire constitutes a perfect role model for many educators who feel compelled to be involved in the public sphere." This is not intended to undervalue theoretical thinking or academic work, but to recognize that, at some particular historical junctures, it is necessary to make difficult choices and to be consistent with one's values and principles through committed action. In this instance, since its modest beginnings in 1980, the political party that Freire helped to build had won its first municipal elections, and he understood that his primary role at that moment was not in the university but in the new administration, making a contribution to the democratization and improvement of the educational system. The second message that Freire's choice imparts to twenty-first-century educators is an attitude of noncomplacency and a disposition to accept new challenges. At that time Freire could have easily rested on his laurels, devoting the last years of his life to enjoying the rewards of fame and to writing on whatever topic he wanted. He did not. He took a risk, a risk that entailed the potential of failure.

The third message is about the importance of making an effort to connect theory with practice. It is easier to pontificate about what should be done—in education as in any other area—than to actually do it, and Freire's choice tells us that when an opportunity arises to put one's ideas to the test, it is worth taking it and making a serious attempt to "walk the talk." The fourth message has to do with the state. Some critical educators understand the role of the state in capitalist democracies to be merely a tool of domination in the hands of the oppressors, without realizing that it is also an arena of confrontation and negotiation among competing interests and political projects. Those critical educators and the social movements in which they participate tend to distrust the state apparatus and therefore engage with it only in oppositional and confrontational terms. In doing so, they miss important opportunities to advance redistributive and democratic policies and practices. As O'Cadiz et al. (1998:45) observed in their analysis of Freire's experience in public administration, educational policymaking in Sao Paulo illustrates the tensions between the state's reproductive functions and the state as a site in the struggle for greater democracy. Hence, Freire shows that it is possible to keep one foot inside the system and one foot outside, engaging simultaneously with government policies and programs and with the daily struggles of social movements and local communities. As he used to say in relation to this, it is important to be at the same time "tactically inside" and "strategically outside" (Freire, quoted in Gadotti 2003:224).

Taken together, these messages could be summarized in one sentence: Freire did not take the easier route. He abandoned the safe and orderly realm of theory, criticisms, and recommendations where it was relatively easy to avoid the conflicts and the messiness of public administration. Instead, he chose the path of civic and political engagement and with it accepted the challenges of attempting educational reform in difficult circumstances. To a great extent, given that he always sought coherence between discourse and practice, he had no other choice. He recognized that he had to accept Mayor Erundina's invitation in order to fulfill everything he had ever said and done: "it was the only way to go," he recalled (Freire 1993b:58). During his tenure as secretary, as I mentioned in Chapter 1, Freire was offered a loan by the World Bank to carry out his projects of curriculum reform and teacher training. Again, the easiest way for him to proceed would have been to accept the loan and use the fresh funds to implement some of his favorite projects without regard for the debt that he would leave to the next generations. His choice, however, was to offer his resignation to the mayor if the loan were approved (C. A. Torres 2002: 379–80). In sum, when we talk about the legacy of Paulo Freire for twenty-first-century educators, we are not talking exclusively about his ideas and his work, but also about his personal traits. Fátima Freire (Paulo's youngest daughter) made a reference to some of these traits when she was speaking about her father's legacy at a conference held in Ireland: "It is a legacy that is both difficult and rich at the same time. I see it as a source of energy and empowerment for the world in the process of enabling transformation. What I learned from my father was to never stop being curious and to never stop questioning" (quoted on S. Brown 2001). As an inspirational figure, then, Freire provides to younger generations of educators a source of energy and empowerment, and at the same time acts as a role model by enacting certain personal dispositions, such as curiosity, honesty, love, humility, hope, and a critical attitude toward reality, combined with indignation about injustice and a commitment toward justice. This inspirational impact should not be underestimated.

Reinventing Freire for the twenty-first century

As mentioned in Chapter 3, Freire did not want to have disciples who treated his texts as sacred scriptures. He emphasized on several occasions that his ideas should not be blindly transplanted but creatively adapted according to the specificities of each context. In his response to the authors who contributed articles to the book *Mentoring the Mentor*, Freire (1997b:325–6) addressed the issue of reinventing himself in the North American context, although he noted that his comments could be relevant to any contexts as well. In this piece, entitled "A Response," Freire noted that this reinvention can only occur in connection with the substance of his ideas. To clarify what he meant, he proceeded to describe some of his main principles. One of them was respect for others, which necessarily implied his refusal to accept discrimination, be it racial, gender, class, cultural, or of any other type. A second was his understanding of history as possibility, which implies a rejection of any fatalistic or deterministic view of history. A third was his unconditional love for freedom, and with this, his certainty that human beings can become transformative beings—and not just adaptative ones—with the capacity for decision making and for opposing corrupt systems of social, economic, and political oppression. Last but not least was Freire's deep commitment to democracy, which ensured that there was no possibility of being reinvented through authoritarian practice. Reinventing Freire, then, implies neither changing his substantive ideas nor applying them indiscriminately to any context. He asked those who wanted to reinvent him to actualize those ideas, principles, and aspirations to the particular conditions and to the methodological and tactical requirements of each situation. As an illustration of what he was trying to convey, he provided the following example:

> The way I struggle against machismo in Northeast Brazil cannot be possible the same way that one should fight against machismo in New York City. It may take a different form in terms of tactics and techniques, but it also has to remain true to the substantive idea of fighting against machismo as something unethical and undemocratic. This is what I mean by reinventing me. (Freire 1997b:326)

Freire said that it would be preposterous of him to provide what many North Americans often so anxiously ask for: recipes with techniques and tactics for action. Again, he expected his readers to adapt his ideas to their contexts and making them alive in their historical circumstance. Moreover, he adjured his readers not to treat him as a guru who had answers for every question. Indeed, in his interactions with educators, Paulo Freire always rejected the status of an icon. Returning to his response to North American scholars and practitioners in the book *Mentoring the Mentor,* toward the end of a section entitled "The Search for an Icon Comes out of Fear of Democracy," he said that he was strongly opposed to any movement that would turn him into a guru or an icon because, by accepting such a position of privilege, he would be directly sabotaging his ideas on democracy.

> The idea, then, is not to interact with or engage me and my ideas in binaristic terms—either Paulo Freire the guru or icon or a total rejection of Paulo Freire as proposing ideas that are unworkable in the North American context. The challenge is to engage my theoretical proposals dialogically, and it is through this dialogue that I think we can create possibilities, including the possibility that I can be reinvented in a North American context. (Freire 1997b:328).

As Fischman and McLaren (2000) argued, the choice of either following Freire's ideas blindly or leaving him behind as a relic of the past is a false dilemma. The challenge is to engage in a critical rereading of his work, adapting creatively those ideas to address the particularities of specific contemporary contexts. In other discussions about the reinvention of his proposals, Freire was concerned that his ideas could be easily co-opted, becoming simply a method decontextualized from its larger philosophical and political foundations: "if you do not understand the substantivity of my ideas, it is impossible to speak of reinvention" (p. 325). Again, it is important to remember that Freire's literacy project was not designed to be a teaching method as an end in itself but as part of a larger goal of politicizing learners so they could critically read their context and be able to connect the word with the world. Freire's intention was never to advance a discrete set of prescribed blueprints that provides teachers with quick and easy solutions to problems and challenges they may face in their classrooms. His main goal was to help educators recognize and link the moral, ethical, and political dimensions of education to their daily teaching and learning practices in their classrooms. However, because Freire used the term "pedagogy" to refer to his approach, many people believe that it comprises a teaching method rather than a philosophy or a social theory. It has been claimed that this tendency to reduce Freire's ideas to methods is particularly noticeable in North American educational circles (Araujo Freire and Macedo 1998, Aronowitz 1993, Farahmandpur 2006).

For these reasons, in assessing projects that claim to "reinvent Freire," it is pertinent to consider to what extent they adhere or depart from Freirean philosophical, political, epistemological, and pedagogical foundations, including his four core principles. It is also pertinent to consider to what extent such projects continue Freire's work, remembering that he devoted most of his life to understanding how subordinate groups become hopeless, depoliticized, and disengaged, and how education could contribute to generate hope, critical awareness, and political engagement. In this regard, Da Silva and McLaren (1993:28–49) believe that, if appropriated with prescience and care, Freire's work can inspire and enable teachers to engage in forms of critical practice that interrogate, destabilize, and disorganize dominant power/knowledge relations and, at the same time, develop alternative pedagogies oriented toward the creation of a radical and plural democracy. Likewise, in the last chapter of *Liberating Praxis: Paulo Freire's Legacy for Radical Education and Politics*, Peter Mayo (2004) illustrates how Freire's ideas can be taken up and reinvented in different sites of practice. After describing, analyzing, and reflecting on different projects in which he was personally involved (ranging from parental participation in primary schools to a workers' education program to the transformation of schools into community learning centers and of museums into public spaces for critical reading of the world) Mayo concludes that Freire's thinking is highly relevant for a variety of contemporary institutional and noninstitutional educational settings. Mayo claims that Freire's analysis and proposals can help twenty-first-century educators to perceive public institutions and public spaces as sites of struggle and contestation and to engage in collective projects aimed at revitalizating and democratizing those spaces.

To be sure, attempts to reinvent Freire and to adapt his ideas creatively to different situations and strategies have been around for a while. For instance, in the 1970s, inspired by *Pedagogy of the Oppressed,* Augusto Boal developed the Theatre of the Oppressed. Around the same time, a French organization called INODEP (Ecumenical Institute for the Development of Peoples), stimulated by Freire's generative themes, developed a methodology called *enquête conscientizante* (conscientizing research). Since the 1990s, ActionAid has reinvented Freire's ideas through an approach called REFLECT (Regenerated Freirean Literacy through Empowering Community Techniques), which has been used with over 500 organizations in 70 countries to address a wide range of issues, from peace and reconciliation and community forestry to domestic violence and government accountability. Among REFLECT's core principles are the political nature of education, the creation of democratic spaces, recognition of existing knowledge, linking reflection and action, participatory processes, power awareness, and self-management. Similarly, community organizers working with welfare rights organizations in Quebec (Canada) reformulated Freire's approach to codification by creating something that they called "blank space codification" or "ongoing codification."[5] More recently, in an attempt to adapt Freire's ideas to the North American context, Paul Carr (2010) built on Freire's approach to conscientization to develop a model that attempts to illustrate the stages that people pass through as they seek higher levels of democratic conscientization and a more robust democracy. Carr contends that democratic conscientization is a permanent process that acknowledges differences, power imbalances, hegemonic forces, and the absence of neutrality of political and educational structures. Along the same lines, and based on an empirical study of 10 programs in the United States aimed at advancing the democratic purposes of education, Westheimer and Kahne (2004) identified three main types of "good citizens" implicit in those programs: personally responsible citizens, participatory citizens, and justice-oriented citizens. The last two models, which are the ones favored by the authors, are strongly influenced by Freirean ideals. As educators become more involved in projects aimed at expanding and deepening democracy, the proposals advanced by Carr and by Westheimer and Kahne could provide a helpful framework to guide practice and also be a useful tool for reflecting upon and theorizing about such practice, particularly in relation to educational interventions. Efforts to reinvent Freire in order to assist the project of "democratizing democracy" are not restricted to school environments. Several models of participatory governance that are currently underway in Latin America (including but not confined to participatory budgeting) demonstrate Freire's influence, especially in the attention paid to the educational dimensions of the process and when they attempt to develop the emancipatory side of social pedagogy (Scocuglia 2006, Schugurensky 2006, Nuñez 2007). Mendes (2009) argues that Freirean pedagogy is helpful in developing collectively an alternative paradigm to the neoliberal educational model that is part and parcel of globalization dynamics of the early twenty-first century. She uses the metaphor of the seven sins (gluttony, sloth, wrath, lust, greed, envy, and vanity) to describe the hegemonic logic of global governance and contrasts them with seven key concepts of the Freirean approach: historicity, dialogue, conscientization, emancipation, autonomy, freedom, and hope. For her, the Freirean framework can help to think about education in a different way and assist emancipatory projects aimed at expanding and deepening democracy. In another attempt to reinvent Freire, Murrell (1997:31) claims that his framework provides the basis for the realization of an African American emancipatory pedagogy for the twenty-first century: "A Freirean theory views education as essential and integral to black people's continuing struggle for humanity in American society." For Murrell, Freire's ideas are relevant because they bring structure and agency together, allowing African Americans to see how their practices of self-determination shape and are shaped by the dominant culture, thereby enabling them to move beyond a dualistic conception of schooling that is only about assimilation or resistance. This approach also enables African Americans to understand resistance to oppression in broader terms than overt political action and hence can also include cultural expressions such as rap music. It is also relevant, says Murrell, because it recognizes the need for oppressed people to appropriate the dominant knowledge for the purpose of negotiating societal codes, but at the same time helps them to reclaim their own voices and histories and increase their power to change the world and contribute to the project of humanization. Along similar lines, Wattsa and Abdul-Adilb (1998) describe a program based

on Freire's ideas called "Young Warriors" for building critical consciousness that includes action research and rap video, and Apple (2003)
argues that Freire's work is useful for understanding the politics of race
in contemporary US education. I would add that this applies not only to
African Americans but also to other racialized groups that suffer
discrimination and oppression.

An unexpected area that has seen some efforts to reinvent Freire is
spiritual education, because he seldom discussed this topic in his books.
However, Dallaire (2001) advanced a proposal for today's spiritual
education that he labels "contemplation-in-liberating praxis." Dallaire's
project integrates Freirean critical praxis (critical engagement in political and social action to improve our societies) and contemplation (a
method to analyze the wholeness of ourselves, of all cosmic existence,
and the interconnectedness of all) as a method for today's spiritual education. Another unexpected area that has seen some efforts to reinvent
Freire is the one known as pedagogy for the oppressor, pedagogy for the
privileged, or pedagogy for the non-poor (Lange 1998, Schapiro 1999,
Goodman 2000, Darder 2002, Allen 2002, Curry-Stevens 2004, Graden
2008). This is somewhat unexpected because Freire's framework seems
to imply that educators (particularly popular educators) should focus
their educational and political energies on working exclusively with the
oppressed. In her work on pedagogy for the privileged, Curry-Stevens
(2004) argues that there is room to educate critically those who might
otherwise be perceived as right-leaning enemies in order to transform
them into allies, which seems an important bridge to build in any truly
transformative endeavor. She acknowledges Freire's warnings of co-
optation by conservatives, but claims that the principles of dialogism
that he has formulated should open up space for transformation of at
least some conservative or nonleftist groups. Along the same lines, Allen
(2002) proposes a "pedagogy of the oppressor" that emphasizes the
radical task of identifying as the oppressor in order to divest oneself of
one's complicity with dehumanization and form solidarity with the
relatively oppressed. Likewise, Antonia Darder (2002:62) suggested the
necessity of a pedagogy of privilege that would help oppressors to better
understand their location in the social structure and eventually lead
them to join the struggle for transforming such a structure, and Graden
(2008) reported that this approach is helpful for educators dealing with

privileged, conservative students to gain greater self-awareness and understanding of their society, and provides them with some of the tools necessary to transform the world (Graden 2008). I am aware, from personal conversations, that some members of the popular education movement have reservations about such a "pedagogy of privilege" because in their view, given the scarce resources of the movement, it makes sense (for ethical and practical reasons) to dedicate those limited resources to educate and organize the oppressed rather than to try to "convert" the oppressors. In my view, it is not an either/or situation. On the contrary, I see them as complementary dynamics. As Freire (1997a:87) observed in relation to this issue in one of his last publications, "it is necessary for the oppressor to convert to the cause of the oppressed, and for the oppressed to commit to their own fight for liberation." Today, Freire's influence extends the field of education, and it can be observed in many areas, including sociology, development studies, political theory, social work, theology, philosophy, cultural studies, anthropology, language studies, and communications (Mayo 2004). His approaches are also being reinvented in the realm of the arts. In addition to several variations of Theatre of the Oppressed, Freire's ideas nurtured initiatives such as "Videogames of the Oppressed" (Frasca 2001), "Photography of the Oppressed" (Grace 2009) and critical social learning in arts-informed community education (Grace and Wells 2011). Freire's perspectives are also being reinvented in the fields of participatory research, peace education, environmental education, participatory democracy, public administration, and human resource management. For instance, in relation to the last two areas, a recent issue of the journal *Administrative Theory and Praxis* (September 2010) devoted an entire section to Freire to examine the potential of his ideas for public administration practice, from disaster management and participatory dialogue to human resource management and performance appraisals (Eagan 2010, Jenkins and Nowell 2010, Salm and Ordway 2010, Boyd 2010).

Nuñez (2007) reported that some people have claimed that revisiting Freire's ideas is nothing else than pure nostalgia for a past that was filled with grand political ideas and radical transformations that are now outdated. Those who assert that Freire's ideas are currently irrelevant argue that today's context is very different from that of the twentieth century in which he wrote and lived. Some things are indeed different (particularly in relation to new technologies) but many are strikingly similar, and most of the educational and social issues that Freire confronted in his work and in his publications are still present today. The "century of education" produced unprecedented increases in educational expansion and school attainment, but these achievements are counteracted by circuits of differential quality that are closely correlated to the socioeconomic status of the students' families. These inequalities in educational opportunities have been compounded by market-oriented educational reforms, a drive toward commercialization of education, an excessive focus on standardization and teaching to the test, and drastic budget cuts across the educational system.[6] In this context, Freire's proposals for a problem-posing, dialogical, inclusive, and democratic education are as valid as in the twentieth century, and his call for a popular, high-quality public school for all still resonates among parents and educators concerned with equality of opportunity. Likewise, many social problems like poverty, oppression, domination, injustice, discrimination, authoritarianism, xenophobia, patriarchy, racism, social inequality, and violence still persist today, in some places with the same virulence as in the twentieth century. Freire's struggle to expand and deepen democracy is far from complete, and the postcolonial dynamics that he denounced decades ago are now intensified, albeit in the new form of neoliberal economic globalization, whose beginning stages concerned him greatly toward the end of his life. Considering these realities, I contend that Freire's vision for a world that is less ugly, less cruel, less authoritarian, more democratic, and more humane is as current as ever, and that his educational and methodological proposals to move in that direction are still useful. This contention is not an arbitrary judgment based on my own opinion. If Freire's ideas were, as some suggest, outdated, by now all his books would be confined to the dust of library archives, only to be read occasionally by a few historians specializing in twentieth-century education. This is certainly not the case. In the twenty-first century, his books are still reprinted and widely read in different languages by new generations of educators, scholars, and activists around the world. Moreover, as mentioned before, a plethora of books, journal articles, dictionaries, dissertations, and conference proceedings dealing with his ideas are continuously being published, some written by authors who agree with them and some by those who disagree, a strong sign that those ideas are still generating healthy debate.

The triangle of transformation: education, politics, and humanization

As we approach the end of the book, I would like to summarize Freire's proposal for social transformation using three key concepts: education, politics, and humanization. By this I mean that what Freire proposed is, fundamentally, a political-pedagogical project aimed at humanization. He became known for his method to teach adult literacy, but what he developed was not just a method. It was a political pedagogy predicated on critical reflection and collective transformative action in order to develop more democratic, just, and happier societies. The triangle of transformation, then, embraces: (a) the direction of Freire's transformative project (humanization), (b) the main social activity to move in that direction (education), and (c) the recognition of the power dynamics and ideological struggles related to the social forces opposing and supporting those changes (politics). Indeed, Freire's main contribution to education for social transformation does not reside in the efficacy and creativity of his literacy methods. Certainly the generative word approach represented an important breakthrough, but in terms of Freire's enduring legacy, his main contribution is to be found in his broad and deep understanding of education, in his discussions about the political nature of education, and in the development of a humanizing pedagogy that is not restricted to a particular place or time and that can be adapted to different contexts (Bimbi 1971, Araujo Freire and Macedo 1998:8). This, in essence, is Freire's triangle of transformation: a framework that allows us to navigate the pedagogical, the political, and the ethical dimensions of social transformation. It is a proposal for a humanistic education guided by an emancipatory project that is political in nature. As Giroux (2010) points out, central to Freire's politics and pedagogy is a philosophical vision of a liberated humanity.

Education, says Freire, cannot be separated from politics, divorced from the material world and the power that constitutes it. It cannot be thought of as an independent activity that occurs in a vacuum. It is an arena where hegemonic values, ideals, standards, and practices are imposed by dominant groups, but not automatically or mechanically. For this reason, it is also a place where counterhegemonic values and practices occur. This tension between reproduction and transformation, which comes about under concrete historical conditions and larger social dynamics of reproduction and change, constitutes the core of the political nature of education. At the same time, political practices, understood as collective struggles to change the world, are important sources of learning. Hence the double relation between education and politics that is important to consider in any transformative project: education is political, and politics are educational. If we now enter the third element of the triangle, Freire (1985a) argued that humanistic education is a utopian project of the oppressed, one in which they denounce dehumanizing processes and announce a new world. When Freire talks about humanization, he is talking from a standpoint of radical democratic humanism. The process of humanization, as proposed by Freire, requires hope, human agency, dialogue, and communion. For him, to be human is to be able to both understand the world and take action to change that world. It is in taking that action, in the transit from objects to subjects, where we become full human beings. Freire's proposal for humanization is deeply rooted in his faith in human beings to overcome their limits, in their capacity to define the future collectively, and in their commitment and resolve to enact their agency. It is this sense of humanization through praxis that defines Freire's ontology and underlies his epistemology and pedagogy (Glass, 2001, Roberts, 2003). Contrary to dehumanization, which is a political project that preserves a status quo characterized by alienation and domination, humanistic education aims at challenging oppressive structures and dynamics and, ultimately, at the radical transformation of the world. Freire's project of humanization is not about the oppressed replacing the oppressors, but about the collective creation, in communion, of a new world that is less ugly and more human, one without exploitation, exclusions, or power hierarchies. For him, full human development can only occur in a society based on freedom and equality for all, not only for some. He emphasized that this should be regarded not as an abstract ideal but as a historical challenge that requires concrete critical reflection and transformative actions, and warned that these actions are sooner or later going to be in tension with other actions that run in the opposite direction, that is, the self-preservation of the system: "It seems important here to emphasize what is most obvious—the interrelationship of dehumanization and humanistic education. Again, both require action from men and women to maintain or modify their respective realities. We emphasize this to overcome idealistic illusions and pipe dreams of an eventual humanistic education for humankind without the necessary transformation of an oppressive and unjust world" (Freire 1985a:113). In short, Freire understood humanization as a permanent process of denunciation and annunciation, that is, denouncing and analyzing a dehumanizing reality while dreaming of a different reality and working collectively toward it by trying things that had not been tried before (untested feasibility). This transformative process is both a pedagogical and a political project. Given widening economic and educational disparities, I suggest that his calls to increase our understanding of the connections between education and politics and of the role of education in social change, as well as his proposals aimed at promoting critical inquiry, dialogue, democracy, and freedom, are as relevant today as they were in the twentieth century.

In reinventing Freire for the twenty-first century, though, it is important to stress again that his project of humanization should not be understood as an anthropocentric project. It is true that most of his texts focused on human liberation from oppression without paying enough attention to environmental issues. This should not be surprising if we consider the historical context and the circumstances in which he worked. In the last years of his life, however, Freire dealt with debates and themes that he had not addressed in earlier books, including ecology and the environment. Interestingly, on April 17, 1997, just a few days before he passed away, Freire was talking about ecopedagogy. In an interview at the Paulo Freire Institute, he talked of his love for the Earth, animals, and plants: "I want to be remembered as somebody who loved men, women, plants, animals, the Earth." In one of his last books, Freire (1997a) speaks of the pleasure of breathing pure air, the joy of swimming in an unpolluted river, of stepping on grass or the sand on the beach, and criticized the capitalist logic that gives no value to those free pleasures, substituting the happiness of satisfying human needs for satisfying the profit motive. In his posthumous publication *Pedagogy of Indignation*, Freire did not separate human needs from the needs of the planet. He called for including the lifeworld in radical progressive politics and for the defense of "fundamental ethical principles, such as respect for the life of human beings, the life of other animals, of birds, and for the life of rivers and forests." Then, he added: "I don't believe in loving among human beings if we do not become capable of loving the world. Ecology has gained tremendous importance at the end of the century. It must be present in any educational practice of a radical, critical, and liberating nature (Freire 2004:47). Unfortunately, Freire did not live enough years to develop further his preliminary ideas on ecopedagogy and its role in the project of humanization. It is now up to twenty-first-century educators to continue that work. The same could be said about other areas that he did not have time to elaborate upon but need further development and refinement, such as peace education, spiritual education, pedagogy for the privileged, or education for participatory democracy.

I would like to end this section with a cautionary note. This may seem obvious, but it is nonetheless important to remember that not all that is said or done in the name of Paulo Freire should be read literally as work that would be endorsed by him if he were alive. In this regard, about a decade ago, Moacir Gadotti (2001:56) predicted that Freire's ideas "will continue developing in many—and perhaps sometimes irreconcilable—directions," and added that "he will be unable to control this and cannot be held responsible for what happens." In this regard, when analyzing concrete pedagogical interventions that are supposedly guided by Freire's ideas, two distinct types of distortions may be observed. A pedagogical distortion is particularly noticeable among certain progressive groups that share Freire's general political orientation and his concern for democracy and social justice but in their day-to-day educational practices tend to use a banking model of knowledge transmission. The content of instruction may be consistent with Freire's understanding of social reality, but it is contradicted by a methodological approach in which the teachers act as enlightened leaders who preach from the podium and impart lessons as if they were "revealed truths," paying lip service to the dialogical and constructivist dimensions of Freire's approach. He emphasized that education is political, but this should not be interpreted as an endorsement of top-down strategies and indoctrination. On the contrary, Freire always warned against slogans and propaganda and was always critical of any type of authoritarianism and dogmatism, whether it came from a conservative right or from a sectarian left.

The other kind of distortion is ideological. Indeed, throughout the years, Freire's approach has been appropriated and co-opted, applying some of his methodological tools but emptying them of their content and their progressive political orientation (Blackburn 2000, McLaren 2010, Brookfield and Holst 2011). Freire's proposals can be—and have been—domesticated and manipulated by people with very different educational and political agendas. Some local, regional, and national literacy campaigns officially have claimed to be based in Freire's proposals (probably only to gain legitimacy) when in reality they were doing something else and for different—sometimes opposite—purposes. For instance, in the 1980s, the military governments of Brazil and Guatemala carried out literacy campaigns that applied selectively Freire's method of the generative word, a paradox if we consider that Freire was sent to exile by a military regime that considered his approach subversive (Kidd and Kumar 1981, Estrella 1998). In short, in the case of the methodological distortion the content may be reasonably aligned with an emancipatory project but the pedagogical approach is clearly antidialogical, whereas in the case of the ideological distortion some of the methods may be aligned with problem-posing education but devoid the process of its social justice orientation. Whereas in the first case there is an overemphasis on the political dimension over the pedagogical one, the second situation privileges the pedagogical dimension at the expense of the political one. In order to avoid these distortions it is necessary to remember that the Freirean project of humanization is both pedagogical and political. Metaphorically speaking, the pedagogical and the political are the two tracks over which the train of humanization can transit.

Concluding remarks

Why are Freire's books still popular, relevant, and influential today, in some cases several decades after their publication? In previous chapters I advanced several reasons, but here I would like to highlight three: his universal thematic, his cross-disciplinary approach, and his combination of denunciation and annunciation. First, the topics addressed by Freire (oppression, emancipation, hope, indignation, political awareness, educational relations, democracy) are general in nature and appeal to readers in different parts of the world, regardless of their particular circumstances. Second, through the variety of the themes that he explored and his interdisciplinary approach, his works appeal not only to readers in the field of education but also in several other disciplines and perspectives, including political science, sociology, anthropology, postcolonial theory, liberation theology, international development, health, social work, urban planning, communications, feminism, and agricultural extension. Third, in addressing those issues, Freire articulated a language of critique and a language of possibility, expressed not only in his denunciation of banking education and in his appeal for an emancipatory education, but also in other social expressions of the tension between oppression and liberation. In doing so, he offered a framework that challenges the status quo but at the same time provides viable alternatives. This is, in my view, the essence of Freire's contribution to educators disenchanted with the current state of affairs and interested in social justice: a framework that brings together education and politics for the project of humanization and offers tools to move from the here and now to a brighter future.

Freire's educational ideas did not arise overnight. He built them over decades by studying methodically the ideas of many who preceded him, by listening to workers and peasants, by engaging in dialogue with colleagues, and by reflecting on his own practice. In this regard, Guilherme (2002:31) argued that Freire represents a later phase of the evolution of education in the twentieth century that culminated in the recognition of schools (and other educational institutions, I would add) as main cultural and political agencies that act as a basis for the future of democratic societies. In the history of influential educational thinkers, Paulo Freire constitutes an anomaly. A quick glance at the list of books of this *Library of Educational Thought* and similar collections would reveal that for many centuries the most influential educational writings were produced in the global north, and eventually were read in the global south. The reverse path has been rather insignificant. Paulo Freire is one of the few exceptions. For some reason, this twentieth-century Brazilian educator managed to send a universal message that still resonates in many regions of the world. His ideas attracted wide international interest from the beginning of his career when he was coordinating literacy circles in Pernambuco in the early 1960s, and as we embark on the second decade of the twenty-first century the interest is far from fading.

Revisiting Freire's ideas is more than just a nostalgic trip to the past. I believe that most of his contributions are still relevant, for at least three reasons. First, a review of the literature reveals that several subfields of educational theorizing and inquiry have sprung up around his ideas (Au 2009:225), and the substantial amount of scholarly work on Freire indicates that his analytical framework is still helpful to understand the relations between education and societal dynamics. Moreover, the increasing body of comparative work that contrasts the ideas of Freire with those of other thinkers is contributing to the placement of his work in a larger perspective and to the creation of new and insightful syntheses. In universities, Freire's texts are used not only in teacher education programs but have also been incorporated in a variety of disciplines, including nursing, early childhood, public health, rural extension, adult education, urban planning, community development, sociology, public administration, music education, mathematics, physics, theology, philosophy, social work, international development, feminist studies, educational psychology, educational gerontology, public affairs, drama, and literature. Second, several of his proposals for pedagogical interventions are still relevant to address contemporary education issues. Today, educational practitioners from all over the world interested in social justice are attempting to apply Freirean pedagogy in a variety of contexts and professional fields. Outside of universities, his ideas have been applied by schoolteachers, adult educators, church leaders, counselors, health professionals, psychologists, artists, social workers, prison rehabilitation workers, language learning specialists, and social activists, among others. His influence is particularly strong in critical pedagogy, popular education, and participatory research movements. In short, the interest on Freirean theory and practice shows no signs of fading and bids fair to flourish further (Ander 1993, Findsen 2007, Laverty 2008, Weiler 1996, Gadotti and Torres 2009, Roberts 2000 and 2010). Third, Freire's life and work are a source of inspiration for twenty-first-century progressive educators interested in social transformation. This should not be underestimated. Many community groups, educational institutions, and social movements engage in difficult work every day, motivated by what Paulo Freire represents: a commitment to the project of humanization. Indeed, the strength of Freire's work resides not so much in his theory of knowledge but in his belief that it is possible and necessary to change things in order to build collectively a better world, and his insistence on hope and utopias draws inspiration among educators and noneducators alike. What has attracted several generations of progressive educators to Freire is not only an intellectual interest for his scholarship but his political vision, his personal conduct, the manner in which he located his work within an ethics of pragmatism, love, and solidarity (Gadotti 2001, McLaren and Giroux 1994).

Freire was a paradigm shifter who had the courage to take the road less traveled. His methodological innovations (especially generative words and themes) opened a new era in literacy training and improved significantly the efficiency and efficacy of the process. This is no small feat, but his main legacy for twenty-first-century education is not just a literacy method or a set of techniques but a pedagogical approach based on key pillars: the political nature of education, problem-posing education, democratic teacher-student relations, conscientization through dialogue, recognition of the knowledge and experience of learners and communities, and cocreation of new knowledge. It is an approach that is praxis-oriented and thus asks for a constant relation between theory and practice, between local pedagogical interventions and emancipatory projects, and between educational change and social transformation. (Farahmandpur 2006, Bhattacharya 2008, Bartlett 2008). As Gadotti (2003) observed, the success of the Freirean literacy process depended less on the specific techniques than on the inclination and capacity of the educator to respect the dignity of the learners and to walk together with them. Contrary to some people's expectations, this approach cannot be downgraded to a method or to step-by-step formulas ready to be applied in any context. As Giroux (2010:10) noted, to demand a "how to" manual for change distorts the essence of Freire's pedagogical and philosophical proposal:

> Paulo offered no recipes for those who felt in need of instant theoretical and political fixes. I was often amazed at how patient he always was in dealing with people who wanted him to provide menu-like answers to the problems they raised about education, not realizing

that they were undermining his insistence that pedagogy is defined by its context and must be approached as a project of individual and social transformation—that it can never be reduced to a method.

What Freire's pedagogy provides, instead, is an ethical compass, a conceptual framework, and a set of analytical tools and theoretical concepts that can assist educators and learners in explaining and transforming the world, as well as feelings of inspiration, agency, and hope to embark in that process in the first place. Freire prompts us to ask ourselves three key questions: Are we happy with the world in which we live? Can we imagine a world that is more inclusive and democratic, where equality, freedom, happiness, and full human development are not just empty words? If so, what role can education play in moving us in that direction? I suggest that Freire's triangle of transformation can assist us in addressing these questions, both at the theoretical and at the practical level. In revisiting Freire's works, it is important to remember that they were produced in a particular sociopolitical moment, and should be interpreted in that context. The worst favor we can do to Freire is to read his texts as sacred scriptures, to freeze his ideas in time, to convert him into an infallible deity, and to reduce Freirean studies to an orthodox church that only accepts established dogma and does not accept the possibility of disagreement. Freire always insisted: "Please do not follow me; reinvent me." Reinventing Freire's ideas, respectfully and creatively, can make an important contribution to the collective efforts around the world for a more democratic education and a more democratic society that has freedom and equality at its core.

Notes

1 The episode took place in 1973 in Lima. Freire and his colleagues asked people questions, but requested the answers in the form of photographs. When they asked "What is exploitation?" some people took pictures of landlords, grocers, or policemens but one child took a photo of a nail on a wall. This made no sense to adults, but it was clear to other children. In the dialogue, the children explained that many of them worked in the shoeshine business and that their clients were in the city, not in the barrio where they lived. Because their boxes were too heavy for them to carry, they had to rent

a nail on a wall (normally in a shop), where they could hang them for the night. That photograph of the "nail on the wall" generated discussions about other forms of institutionalized exploitation, and about ways to overcome them (Boal 1979:123, Singhal 2007:1).

2 See www.youtube.com/watch?v=1b0ECKAKyfM. Last accessed January 30, 2011.

3 The first forum was held in Sao Paulo in 1998, the second in Bologna in 2000, the third in Los Angeles in 2002, the fourth in Porto in 2004, the fifth in Valencia in 2006, the sixth again in Sao Paulo in 2008, the seventh in Praia (Cabo Verde) in 2010, and the next will be in Los Angeles in 2012.

4 The original French title was *Education et Transformation Sociale: Interrogeons nos pratiques. Croisement des savoirs et des pratiques autour de Paulo Freire.*

5 At the beginning of the discussion, the codification only had a few entries that reflected important aspects of their lives. As the discussion ensues and participants reflect on their experiences, new key words are added (Campfens 1999).

6 Regrettably, these cuts to education have come at the same time that military expenditures have increased. During the first decade of the twenty-first century, global military expenditures have increased by almost 50 percent, and less than 1 percent of those expenditures (0.5 percent, to be exact) would be sufficient to provide basic education to the entire population of the planet.

References

Abdi, A. (2001), "Identity in the philosophies of Dewey and Freire: Select analyses." *Journal of Educational Thought/Revue De La Pensee Educative* 35, (2), 181–200.

Accorinti, S. (2002), "Matthew Lipman y Paulo Freire: Conceptos para la libertad." *Utopia y Praxis LatinoAmericana: Revista Internacional de Filosofia Iberoamericana y Teoria Social* 7, (18), 35–56.

Ahmadifar, G. H. (2000), "Impact of culture circles on minority high school students in mathematics." Ph.D. thesis, The University of Oklahoma.

Alim, H. S. (2004), "You know my steez: An ethnographic and sociolinguistic study of styleshifting in a black American speech community." *American Speech* 79, (2), 167–93.

Al-Kahtany, A. H. (1996), "Literacy from a linguistic and a sociolinguistic perspective." *International Review of Education* 42, (6), 547–62.

Allen, R. L. (2002), "Pedagogy of the oppressor: What was Freire's theory for transforming the privileged and powerful?" Paper presented at the Annual Meeting of the American Educational Research Association. New Orleans, LA, April 1–5.

Allman, P. (1988), "Gramsci, Freire and Illich: Their contributions to education for socialism," in T. Lovett (ed.), *Radical Approaches to Adult Education.* London: Routledge, 85–113.

—(1994), "Paulo Freire's contributions to radical adult education." *Studies in the Education of Adults* 26, (2), 144–61.

—(1999), *Revolutionary Social Transformation: Democratic Hopes, Political Possibilities and Critical Education.* Westport, CT: Bergin & Garvey.

—(2010), *Critical Education against Global Capitalism: Karl Marx and Revolutionary Critical Education.* Rotterdam: Sense Publishers.

Allman, P., Mayo, P., and Cavanagh, C. (1998), "The creation of a world in which it will be easier to love." *Convergence* (Toronto, Ont.), 31, (1–2), 9–16.

Alschuler, L. R. (1992), "Oppression and liberation: A psychopolitical analysis according to Freire and Jung." *Journal of Humanistic Psychology* 32, (Spring), 8–31.

Alvarado, M. (2007), "José Martí y Paulo Freire: aproximaciones para una lectura de la pedagogía crítica. Revista electrónica de investigación educativa." 9, (1), available at http://redie.uabc.mx/vol9no1/contenido-alvarado.html.

Amorim, R., and Berkenbrock, M. (2007), "Freire, Dussel and Kohlberg: From vulnerability to autonomy." *Contrapontos* 7, (3), 615–27.

Ander, K. (1993), *Education for Critical Consciousness: A Theory of Empowerment for Public Health Nurses*. Washington, DC: University of Washington.

Andreola, B. A. (1993), "Action, knowledge and reality in the educational work of Paulo Freire." *Educational Action Research* 1, (2), 221–34.

Apple, M. (2003), "Freire and the politics of race in education." *International Journal of Leadership in Education* 6, (2), 107–18.

—(2008), "Introduction to essays in honor of Paulo Freire," in M. Shaughnessy, E. Galligan, and R. H. de Vivas (eds), *Pioneers in Education: Essays in Honor of Paulo Freire*. New York: Nova.

Apple, M., Gandin, L. A., and Hypolito, A. M. (2001), "Paulo Freire, 1921–1997," in Joy A. Palmer (ed.), *Fifty Modern Thinkers on Education: From Piaget to the Present*. New York: Routledge, 128–32.

Araujo Freire, A. M. (1998), *Nita e Paulo: Cronicas de amor*. São Paulo: Olho de Agua.

—(2002), "Preface: The Freirean legacy," in J. Slater, S. Fain, and C. Rossatto (eds), *The Freirean Legacy: Educating for Social Justice*. New York: Peter Lang.

—(2006), *Paulo Freire: Uma história de vida*. Indiaiatuba: Villa de Letras.

—(2008), "Bibliografía de Paulo Freire," in Danilo Streck, Euclides Redin and Jaime Zitkoski (eds), *Dicionário Paulo Freire*. Belo Horizonte: Auténtica, 433–8.

Araujo Freire, A. M. (ed.) (2001), *A pedagogia da libertação em Paulo Freire*. São Paulo: UNESP.

Araujo Freire, A. M., and Donaldo Macedo (1998), "Introduction," in A. M. Araujo Freire and Donaldo Macedo (eds), *The Paulo Freire Reader*. New York. Continuum.

Aronowitz, Stanley (1993), "Paulo Freire's radical democratic humanism," in P. McLaren and P. Leonard (eds), *Paulo Freire: A Critical Encounter*. New York: Routledge, 8–23.

Atack, Iain (2009), "Peace studies and social change: The role of ethics and human agency." *Development Education Review* 9, 39–51.

Au, Wayne (2007), "Epistemology of the oppressed: The dialectics of Paulo Freire's theory of knowledge." *Journal for Critical Education Policy Studies* 5, (2), www.jceps.com/index.php?pageID=article&articleID=100.

—(2009), "Fighting with the text: contextualizing and reconceptualizing Freire's critical pedagogy," in Michael Apple, Wayne Au, and Luis Armando Gandin (eds), *The Routledge International Handbook of Critical Education*. New York: Routledge, 221–31.

Au, Wayne, and Apple, M. (2007), "Freire, critical education, and the environmental crisis." *Educational Policy* 21, (3), 457–70.

Austin, R. (1997), "Freire, Frei, and literacy texts in Chile, 1964–70," in C. A. Torres and A. Puiggrós (eds), *Latin American Education*. Boulder, CO: Westview, 323–48.

Ayers, William (1987), "Review of a pedagogy for liberation." *Teachers College Record* 89, (1), 162–3.

Baatjes, I., and Mathe, K. (2004), "Adult basic education and social change in South Africa, 1994–2003," in L. Chisholm (ed.), *Changing Class: Education and Social Change in Post-apartheid South Africa*. Pretoria: Human Sciences Research Council, 393–420.

Balke, Tom (1986), "Review of *The Politics of Education: Culture, Power and Liberation*." *Studies in the Education of Adults* 18, 47–8.

Baltodano, Charlotte (2009), "A Freirean analysis of the process of conscientization in the Argentinean Madres Movement," in Ali Abdi and Dip Kappor (eds), *Global Perspectives on Adult Education*. New York: Palgrave, 221–38.

Bambozzi, Enrique (2000), *Pedagogía Latinoamericana: teoría y praxis en Paulo Freire. Córdoba*. Editoral de la Universidad Nacional de Córdoba.

Barndt, Deborah (1998), "The world in a tomato: revisiting the use of 'codes' in Freire's problem-posing education." *Convergence* XXXI, (1–2), 62–74.

Bartlett, Leslie (2005), "Dialogue, knowledge, and teacher-student relations: Freirean pedagogy in theory and practice." *Comparative Education Review* 49, (3), 344–64.

—(2008), "Paulo Freire and peace education." *Encyclopedia of Peace Education*. New York: Teachers College, Columbia University.

Basu, S. J. (2006), "How urban youth express critical agency in a 9th grade conceptual physics classroom." Ph.D. thesis, Columbia University.

Bataille, L. (ed.) (1976), *A Turning Point for Literacy: Adult Education for Development. The Spirit and Declaration of Persepolis*. London: Pergamon Press.

Bazata, Bonnie, Erin Cressy, Joy Evans, Sarita Fritzler, Adriana Lopez, Razia Stanikzia, and Kimberly Warren (2007), "The catalyst trip: A journey of transformation." *Diversity & Democracy* 10, (3), 14–16, available at www.diversityweb.org/DiversityDemocracy/vol10no3/bazata.cfm.

Becker, Fernando (1983), "Da ação a operação: O caminho da aprendizagem em Jean Piaget e Paulo Freire." Doctoral dissertation, Universidade de São Paulo.

Bennett, J. N. (1996), "Participation, persistence, and progression: Motivating factors in the success of Hispanic community college students who moved from mastering English as a Second Language to a certificate or degree program." Ed.D. thesis, Oregon State University.

Berger, Peter (1974), *Pyramids of Sacrifice*. New York: Basic Books.

Berthoff, Ann (1986), "Paulo Freire's liberation pedagogy." *Language Arts* 67, (4), 362–9.

Betto, Frei (2010), "Educación popular." Presentation at the IV National Conference of Popular Educators. La Habana, November 10.

Beveridge, D. M. (1984), "Adult Education in a local church in Midwest U.S.A.: A case study based on Paulo Freire's Theory of Conscientization." Ph.D. thesis, University of Wisconsin—Madison.

Bhattacharya, Asoke (2008), "Paulo Freire: The Rousseau of the twentieth century," in M. Shaughnessy, Elizabeth Galligan, and Romelia Hurtado de Vivas (eds), *Pioneers in Education: Essays in Honor of Paulo Freire*. New York: Nova.

—(2010), *Education for the People. Concepts of Grundtvig, Tagore, Ghandi and Freire*. Rotterdam: Sense Publishers.

Bimbi, Linda (1971), Preface to the Italian edition of *Pedagogy of the Oppressed*. (La pedagogia degli oppressi.) Milano: Mondadori.

Blackburn, James (2000), "Understanding Paulo Freire: Reflections on the origins, concepts, and possible pitfalls of his educational approach." *Community Development Journal* 35, (1), 3–15.

Blier, H. M. (2002), "Like mining for precious stones: The wisdom and work of exemplary teachers." Ph.D. thesis, Emory University. Boal, Augusto (1979), *Theatre of the Oppressed*. London: Pluto Press.

Borg, Carmel, and Peter Mayo (2000), "Reflections from a third age marriage. A pedagogy of hope, reason and passion. An interview with Ana Maria (Nita) Araujo Freire." *McGill Journal of Education* 35, (2), 105–20.

—(2002), "Making sense of a postcolonial context: A Freirean perspective." *Journal of Postcolonial Education* 1, (1), 101–25.

Boshier, R. (1999), "Freire at the beach: Remembering Paulo in the bright days of summer." *Studies in Continuing Education* 21, (1), 113–25.

Boston, Bruce (1972), "Paulo Freire," in Stanley Grabowski (ed.), *Paulo Freire: A Revolutionary Dilemma for the Adult Educator*. Syracuse, NY: Syracuse University Publications in Continuing Education.

Boughton, Bob (2008), "East Timor's national literacy campaign and the struggle for a post-conflict democracy." Paper presented to the 17th Biennial Conference of the Asian Studies Association of Australia. Melbourne, July 1–3.

Bower, T. R. (2003), "Identifying current uses of philosophies of critical pedagogy in religious education." Doctoral thesis, Presbyterian School of Christian Education.

Bowers, C. A. (1983), "Linguistic roots of cultural invasion in Paulo Freire's pedagogy." *Teachers College Record* 84, (4), 935–53.

—(2003), "The constructivism of John Dewey and Paulo Freire: A Trojan horse of Western imperialism?" Paper presented at the Conference "Lifelong Citizenship Learning, Participatory Democracy and Social Change." Ontario Institute for Studies in Education, Toronto, October 17–19.

—(2007), "A response to McLaren's revisionist interpretation of Freire." *Capitalism Nature and Socialism* 18, (1), 109–18.

—(2008), "Why a critical pedagogy of place is an oxymoron." *Environmental Education Research* 14, (3), 325–35.

Bowers, C. A., and Apffel-Marglin, F. (eds) (2005), *Rethinking Freire: Globalization and the Environmental Crisis.* Mahway, NJ: Lawrence Erlbaum.

Bowers, Rick (2005), "Freire (with Bakhtin) and the Dialogic Classroom Seminar." *Alberta Journal of Educational Research* 51, (4), 368–78.

Boyd, Neil (2010), "Oppression in the mundane of management. An example from human resources." *Administrative Theory and Practice* 32, (3), 445–49.

Brady, Jeanne (1994), "Critical literacy, feminism, and a politics of representation," in Peter L. McLaren and Colin Lankshear (eds), *Politics of Liberation. Paths from Freire.* New York: Routledge.

Brantlinger, A. (2007), "Geometries of inequality: Teaching and researching critical mathematics in a low-income urban high school." Ph.D. thesis, Northwestern University.

Brazil, A. (2007), "Correctional education: A theoretical analysis for change." Master's thesis, Mount Saint Vincent University.

Bridges-Johns, Cheryl (1993), *Pentecostal Formation: A Pedagogy among the Oppressed.* United Kingdom: Sheffield Academic Press.

Brookfield, Stephen, and John Holst (2011), *Radicalizing Learning: Adult Education for a Just World.* San Francisco, CA: Jossey Bass.

Brown, Cynthia (1974), "Literacy in 30 hours: Paulo Freire's process in North East Brazil." *The Urban Review* 7, (3), 245–56.

Brown, Sharon (2001), "Paulo Freire in modern times. Dublin hears how to change the world." Changing Ireland Project, available at www.changingireland.ie/tft.html.

Bugbee, John (1973), "The Freire approach to literacy review and reflections." *Literacy Discussion* 4, (4), 415–37.

—(1975), "Reflections on Griffith, Freire and beyond." *Literacy Discussion* 5, (4), 151–60.

Butte, Susanne (2010), "Freire: Informal education as protest." *Journal for Critical Education Policy Studies* 8, (1), 162–180.

Butterwick, S. J. (1987), *Learning Liberation: Comparative Analysis of Feminist Consciousness Raising and Freire's Conscientization Method.* Master's Thesis, University of British Columbia.

Byam, L. D. (1996), "ZACT: Theatre for development in Zimbabwe." Ph.D. thesis, New York University.

Calvo Muñoz, Carlos (2006), "La presencia sutil del maestro: la influencia de Paulo Freire en mi formación." *Revista Universidad EAFIT* 42, (143), 32–40.

Campfens, Hubert (1999), *Community Development around the World. Practice, Theory, Research, Training.* Toronto: University of Toronto Press.

Cardoso, Fernando, and Enzo Faletto, (1969), *Dependencia y desarrollo en América Latina.* Mexico: Siglo XXI.

Carnoy, Martin (2004), Foreword to *Pedagogy of the Heart*. New York: Continuum, 7–20.

Carr, Paul (2010), "Re-thinking normative democracy and the political economy of education." *Journal for Critical Education Policy Studies* 8, (1), 1–40.

—(2011), *Does Your Vote Count? Critical Pedagogy and Democracy*. New York: Peter Lang.

Castells, Manuel, Ramón Flecha, Paulo Freire, Henry Giroux, Donaldo Macedo and Paul Willis, Paul (1999), *Critical Education in the New Information Age*. Lanham, MD: Rowman and Littlefield.

Caulfield, Peter (1991), "From Brazil to Buncombe County." *Educational Forum* 55, (4), 307–17

CEAAL (1985), *Paulo Freire en Buenos Aires*. Buenos Aires: Consejo de Educación de Adultos de América Latina.

Cheng, Yinghong, and Patrick Manning (2003), "Revolution in education: China and Cuba in global context, 1957–1976." *Journal of World History* 14, (3), 359–91.

Chew, Esyin, and Norah Jones (2007), "The marriage of Freire and Bloom: An assessment prototype for pedagogy of the oppressed and higher order thinking." Proceedings of the 11th International Computer Assisted Conference, July 10–11. Loughborough University, Loughborough, 117–25.

CIDC (Centro de Investigaciones y Desarrollo Cultural) (1990), *Paulo Freire conversando con educadores*. Roca Viva: Montevideo.

Cintra, Eliseu (1998), *Paulo Freire entre o grego e o semita*. Porto Alegre: EDIPURCS.

Clare, R. C. (2000), "The Ethical Choices Workshop: A Freirean pedagogy for the North American middle class." Ed.D. thesis, Columbia University, Teachers College.

Clarke, Patrick (1998), "Translator's notes," in P. Freire (ed.), *Pedagogy of Freedom*. Rowman and Littlefield, ix–x.

Clovis, Jose and Daniel Schugurensky (2005), "Three dimensions of educational democratization: The Citizen School project of Porto Alegre." *Our Schools/Our Selves* 15, (1), 41–58.

Coben, Diana. (1998), *Radical Heroes: Gramsci, Freire, and the Politics of Adult Education*. New York: Garland.

Collins, Colin Bryan (1974), "The ideas of Paulo Freire and an analysis of black consciousness in South Africa." Unpublished thesis, University of Toronto.

Collins, Denis (1973), "Two utopians: a comparison and contrast of the educational philosophies of Paulo Freire and Theodore Bremeld." Ph.D. thesis, University of Southern California.

—(1977), *Paulo Freire, His Life, Works, and Thought*. New York: Paulist Press.

—(1998), "From oppression to hope: Freire's journey towards utopia." *Anthropology & Education Quarterly* 29, (1), 115–24.

Collyer, J. R. (1996), "Independent and inclusive leadership experiences in relation to critical consciousness and social structure." Ph.D. thesis, The Fielding Institute.

Cooper, Gillian (1995), "Freire and Theology." *Studies in the Education of Adults* 27, (1), 66–78.

Craig, G. (1981), "The Development of a Freire-Based Literacy/conscientization Program for Low-Literate Women in Prison." Ph.D. thesis, Pennsylvania State University.

Crouse, T. (2000), "Higher education in prisons: A historical analysis." M.A. thesis, University of Ottawa.

Cuadernos de Educación (1972), "Entrevista con Paulo Freire." *Cuadernos de Educación* 26, 1–10.

Curle, A., Freire, P., and Galtung, J. (1976), "What can education contribute towards peace and social justice?" in Magnus Haavelsrud (ed.), *Education for Peace, Reflection, and Action*. Guilford: IPC Science and Technology, 64–97.

Curzon-Hobson, Aidan (2002), "Higher education in a world of radical unknowability: An extension of the challenge of Ronald Barnett." *Teaching in Higher Education* 7, (2), 179–91.

Da Silva, Maria (2005), "Freire e Durkheim: (Des)encontro de olhares e de práticas." Paper presented at V Coloquio Internacional Paulo Freire. Recife, September 19–22.

Da Silva, Tomas Tadeu, and Peter McLaren (1993), "Knowledge under siege: The Brazilian debate," in Peter McLaren and P. Leonard (eds), *Paulo Freire: A Critical Encounter*. New York: Routledge, 36–46.

Da Silva Sousa, Aline (2009), "Pestalozzi e Paulo Freire: Caminhos Que Se Cruzam Na Práxis Educativa Popular." Paper presented at the Encontro de Pesquisa Educacional do Norte e Nordeste. Universidade Federal da Paraiba, July 5–8.

Dagostino-Kalniz, V. (2008), "Toward a being based liberatory educational paradigm: A dialogical encounter between Paulo Freire and Erich Fromm." Ph.D. thesis, University of Toledo.

Dale, John, and Emery Hyslop-Margison (2010), *Paulo Freire: Teaching for Freedom and Transformation: The Philosophical Influences on the Work of Paulo Freire*. London: Springer.

Dallaire, Michael (2001), *Contemplation in Liberation: A Method for Spiritual Education in the Schools*. New York: Edwin Mellen Press.

Darder, Antonia (2002), *Reinventing Paulo Freire: A Pedagogy of Love*. Cambridge: Westview Press.

—(2003), "Teaching as an act of love: reflections on Paulo Freire and his contributions to our lives and our work," in Antonia Darder, Marta

Baltodano, and Rodolfo Torres (eds), *The Critical Pedagogy Reader*. New York: Routledge, 497–510.

Darder, Antonia, Marta Baltodano, and Rodolfo Torres (2003), "Critical pedagogy: An introduction," in Antonia Darder, Marta Baltodano, and Rodolfo Torres (eds), *The Critical Pedagogy Reader*. New York: Routledge, 1–23.

Darnell, S. B. (1981), "A study of adult development through learning in general education courses." Ph.D. thesis, The Union for Experimenting Colleges and Universities.

De Castro, Sandro, and Gomercindo Ghiggi (2009), "Autoridade e liberdade na práxis educativa Paulo Freire e o conceito de autonomia." *Saberes* 2, (3), 80–93.

De Sanctis, Filippo (1977), "A victory for Italian workers: The 150 hours." *Prospects* 7, (2), 280–87.

Demetrion, G. (1997), "Student goals and public outcomes: The contribution of adult literacy education to the public good." *Adult Basic Education* 7, (3), 145–64.

Dewey, John (1916) [1964], *Democracy and Education*. New York: Free Press.

Dillon, David (1985), "Reading the world and reading the word. An interview with Paulo Freire." *Language Arts* 62, 15–21.

Dorvlo, Leonard (1993), *Adult Literacy Teaching in Ghana: Adapting the Freirean Approach and Technique*. Accra: Ghana Universities Press.

Dos Reis, Mericio (2004), "The involvement of men in solving gender issues in Timor Leste." International Area Studies Conference No. 9, Tokyo, Japan.

Druliner, Marcia (1992), "Gutierrez's theology and Freire's pedagogy with implications for Christian education." Ph.D. thesis, Marquette University.

Durnan, Deborah (2005), "Popular education and peacebuilding in Timor Leste." Master's thesis, University of New England.

Eagan, Jennifer (2010), "Paulo Freire's *Pedagogy of the Oppressed*." Forum Section, *Administrative Theory and Practice* 32, (3), 429–30.

Egerton, John (1973), "Searching for Freire." *Saturday Review of Education* 1, (3), 32–5.

Elias, John (1994), *Paulo Freire: Pedagogue of Liberation*. Malabar: Krieger.

—(1976), *Conscientization and Deschooling: Freire's and Illich's Proposals for Reshaping Society*. Philadelphia, PA: Westminster Press.

Elias, John and Sharan Merriam (1980), *Philosophical Foundations of Adult Education*. Huntington, NY: Krieger Publishing.

Ellsworth, E. (1989), "Why doesn't this feel empowering? Working through the repressive myths of critical pedagogy." *Harvard Educational Review* 59, 297–324.

Entwistle, Harold (1989), *Antonio Gramsci: Conservative Schooling for Radical Politics*. Boston, MA: Routledge.

Epstein, Erwin (1972), "Blessed be the oppressed—and those who can identify with them: a critique of Paulo Freire's Conscientizacao." Paper presented at a meeting of the American Educational Studies. Chicago, February 23 (p. 7).

Escobar, Miguel, Alfredo Fernández, Gilberto Guevara Niebla, and Paulo Freire (1994), *Paulo Freire on Higher Education: A Dialogue at the National University of Mexico SUNY series, Teacher Empowerment and School Reform.* Albany, NY: State University of New York Press.

Esteva, Gustavo, Stuchul, D., and Prakash M. (2005), "From pedagogy for liberation to liberation from pedagogy," in C. A. Bowers and F. Apffel-Marglin (eds), *Rethinking Freire: Globalization and the Environmental Crisis.* Mahway, NJ: Lawrence Erlbaum Associates, 82–98.

Estrella, Antonio (1998), "La práctica alfabetizadora y educativa de Freire en una perspectiva utópica." *Diálogos* 15–16, 14–19.

Evenson, M. C. (1995), "Rethinking the heroic: Demystification and revision of history in the Nuevo Teatro." Ph.D. thesis, University of Wisconsin—Madison.

Ewert, David (1977), "Freire's concept of critical consciousness and social structure in rural Zaire." Unpublished doctoral dissertation, University of Wisconsin—Madison.

Facundo, Blanca (1984), *Freire Inspired Programs in the United States and Puerto Rico: A Critical Evaluation.* Washington, DC: The Latino Institute.

Farahmandpur, Ramin (2006), "Review of pedagogy of indignation, by Paulo Freire," in G. Glass and Gustavo Fischman (eds), *Education Review: a Journal of Book Reviews,* retrieved from www.edrev.info/reviews/rev454.htm (accessed June 10, 2009).

Feinberg, Walter and Torres, C. A. (2007), "Democracy and education: John Dewey and Paulo Freire," in J. Zajda (ed.), *Education and Society.* Australia: James Nicholas.

Fetterman, David (1986), "Review of *The Politics of Education.*" *American Anthropologist* 88, (1), 253–4.

Filax, Gloria (1997), "Resisting resistors: resistance in critical pedagogy classrooms." *The Journal of Educational Thought* 31, (3), 259–70.

Findsen, B. (1998), "Freire as an adult educator: An international perspective." *New Zealand Journal of Adult Learning* 26, (1), 9–22.

—(2007), "Freirean philosophy and pedagogy in the adult education context: The case of older adults' learning." *Studies in Philosophy and Education* 26, (6), 545–59.

Fiore, Kyle, and Nan Elsasser (1987), "Strangers no more: A liberatory literacy curriculum," in Ira Shor (ed.), *Freire for the Classroom: A Sourcebook for Liberatory Teaching.* Portsmouth: Heinemann, 87–104.

Fischman, Gustavo, and Peter McLaren (2000), "Schooling for democracy: toward a critical utopianism." *Contemporary Sociology* 29, (1), 168–79.

—(2009), "Un/taming Freire's *Pedagogy of the Oppressed*," in Michael Apple, Wayne Au, and Luis Armando Gandin (eds), *The Routledge International Handbook of Critical Education*. New York: Routledge.

Fischman, Gustavo, and Sandra Sales (2010), "Formação de professores e pedagogias críticas: é possível ir além das narratives redentoras?" *Revista Brasileira de Educação* 15, (43), 7–20.

Fisher, J. S. (1980), "Political education: The views of Michael Oakeshott and Paulo Freire." Ph.D. thesis, Claremont Graduate University.

Flecha, Ramón (2004), "La pedagogía de la autonomía de Freire y la educación democrática de personas adultas." *Revista interuniversitaria de formación del profesorado* 7, (1), 27–44.

—(2007), "La presencia de Paulo Freire en España." *Revista Interamericana de Educación de Adultos* 29, (1), 70–6.

Fletcher, P. (1979), *Paulo Freire and Concientizacion in Latin America*. Stanford, CA: Center for Latin American Studies.

Fonvieille, Raymond (ed.) (1997), Paulo Freire et Janusz Korczak. Deux pédagogues pour les exclus. Revue d'analyse institutionnelle 1, (1), 27–30.

Fortes, Daniele (2007), *A aprendizagem em Freire e Piaget*. Bauru: Universidade Estadual Paulista Julio de Mequita Filho.

Foy, Rena (1971), "Review of *Pedagogy of the Oppressed*." *Educational Studies* 2, (3–4), 92–3.

Frankestein, Marily, and Arthur Bowell (1994), "Towards liberatory mathematics. Paulo Freire's epistemology and ethnomathematics," in Peter L. McLaren and Colin Lankshear (eds), *Politics of Liberation. Paths from Freire*. New York: Routledge, 74–99.

Frasca, Gonzalo (2001), Videogames of the Oppressed: Videogames as a means of critical thinking and debate." M.A. thesis, Georgia Institute of Technology.

Fraser, James (1997), "Love and history in the work of Paulo Freire," in P. Freire, with J. W. Fraser, D. Macedo, T. McKinnon, and W. T. Stokes (eds), *Mentoring the Mentor: A Critical Dialogue with Paulo Freire*. New York: Peter Lang, 303–29.

Freire, Madalena (1983), *A paixão de conhecer o mundo: relatos de uma professora*. Rio de Janeiro: Paz e Terra.

Freire, Paulo (1959), *Educação e atualidade brasileira*. Recife: Universidade Federal do Recife.

—(1963), "Conscientização e Alfabetização: Una Nova Visão do Processo." *Revista Estudos Universitários*, Universidade do Recife, (4), 5–23.

—(1967), *La educación como práctica de la libertad*. México: Siglo XXI.

—(1970a), "Cultural Action for Freedom." *The Harvard Educational Review*, monograph series No. 1. Cambridge: Center for the Study of Development and Social Change.

—(1970b), *Pedagogy of the Oppressed*. New York: Continuum

—(1971), "To the coordinator of a Culture Circle." *Convergence* 4, (1), 61–2.

—(1972a), *Conscientizing as a Way of Liberation.* Washington, DC: LADOC, 2–29.

—(1972b), "A letter to a theology student." *Catholic Mind* 70, (1265), 6–8.

—(1973), *Education for Critical Consciousness.* New York: Continuum.

—(1974), "When I met Marx I continued to meet Christ on the corner of the street." Interview with Barry Hill. *The Age Newspaper.* Melbourne, Australia, April 19.

—(1975a), "Pilgrims of the obvious." *Risk* 11, (1), 12–17.

—(1975b), "Are adult literacy programs neutral?" Presentation at the International Symposium for Literacy, Persepolis. Hamburg: UNESCO Institute for Lifelong Learning, September 3–8.

—(1978a), *Fundamentos revolucionarios de pedagogía popular.* Buenos Aires: Editora 904.

—(1978b), *Pedagogy in Process: The Letters to Guinea Bissau.* New York: Seabury.

—(1979), "To know and to be." *Indian Journal of Youth Affairs* 70, 6–8, June.

—(1980), *Conscientização. Teoria e prática da libertação.* São Paulo: Centauro Editora, 3rd edition.

—(1981), The People Speak Their Word: Learning to Read and Write in Sao Tome and Principe. *Harvard Educational Review* 51, (1), 2 7–30.

—(1982), "Creating alternative research methods: Learning to do it by doing it," in B. Hall, A. Gillette, and R. Tandon (eds), *Creating Knowledge: A Monopoly? Society for Participatory Research in Asia.* New Delhi, India: New Delhi Press.

—(1983), "The importance of the act of reading." *Journal of Education* 165, (1), 5–11.

—(1984a), "Un mensaje a los alfabetizadores. Entrevista por Tomás Miklos." *Revista Educación de Adultos* 2, (3), 41–2.

—(1984b), "Le monde et le mot." *Le courier de l'Unesco* 37, (2), 29–31.

—(1984c), "Education, liberation and the church." *Religious Education* 79, (4), 524–45.

—(1985a), *The Politics of Education: Culture, Power and Liberation.* London: Macmillan.

—(1985b), "Intervención de Paulo Freire en Centro Cultural San Martín de Buenos Aires," in *Paulo Freire en Buenos Aires.* Buenos Aires: Consejo de Educación de Adultos de América Latina, 11–20.

—(1987), "Letter to North-American teachers," in Ira Shor (ed.), *Freire for the Classroom: A Sourcebook for Liberatory Teaching.* New Hampshire: Boynton/Cook, 211–14.

—(1989), *Learning to Question.* New York: Continuum.

—(1991), *A educação na cidade.* São Paulo: Cortez.

—(1993a), Foreword, in P. McLaren and P. Leonard (eds), *Paulo Freire: A Critical Encounter.* New York: Routledge, ix–xii.

—(1993b), *Pedagogy of the City.* New York: Continuum.

—(1994a), "Obrigado, Professora: Eunice Vasconcelos." *Nova Escola* 57, 62–3, December.

—(1994b), *Pedagogy of Hope*. New York: Continuum.

—(1995), "Learning to read the world. Paulo Freire in conversation with Carlos Alberto Torres," in C. A. Torres (ed.), *Education and Social Change in Latin America*. Australia: James Nicholas Publishers, 175–82.

—(1996), *Letters to Cristina. Reflections on My Life and Work*. New York: Routledge.

—(1997a), *Pedagogy of the Heart*. New York: Continuum.

—(1997b), "A response," in P. Freire, with J. W. Fraser, D. Macedo, T. McKinnon, and W. T. Stokes (eds), *Mentoring the Mentor: A Critical Dialogue with Paulo Freire*. New York: Peter Lang, 303–29.

—(1998a), *Politics and Education*. Berkeley, CA: UCLA.

—(1998b), *Pedagogy of Freedom. Ethics, Democracy and Civic Courage*. New York: Rowman and Littlefield.

—(1998c), *Teachers as Cultural Workers, Letters to Those Who Dare Teach*. Boulder, CO: Westview.

—(2004), *Pedagogy of Indignation* (organized by Nita Araujo Freire). Boulder, CO: Paradigm Publishers.

—(2006), *Pedagogia da Tolerância* (organized by Nita Araujo Freire). São Paulo: UNESP.

—(2007), *Daring to Dream: Toward a Pedagogy of the Unfinished* (organized by Nita Araujo Freire). Boulder, CO: Paradigm Publishers.

Freire, Paulo, Frei Betto, and Ricardo Kotscho (1985), *Essa escola chamada vida*. São Paulo: Attica.

Freire, Paulo, Claudius Ceccon, Rosiska Dary de Oliveira, and Miguel Darcy de Oliveira (1983), *Vivendo e aprendendo: experiências do IDAC em educação popular*. São Paulo: Brasiliense.

Freire, Paulo and Antonio Faundez (1989), *Learning to Question: A Pedagogy of Liberation*. New York: Continuum.

Freire, Paulo, with Fraser, J. W., Macedo, D., McKinnon, T., and Stokes, W. T. (eds) (1997), *Mentoring the Mentor: A Critical Dialogue with Paulo Freire*. New York: Peter Lang.

Freire, Paulo, with Moacir Gadotti, Sergio Guimaraes, and Isabel Hernandez (1988), *Pedagogía, Diálogo y Conflicto*. São Paulo: Cortez.

Freire, Paulo and Sergio Guimaraes (1984), *Sobre Educação: diálogos*. Rio de Janeiro: Paz e Terra.

Freire Paulo and Ivan Illich (1975), *Diálogo*. Buenos Aires: Búsqueda.

Freire, Paulo and Donaldo Macedo (1987), *Literacy: Reading the Word and the World*. South Hadley: Bergin & Garvey.

—(1996), "A dialogue: Culture, language and race," in Pepi Leistyna, Arlie Woodrum, and Stephen Sherblom (eds), *Breaking Free: The Transformative Power of Critical Pedagogy*. Cambridge: Harvard Education Review, 199–228.

Freire, Paulo and Ira Shor (1987), *Pedagogy for Liberation. Dialogues on Transforming Education.* London: Macmillan

Freire, Sandra Ferraz de Castillo Dourado (2000), "Dialogue: The intersection between Freire and Vygotsky." M.Ed. thesis, Michigan State University.

Friedenberg, Edgar (1971), "Review of *Pedagogy of the Oppressed.*" *Comparative Education Review* 15, (3), 378–80.

Fundación para la Innovación Agraria (2009), *Resultados y lecciones en alfabetización digital rural: escuelas de informática y ciudadanía.* Chile: Ministerio de Agricultura.

Furter, Pierre (1985), "Profiles of educators." *Prospects* 15, (2), 301–9.

Gadotti, Moacir (1994), *Reading Paulo Freire. His Life and Work.* New York: State University of New York Press.

—(1996), "A Voz do Biógrafo Brasileiro: A Prática à Altura do Sonho," in M. Gadotti and C. A. Torres (eds), *Paulo Freire: Uma Bio-bibliógrafia.* São Paulo: Instituto Paulo Freire-UNESCO-Cortez Editora.

—(2001a), *Um Legado de Esperança.* São Paulo: Cortez.

—(2001b), "Review of Chapter 2: The work of Paulo Freire," in Liam Kane (ed.), *Popular Education and Social Change in Latin America.* London: Latin American Bureau.

—(2003), *Perspectivas actuales de la educación.* Buenos Aires: Siglo XXI.

—(2008), "Paulo Freire and the culture of justice and peace: The perspective of Washington vs. the perspective of Angicos," in C. A. Torres and P. Noguera (eds), *Social Justice Education for Teachers. Paulo Freire and the Possible Dream.* Rotterdam: Sense Publishers, 147–60.

Gadotti, Moacir, Margarita Gomez, and Lutgardes Freire (eds) (2003), *Lecciones de Paulo Freire. Cruzando fronteras: experiencias que se completan.* Buenos Aires: CLACSO.

Gadotti, Moacir and Carlos A. Torres (1997), "Paulo Freire: A homage." *Taboo: The Journal of Culture and Education* 11, 96–101.

—(2009), "Paulo Freire: Education for development." *Development and Change* 40, (6), 1255–67.

Gajardo, Marcela (1998), "Despedida a Paulo Freire." *Convergence XXXI* (1–2), 40–8.

Gandin, L. A., and Apple, M. (2002), "Challenging neo-liberalism, building democracy: Creating the citizen school in Porto Alegre, Brazil," *Journal of Education Policy* 17, (2), 259–79.

—(2003), "Educating the state, democratizing knowledge: The citizen school project in Porto Alegre, Brazil," in M. Apple (ed.), *The State and the Politics of Knowledge.* New York: Routledge, 193–219.

Garrido, Danilo (2005), "Paulo Freire y la educación superior." Master's thesis, Universidad de San Carlos de Guatemala.

Gee, James (1997), "Dilemmas of literacy: Plato and Freire," in P. Freire, with J. W. Fraser, D. Macedo, T. McKinnon, and W. T. Stokes (eds), *Mentoring the Mentor: A Critical Dialogue with Paulo Freire*. New York: Peter Lang, 229–41.

Geribello, Wanda (1977), *Anisio Teixeira. Análise e sistematização de sua obra*. São Paulo: Atlas.

Gerhardt, Heinz-Peter (1989), "Pourquoi l'alphabétizasion? Pluralité des approches culturelles." *Perspectives* 19, (4), 535–51.

—(1993), "Paulo Freire." *Prospects: The Quarterly Review of Comparative Education* XXIII, (3/4), 439–58.

Ghiggi, Gomercindo, and Sandro De Castro (2009), *Origens e concepçoes de autoridade e educacao para a liberdade en Paulo Freire: (re)visitando intencionalidades educativas*. São Luis: EDUFMA.

Gibson, Richard (1994), "The Promethean literacy: Paulo Freire's pedagogy of reading, praxis and liberation." Doctoral dissertation, The Pennsylvania State University.

—(1999), "Paulo Freire and pedagogy for social justice." *Theory and Research in Social Education* 27, (2), 129–59.

—(2007), "Paulo Freire and the revolutionary pedagogy for social justice," in Wayne Ross and Rich Gibson (eds), *Neoliberalism and Education Reform*. New Jersey: Hampton Press.

—(2008), "The dead end at Freire." Paper presented at the Annual Conference of the Canadian Society for the Study of Education. University of British Columbia. Vancouver BC, June 2.

Giroux, Henry (1985), "Introduction," in Paulo Freire, *The Politics of Education: Culture, Power and Liberation*. Massachusetts: Bergin & Garvey Publishers.

—(1993), "Paulo Freire and the politics of postcolonialism," in Peter McLaren and Peter Leonard (eds), *Paulo Freire: A Critical Encounter*. London: Routledge.

—(1994), "Paulo Freire and the rise of the border intellectual," in *Disturbing Pleasures: Learning Popular Culture*. New York: Routledge.

—(2010), "Lessons from Paulo Freire." *The Chronicle of Higher Education* 57 (9), http://chronicle.com/article/Lessons-From-Paulo-Freire/124910/

Giroux, Henry and Peter McLaren (1997), "Paulo Freire, postmodernism and the utopian imagination: A Blochian reading," in Jamie Owen and Tom Moylan (eds), *Not Yet: Reconsidering Ernst Bloch*. London: Verso, 138–64.

Glass, Ron (2001), "On Paulo Freire's philosophy of praxis and the foundations of liberation education." *Educational Researcher* 30, (2), 15–25.

—(2009), "Re-imagining and re-creating the 'public' and the 'education' in public education: A Freirean approach using digital stories." Paper presented at the Transformative Learning Centre. University of Toronto, March 25.

Godonoo, Prosper (1998), "Tribute to Paulo Freire: His influence on scholars in Africa." *Convergence* 31, (1–2), 30–9.

Goldmann, Lucien (1966), *Sciences humaines et philosophie. Suivi de structuralisme génétique et création littéraire.* Paris: Gonthier.

Gomez, Margarita (2009), "Emmanuel Levinas and Paulo Freire: The ethics of responsibility for the face-to-face interaction in the virtual world." *International Journal of Instruction* 2, (1), 27–58.

Goodman, Diane (2000), *Promoting Diversity and Social Justice: Educating People from Privileged Groups.* London: Sage Publications Ltd.

Gottlieb, Esther E., and Thomas J. La Belle (1990), "Ethnographic contextualization of Freire's discourse." *Anthropology & Education Quarterly* 21 (1), 13–18.

Grabowski, Stanley (ed.) (1972), *Paulo Freire: A Revolutionary Dilemma for the Adult Educator.* Syracuse, NY: Syracuse University Publications in Continuing Education.

Grace, André and Kristopher Wells (2011). Using Freirean pedagogy of just ire to inform critical social learning in arts-informed community education for sexual minorities. In Sharan Merriam and André Grace (eds), *Contemporary Issues in Adult Education*. San Fco: Jossey-Bass, 436-458.

Grace, Daniel (2009), "Photography of the oppressed: The pedagogical possibilities of democratizing image construction and dissemination." Policy Brief. Centre for International and Security Studies, York University, retrieved from www.yorku.ca/yciss/research/documents/DDCSPolicyBriefDanielGrace.pdf

Graden, Dale (2008), "Notes from a fan: Paulo Freire comes to Idaho." *International Journal of Critical Pedagogy* 1, (2), 98–114.

Griffith, William (1972), "Paulo Freire," in Stanley Grabowski (ed.), *Paulo Freire: A Revolutionary Dilemma for the Adult Educator.* Syracuse, NY: Syracuse University Publications in Continuing Education.

Grollios, Georgios (2009), *Paulo Freire and the Curriculum.* Boulder, CO: Paradigm.

Gronholm, Chris (1999), "Revisiting Freire's radical tradition. A dialogue with editors," in Chris Gronholm and Jozsef Katus (eds), *Issues of Education and Civil Society.* Helsinki: Fonda, 159–68.

Gruenewald, D. A. (2003), "The best of both worlds: A critical pedagogy of place." *Educational Researcher* 32, (4), 3–12.

Guilherme, Manuela (2002), *Critical citizens for an Intercultural World: Foreign Language Education as Cultural Politics.* Clevedon: Cromwell Press.

Guo, Shibao (1998), "Freire's critical literacy theory and adult literacy education in China." Comparative and International Education Society (CIES) Conference, Western Region. The University of British Columbia, Vancouver. June 11–13.

Hall, Budd (1998), "'Please don't bother the canaries': Paulo Freire and the International Council for Adult Education." *Convergence* XXXI, (1–2), 95–103.

Harasim, Linda (1983), "Literacy and national reconstruction in Guinea-Bissau: A critique of the Freirean literacy campaign." Ph.D. thesis, University of Toronto.

Harman, David (1971), "Review of *Pedagogy of the Oppressed.*" *Saturday Review*, 44–5, June 19.

Haymes, Stephen (2002), "Race and Freire's *Pedagogy of the Oppressed.*" *Radical Philosophy Review* 5, (1/2), 165–75.

Hedeen, Timothy (2005), "Dialogue and democracy, community and capacity: Lessons for conflict resolution education from Montessori, Dewey, and Freire." *Conflict Resolution Quarterly* 23, (2), 185–202.

Hirsch, Judy (1986), "Using critical pedagogy for democratic empowerment in teacher education: A comparison of the theories of Freire and Feuerstein." Paper presented at the Fourth International Conference on Critical Thinking and Educational Reform. Sonoma State University, August 3–6.

—(1993), "Assessment and remediation of cognitive skills: Combining the theories of Feuerstein and Freire," in Riva Heft and Olivia Rovinescu (eds), *Dimensions of Literacy in a Multicultural Society*. Montreal: Concordia University.

Holst, John (2002), *Social Movements, Civil Society, and Radical Adult Education*. Westport, CT: Bergin & Garvey.

—(2006), "Paulo Freire in Chile, 1964–1969: *Pedagogy of the Oppressed* in its sociopolitical economic context." *Harvard Educational Review* 76, (2), 243–70

hooks, b. (1993), "bell hooks speaking about Paulo Freire: The man, his work," in P. McLaren and P. Leonard (eds), *Paulo Freire: A Critical Encounter*. London: Routledge, 146–54.

Horton, Myles, and Paulo Freire (1990), *We Make the Road by Walking. Conversations on Education and Social Change*. New York: Continuum.

Houden, L. L. (1997), "Co-creating sacred space: The use of theatre in the transformation of conflict." Ph.D. thesis, The Fielding Institute.

Hudalla, Justin (2005), "Transforming my curriculum, transforming my classroom: Paulo Freire, James Banks, and social justice in a middle school classroom." EdChange and Multicultural Pavilion, available at www.edchange.org/multicultural/papers/hudalla.pdf.

Hussey, Peter (1999), *The Jesus of Rio Syndrome*. Dublin: The Adult Learner, 44–51.

Illich, Ivan (1970), Kann Gewalt Christlich Sein? *Der Spiegel* No. 9, February 23.

—(1971), *Deschooling Society*. New York: Harper & Row.

—(1982), *Gender*. New York. Pantheon.

Irwin, Jones (2009), "Repositioning Paulo Freire's educational philosophy: Critical pedagogy, the Birmingham School and the problem of popular cultural dissent." Paper presented to the Philosophy of Education Society of Great Britain Conference. Oxford University, April.

—(2011), *Paulo Freire's Philosophy of Education: Origins, Developments, Impacts and Legacies*. New York: Continuum.

Isaacs, Charles (1972), "The praxis of Paulo Freire: A critical interpretation." *Critical Anthropology* 2, (2), 5–30.

Janmohaded, A. R. (1994), "Some implications of Paulo Freire's border pedagogy," in H. Giroux and P. McLaren (eds), *Between Borders: Pedagogy and the Politics of Cultural Studies*. London: Routledge, 242–52.

Jay, Gregory, and Gerald Graff (1995), "A critique of critical pedagogy," in Michael Banibe and Gary Nelson (eds), *Higher Education under Fire*. New York: Routledge.

Jenkins, Pamela, and Branda Nowell (2010), "Humanistic perspectives on the policy and praxis of disaster management: Reflections on Freire and recovery post-Katrina." *Administrative Theory and Practice* 32, (3), 431–37.

Joldersma, Clarence (2001), "The tension between justice and freedom in Paulo Freire's epistemology." *Journal of Educational Thought* 35, (2), 129–48.

Juma, Ali, Pescador, O. A., Torres, C. and Van Heertum, R. (2008), "The educational praxis of Paulo Freire: Translations and interventions," in Michael Shaughnessy, E. Galligan, and R. Hurtado de Vivas (eds), *Pioneers in Education: Essays in Honor of Paulo Freire*. New York: Nova, 85–100.

Jung, Shu-hwa (2008), "The journey to transform: Theatre in education and paradigm shifting." Ph.D. thesis, Exeter University.

Kadt, E. de (1970), *Catholic Radicals in Brazil*. London. Oxford University Press.

Kahn, R. (2005), "Book review of *Rethinking Freire: Globalization and the Environmental Crisis*," available at http://independent.academia.edu/RichardKahn/Papers/141437/Book-Review-of-Rethinking-Freire—Globalization-and-the-Environmental-Crisis-by-C—A—Bowers-and-F—Apffel-Marglin.

Kahn, Richard and Douglas Kellner (2008), "Paulo Freire and Ivan Illich: Technology, politics, and the reconstruction of education," in C. A. Torres and P. Noguera (eds), *Social Justice Education for Teachers. Paulo Freire and the Possible Dream*. Rotterdam: Sense Publishers, 13–34.

—(2010), *Critical Pedagogy, Ecoliteracy, and Planetary Crisis: The Ecopedagogy Movement*. New York: Peter Lang.

Kane, Liam (2001), *Popular Education and Social Change in Latin America*. London: Latin American Bureau.

Kanpol, Barry (1997), *Issues and Trends in Critical Pedagogy*. New Jersey: Hampton Press.

Kavaya, Martinho, and Gomercindo Ghiggi (2008), *Educação comunicativa angolana na realidade "ondjangotchiwiana": diálogos com Paulo Freire*. Benguela: Universidade Católica de Angola em Benguela.

Kester, Kevin (2010), "Assessing the impact of peace education training programs: A case study of UNESCO-APCEIU." M.A. thesis, Ontario Institute for Studies in Education, University of Toronto.

Kidd, Ross, and Krishna Kumar (1981), "Co-opting Freire: A critical analysis of peudo-Freirean adult education." *Economic and Political Weekly* 16, (1/2), 27–36.

Kim, M. (2006), "Beyond the politics of technology-enhanced English language teaching in Korea." Proceedings of the Pacific Computer-Assisted Language Learning Association Conference. Nanjing, China, November 16–19.

Kincheloe, Joe (1997), "Beans and Beaujolais: Preface," in Paulo Freire (ed.), *Mentoring the Mentor. Critical Dialogue with Paulo Freire.* New York: Peter Lang.

—(2008), *Critical Pedagogy Primer.* New York: Peter Lang.

Kirkendall, Andrew (2004), "Paulo Freire, Eduardo Frei, literacy training and the politics of consciousness raising in Chile, 1964–1970." *Journal of Latin American Studies* 36, (4), 686–717.

—(2010), *Paulo Freire and the Cold War Politics of Literacy.* Chapel Hill, NC: University of North Carolina Press.

Kirkwood, Gerri, and Colin Kirkwood (2011), *Living Adult Education: Freire in Scotland.* Rotterdam: Sense Publishers.

Klein, Mike (2007), "Peace education and Paulo Freire's method. Towards the democratization of teaching and learning." *Convergence* XL, (1–2), 187–206.

Kleinman, A. S. (1978), "Paulo Freire: An exploratory study." Master's thesis, University of Canterbury.

Knowles, Malcolm (1989), *The Making of an Adult Educator.* San Francisco, CA: Jossey-Bass.

Knudson, Rozanne (1971), "Review of *Pedagogy of the Oppressed.*" *Library Journal* 96, 1261–2, April 1.

Kohl, Herbert (1990), "The making of history: Paulo Freire's pedagogy." *Hungry Mind Review* 13, March.

Kozol, Jonathan (1972), *Free Schools.* Boston, MA: Houghton Mifflin.

Ku, Hok Bun, Sik Chung Yeung, and Pauline Sung-Chan (2005), "Searching for a capacity building model in social work education in China." *Social Work Education* 24, (2), 213–33.

Kubota, R. (1998), "Ideologies of English in Japan." *World Englishes* 17, (3), 295–306.

Ladson-Billings, G. (1997), "I know why this doesn't feel empowering: A critical race analysis of critical pedagogy," in P. Freire, J. Fraser, D. Macedo, T. McKinnon, and W. Stokes (eds), *Mentoring the Mentor.* New York: Peter Lang, 127–41.

Lamb, C. M. (1984), "A rhetorical method for social consciousness-raising addressed to an American middle-class audience (non-poor, inner-outer journey, relinquishment)." Doctoral thesis, The Catholic University of America.

Lange, Elizabeth (1998), "Fragmented ethics of justice, Freire, liberation theology and pedagogies for the non-poor." *Convergence* XXXI, (1–2), 81–94.

Lankshear, Colin, and Peter McLaren (1993), "Introduction," in C. Lankshear and P. McLaren (eds), *Critical Literacy, Politics, Praxis and the Postmodern*. Albany, NY: State University of New York Press, 1–56.

Lather, Patti (1991), *Getting Smart: Feminist Research and Pedagogy with the Postmodern*. New York: Routledge.

Lau, S. C. (1992), "Adult education in a transition society: The case of Hong Kong." Master's thesis, Michigan State University.

Laverty, Megan (2008), "The role of Freire's 'Banking' analogy in the educational imaginary," in M. Shaughnessy, E. Galligan, and R. Hurtado de Vivas (eds), *Pioneers in Education: Essays in Honor of Paulo Freire*. New York: Nova, 7–23.

Leach, Tom (1982), "Paulo Freire: Dialogue, politics and relevance." *International Journal of Lifelong Education* 1, (3), 185–201.

Leary, C. B. (2005), "The student writer as the citizen in public journalism." Ph.D. thesis, State University of New York at Albany.

Ledwith, Margaret (2005), *Community Development: A Critical Approach*. Bristol: The Policy Press.

Lee, Myung-Joon (2000), "Korea: Improving human rights education in schools," in Asia-Pacific Human Rights Information Center (ed.), *Human Rights Education in Asian Schools*. Osaka: Urano.

Leonard, P. (1993), "Critical pedagogy and state welfare: Intellectual encounters with Freire and Gramsci," in P. McLaren and P. Leonard (eds), *Paulo Freire: A Critical Encounter*. London: Routledge, 155–68.

Leonardo, Zeus (ed.) (2005), *Critical Pedagogy and Race*. Malden, MA: Blackwell.

Lewis, Tyson (2010), "Paulo Freire's last laugh: Rethinking critical pedagogy's funny bone through Jacques Ranciere." *Educational Philosophy and Theory* 42, (5–6), 635–48.

Lindquist, Pia (1994), "Moving from Pinochet to Piaget: Implementation of the interdisciplinary project in the São Paulo public schools." Ph.D. thesis, Stanford University.

—(2009), "Against all odds: Implementing Freirean approaches to education in the United States," in Michael Apple, Wayne Au, and Luis Armando Gandin (eds), *The Routledge International Handbook of Critical Education*. New York: Routledge, 254–66.

Linhares, Celia, and Maria Trindade (eds) (2003), *Compartilhando o mundo com Paulo Freire*. São Paulo: Cortez Editora.

Liu, J. (1998), "Sowing the seeds: Reproduction and education reform in China." *Comparative Education Review* 42, (2), 184–96.

Lownd, Peter (2001), "Freire's life and work." Paulo Freire Institute, available at www.paulofreireinstitute.org/PF-life_and_work_by_Peter.html.

Macedo, Donaldo, and Shirley Stainberg (eds) (2007), *Media Literacy: A Reader*. New York. Peter Lang.

MacEoin, Gary (1972), "Conscientization for the masses." *National Catholic Reporter*, 9–10, March 17.

Mackie, Robert (1980), *Literacy and Revolution: The Pedagogy of Paulo Freire*. New York: Continuum.

Maehira, Yasushi (1994), "Patterns of lifelong education in Japan." *International Review of Education* 40, (3–5), 333–8.

Major, Thenjiwe, and Thalia Mulvihill (2009), "Julius Nyerere (1922–1999), an African philosopher, re-envisions teacher education to escape colonialism." *New Proposals: Journal of Marxism and Interdisciplinary Inquiry* 3, (1), 15–22.

Malagón Plata, Luis (2010), *Ideas pedagógicas de Paulo Freire: pedagogía, política y sociedad*. Guatemala: Editorial Magisterio.

Mandiola, Marcela (2010), "Latin America's critical management? A liberation genealogy." *Critical Perspectives on International Business* 6, (2/3), 62–176.

Manicom, Linzi, and Shirley Walters (forthcoming, 2011), *Feminist Popular Education: Building Pedagogies of Possibility*. New York: Palgrave.

Manke, Mary (1999), "Liberatory education: Myles Horton's 'American' model." Paper presented at the Annual Conference of the American Educational Research Association. Montreal, Canada, April 19–23.

Mann, Bernhard (1995), *The Pedagogical and Political Concepts of Mahatma Gandhi and Paulo Freire: A Comparative Study on Developmental and Strategic Political Education in the Third World*. Hamburg: Krämer.

Manyozo, Linje (2003), "Depoliticising Paulo Freire's liberatory education in Southern Africa's participatory social development advocacy programs." *The Journal of Development Communication* 14, (2), 49–59.

Margonis, Frank (2007), "A relational ethic of solidarity?" *Philosophy of Education* 12, (1), 62–70.

Mariño, Germán (1982), "El nuevo Freire: traducción y críticas a su último trabajo en Africa." *Bogotá: Dimensión Educativa*.

Marsh, D. G. (1996), "Freire, Vygotsky and special education: Towards a mediated metacognitive resource model." Ph.D. thesis, Dalhousie University (Canada).

Martin, D'Arcy (1975), "Reappraising Freire: The potential and limits of conscientization." M.A. thesis, OISE/University of Toronto.

—(1998), "Learning from the South." *Convergence* XXXI, (1–2), 117–27.

Martinez Salazar, Egla (1998), "Freire in the North under Southern eyes." *Convergence* XXXI, (1–2), 128–36.

Mathew, George (ed.) (1980), *A Day with Paulo Freire*. Delhi, India: Indian Society for Promoting Christian Knowledge.

Mayo, Marjorie (1997), *Imagining Tomorrow: Adult Education for Transformation*. Leicester: NIACE.

Mayo, Peter (1994), "Synthesizing Gramsci and Freire: Possibilities for a theory of transformative adult education." Ph.D. thesis, OISE/University of Toronto.

—(1997), "Paulo Freire 1921–1997. An appreciation." *Convergence* XXX, (1), 4–8.

—(1999), *Gramsci, Freire and Adult Education*. London: Zed Books.

—(2000), "Synthesizing Gramsci and Freire. Possibilities for a theory of transformative adult education," in Stanley Steiner, Mark Krank, Peter McLaren, and Robert Baruth (eds), *Freirean Pedagogy, Praxis and Possibilities*. New York: Falmer Press, 249–83.

—(2004), *Liberating Praxis. Paulo Freire's Legacy for Radical Education and Politics*. Rotterdam: Sense Publishers.

—(2006), "Antonio Gramsci and Paulo Freire. Some connections and contrasts," in C. A. Torres and P. Noguera (eds), *Social Justice Education for Teachers. Paulo Freire and the Possible Dream*. Rotterdam: Sense Publishers, 50–68.

—(2007), "Critical approaches to education in the work of Lorenzo Milani and Paulo Freire." *Studies in Philosophy and Education* 26, (6), 525–44.

—(2010), "Nicaragua's pedagogical effort 30 years on." *Truthout*, October 30, www.truth-out.org/nicaraguas-pedagogical-effort-30-years64655.

McCowan, Tristan (2006), "Approaching the political in citizenship education: The perspectives of Paulo Freire and Bernard Crick." *Educate* 6, (1), 57–70.

McDonough, Graham and John Portelli (2004), "Environmental Reflections: Insights from Dewey and Freire." *Journal of Thought* 39, (3), 59–80.

McLaren, Peter (1989), *Life in Schools*. New York: Longman.

—(1996), "Paulo Freire and the Academy: A challenge from the U.S. left." *Cultural Critique* 33, 151–84.

—(2000a), "Paulo Freire's pedagogy of possibility," in S. Steiner, H. Krank, P. McLaren, and R. Bahruth (eds), *Freirean Pedagogy, Praxis, and Possibilities. Projects for the New Millennium*. New York: Falmer Press, 1–22.

—(2000b), *Che Guevara, Paulo Freire and the Pedagogy of Revolution*. Lanham, MD: Rowman and Littlefield.

—(2007), "Conservation, class struggle, or both: A response to C.A. Bowers." *Capitalism Nature Socialism* 18, (1), 99–108.

—(2010), "Foreword: Challenging imperial capital and the struggle for critical consciousness," in Paula Allman (ed.), *Critical Education against Global Capitalism: Karl Marx and Revolutionary Critical Education*. Rotterdam: Sense Publishers, xvii–xxvii.

McLaren, Peter and Ramin Farahmandpur (2002), "Freire, Marx, and the new imperialism: Toward a revolutionary praxis," in Judith Slater, Steven Fain, and César Rossatto (eds), *The Freirean Legacy: Educating for Social Justice*. New York: Peter Lang.

McLaren, Peter and Henry Giroux (1994), "Foreword," in M. Gadotti (ed.), *Reading Paulo Freire. His Life and Work*. New York: State University of New York Press, xiii–xviii.

McLaren, Peter and Donna Houston (2004), "Revolutionary ecologies: Critical pedagogy and ecosocialism." *Educational Studies* 36, 27–44.

McLaren, Peter, and Colin Lankshear (1994), *Politics of Liberation: Paths from Freire*. New York: Routledge.

McLaren, Peter, and Peter Leonard (eds) (1993), *Paulo Freire: A Critical Encounter*. New York: Routledge.

Menconi, Margo (1999), "Grappling with Martin Buber and Paulo Freire: Implications for participatory development." Paper presented at the Participatory Development Forum "Deepening Our Understanding and Practice." Ottawa, August 25–27.

Mendes, Madalena (2009), "Os sete pecados da governação global: Paulo Freire e a reinvenção das possibilidades de uma pedagogia democrática e emancipatória da educação." *Revista Lusófona de Educação* 14, 61–76.

Mezirow, Jack (1996), "Beyond Freire and Habermas: Confusion. A response to Bruce Pietrykowski." *Adult Education Quarterly* 46, (4), 237–39.

Miller, Richard E. (1989), "Teaching Freire and testing Hirsch: Bringing literacy into the classroom." Paper presented at the Annual Meeting of the Conference on College Composition and Communication. Seattle, Washington, March 16–18.

Mills, Theodore, and Bertell Ollman (1978), *Studies in Socialist Pedagogy*. New York: Monthly Review Press.

Misoczky, Maria, Joysi Moraes and Rafael Flores (2009), "Bloch, Gramsci e Paulo Freire: referências fundamentais para os atos da denúncia e do anúncio." *Cadernos EBAPE.BR* 7 (3), 448–71.

Monferrer, Dolors, Isabel Aparicio Guadas, Pascual Murcia Ortiz, and Pep Aparicio Guadas (2006), *Sendas de Freire: opresiones, resistencias y emancipaciones en un nuevo paradigma de vida*. Xàtiva: Institut Paulo Freire de España and Crec.

Monteith, Mary (1977), "Paulo Freire's literacy method." *Journal of Reading* 20, (7), 628–31.

Morris, M. A. (2005), "Utilizing the theories of Mezirow and Freire to foster learning of the principles of health promotion." Master's thesis, University of British Columbia.

Morrow, Raymond, and Carlos A. Torres (2002), *Reading Freire and Habermas: Critical Pedagogy and Transformative Social Change*. New York: Teachers College Press.

Mulenga, Derek (2001), "Mwalimu Julius Nyerere: A critical review of his contributions to adult education and postcolonialism." *International Journal of Lifelong Education* 20, (6), 446–70.

Murrell, Peter (1997), "Digging again the family wells. A Freirean literacy framework as emancipatory pedagogy for African-American children," in Paulo Freire (ed.), *Mentoring the Mentor. Critical Dialogue with Paulo Freire.* New York: Peter Lang.

Nasaw, David (1972), "Reconsidering Freire." *Liberation* 19, (18), 28–32.

Nekhwevha, F. (2002), "The influence of Freire's 'Pedagogy of Knowing' on the South African education struggle in the 1970s and 1980s," in P. Kallaway (ed.), *The History of Education under Apartheid, 1948–1994: The Doors of Learning and Culture Shall Be Opened.* Cape Town: Maskew Miller Longman, 133–34.

New Citizen (1974), "Freire on free space." Interview with Paulo Freire, May 30.

Nicholls, Walter, and Justus Uitermark (2010), "Rules and divides. A comparison of minority politics in Amsterdam and Los Angeles, 1970–2010." Paper presented at the 6th International Seminar of the Research Network: Plurality and Diversity in Urban Context. Leuven University, September 17–18.

Nicolai, André (1960), *Comportement économique et structures socials.* Paris: Presses Universitaires.

Nieto, Sonia (2008), *Dear Paulo: Letters from Those Who Dare to Teach.* Boulder, CO: Paradigm Publishers.

Nkomo (1999), *Pedagogy of domination.* Trenton: Africa World Press.

Nocella, A. J. (2008), "Emergence of disability pedagogy." *Journal for Critical Education Policy Studies* 6, (2), 77–94.

Noguera, Pedro (2008), "Bringing Freire to the hood: The relevance and potential of Freire's work and ideas to inner-city youth," in C. A. Torres and P. Noguera (eds), *Social Justice Education for Teachers. Paulo Freire and the Possible Dream.* Rotterdam: Sense Publishers, 35–50.

Nuñez, Carlos (2007), "The continuing relevance of Paulo Freire's ideas." *Adult Education and Development* 69, 51–78.

Nuryatno, M. (2006), "Education and social transformation: Investigating the influence and reception of Paulo Freire in Indonesia." Ph.D. thesis, McGill University.

—(2009), "Freire and popular education in Indonesia," in Ali Abdi and Dip Kappor (eds), *Global Perspectives on Adult Education.* New York: Palgrave, 107–24.

O'Cadiz, M. (1996), "The politics of schooling in Brazil: A Freirean curriculum reform in the municipal schools of São Paulo." Ph.D. thesis, UCLA.

O'Cadiz, M. P., Torres, C. A., and Lindquist Wong, P. (1998), *Education and Democracy: Paulo Freire, Social Movements and Educational Reform in São Paulo*. Boulder, CO: West View Press.

O'Hara, Maureen (1989), "Person-centered approach as Conscientizaçao. The works of Carl Rogers and Paulo Freire." *Journal of Humanistic Psychology* 29, (1), 11–35.

Ohara,Yumiko, Scott Saft, and Graham Crookes (2001), "Toward a feminist critical pedagogy in a beginning Japanese-as-a-foreign-language class." *Japanese Language and Literature* 35, (2), 105–33.

Ohliger, John, and Anne Hartung (1972), "Quotational bibliography," in Stanley Grabowski (ed.), *Paulo Freire: A Revolutionary Dilemma for the Adult Educator*. Syracuse, NY: Syracuse University Publications in Continuing Education.

Oliveira, Rosiska Darcy de, and Pierre Dominice (1974), *The Pedagogy of the Oppressed. The Oppression of Pedagogy*. Geneva: Institute of Cultural Action.

Olson, David (2001), "Carl Bereiter," in Joy Palmer (ed.), *Fifty Modern Thinkers on Education. From Piaget to the Present*. New York: Routledge.

Olson, Gary (1992), History, praxis and change: Paulo Freire and the Politics of Literacy. *Journal of Advanced Composition* 12, (1), 1–14.

O'Meara, Noel (1988), "A new way of being Church? A case study of the Base Christian Community of Vila Prudente, Brazil." Ph.D. thesis, Fordham University.

O'Meara, Philip (1973), "The Relevance of Freire." Georgetown: Guyana Institute for Social Research and Action.

O'Neill, M. (1986), "Innovative practices in state funded community health agencies: The case of Quebec's community health departments." Ph.D. thesis, Boston University.

Organ, D. A. (2002), "All around one table: Uncovering and preaching the connection between professed faith and community living." D.Min. thesis, Aquinas Institute of Theology.

Otty, N. (2000), "Language, learning and the body: Brecht and Freire in higher education." *Korrespondenzen/Correspondence: Zeitschrift Für Theaterpädagogik/Theatre Pedagogy News Journal* 16, (35–6), 10–16.

Pacheco, Luciana, and Samya Pessoa (2005), "Paulo Freire e Vygotsky: Reflexões Sobre A Educação." Paper presented at the V Colóquio Internacional Paulo Freire. Recife, September 19–22.

Paiva, Vanilda (1980), *Paulo Freire e o nacionalismo-desenvolvimentista*. Rio de Janeiro: Civilização Brasileira.

Paniago, Maria, and Silvia Andrade (2006), O manual didático na pedagogia de Anísio Teixeira e Paulo Freire. Accessed February 6, 2011 www.histedbr. fae.unicamp.br/acer_histedbr/.../NZ7gLTYg.doc

Paulston, Rolland G. (1992), "Ways of seeing education and social change in Latin America." *Latin American Research Review* 27, (3), 177–202.

Payne, L. M. (1998), "Voices through the margins: A qualitative study exploring voice and marginality in the experiences of three women who have physical disabilities." Ph.D. thesis, The University of Tennessee.

Peach, M. L. (1975), "Freire's process of conscientization and an analysis of a community health care attitude survey." M.A. thesis, University of Toronto.

Pérez, Esther (2004), *Freire entre nosotros. Una experiencia cubana de educación popular.* Havana: Editorial Caminos.

Pérez Alarcón, Abiega, Zarco, and Schugurensky (2002), *Nezahualpilli. Educación presscolar comunitaria.* Mexico: Plaza y Valdés.

Pérez Cruz, Felipe (2009), "Paulo Freire y la Revolución Cubana." Paper presented at the XXVIII International Congress of the Latin American Studies Association (LASA). Rio de Janeiro, Brazil, June 11–14.

Perry, P. H. (1991), "Transformation of consciousness and knowledge-making about writing: The philosophies and praxes of Paulo Freire and Peter Elbow." Ph.D. thesis, State University of New York at Stony Brook.

—(2000), *A Composition of Consciousness: Roads of Reflection from Freire and Elbow.* New York: Peter Lang.

Peters, Michael (1999), "Freire and postmodernism," in P. Roberts (ed.), *Paulo Freire, Politics and Pedagogy. Reflections from Aotearoa-New Zealand.* Palmerston North: Dunmore Press, 113–22.

Peters, Michael and Colin Lankshear (1994), "Education and hermeneutics: A Freirean interpretation," in Peter L. McLaren and Colin Lankshear (eds), *Politics of Liberation. Paths from Freire.* New York: Routledge.

Pietrykowski, Bruce (1996), "Knowledge and power in adult education: Beyond Freire and Habermas." *Adult Education Quarterly* 46, (2), 82–97.

Pinkus, A. M. (1994), "Conscientization: An educational model for integrative social work practice. Learners not consumers: 'Making literate experiences that are lived and felt'." Master's thesis, York University, Canada.

Plunkett, Dudley (1986), "Review of *The Politics of Education: Culture, Power and Liberation.*" *British Journal of Educational Studies* 34, (2), 200–2.

Powell, A., and Frankenstein, M. (eds) (1997), *Ethnomathematics: Challenging Eurocentrism in Mathematics Education.* Albany, NY: State University of New York Press.

Prasadam, A. A. (2005), "Beyond conscientization: James E. Loder's transformational model for Christian education in the Indian context and beyond." Ph.D. thesis, Princeton Theological Seminary.

Preiswerk, Matthias (1995), *Educación Popular y Teología de la Liberación.* Buenos Aires: CELADEC.

Price Clemetson, C. L. (1992), "Religious education guidelines and activities for African-American children who are deaf." Ph.D. thesis, School of Theology at Claremont.

Pruyn, M. A. (1996), "The social construction of critical student agency in one adult literacy classroom." Ph.D. thesis, University of California, Los Angeles.

Puiggrós, Adriana (2005), *De Simón Rodríguez a Paulo Freire. Educación para la integración iberoamericana*. Bogotá: Convenio Andrés Bello.

Quinn, P. (2001), "Plato and Freire on knowledge, education and justice." *Skepsis: A Journal for Philosophy and Interdisciplinary Research* 12, 27–36.

Quiroga, Ana (2001), "El universo compartido de Paulo Freire y Enrique Pichon-Riviere." Página 12, June 29, Suplemento Madres de Plaza de Mayo, available at www.pagina12.com.ar/2001/suple/Madres/01–06/01–06-29/index/htm.

Rafferty, Frances (1993), "Literacy man's utopias." *Times Educational Supplement*, 14–15, October 29.

Rafi, Mohammad (2003), "Farewell Freire? Conscientization in early twenty-first century Bangladesh." *Convergence* XXXVI, (1), 41–60.

Ramos, S. F. (1999), "The FotoDialogo Method: Using pictures and storytelling to promote dialogue and self-discovery among Latinas within a community-based organization in Massachusetts." Ed.D. thesis, University of Massachusetts Amherst.

Rasmussen, D. (2005), "Cease to Do Evil, Then Learn to do Good," in C. A. Bowers and F. Apffel-Marglin (eds), *Rethinking Freire: Globalization and the Environmental Crisis*. Mahway, NJ: Lawrence Erlbaum, 115–32.

Reed-Jones, S. (1993), "Voice, text, and context: The social construction of an A.A. group." Ph.D. thesis, University of Southern California.

Reimer, E. (1970), "Does the shoe fit? A background piece on the 'silent majority'." *America* 23, (3), 69–70.

—(1971), *School Is Dead: Alternatives in Education*. Rio de Janeiro: Paz e Terra Penguin.

Rey Leyes, Maria Adela (2003), "Paulo Freire: ¿Pedagogo o político?" Revista Iberoamericana de Educación, available at www.rieoei.org/teo_edu3.htm.

Rhone, L. (2008), "School bullying: A Freirean perspective." Doctoral thesis, West Virginia University.

Rivera, R. (2004), *A Study of Liberation Discourse: The Semantics of Opposition in Freire and Gutierrez*. New York: Peter Lang.

Roberts, Peter (1996), "Rethinking Conscientisation." *Journal of Philosophy of Education* 30, (2), 179–96.

—(2000), *Education, Literacy and Humanization. Exploring the Work of Paulo Freire*. Westport, CT: Bergin & Garvey.

—(2003), "Knowledge, dialogue, and humanization: Exploring Freire's philosophy," in M. Peters, C. Lankshear, and M. Olssen (eds), *Critical Theory and the Human Condition: Founders and Praxis*. New York: Peter Lang, 169–83.

—(2005), "Freire and Dostoevsky: Uncertainty, dialogue, and transformation." *Journal of Transformative Education* 3, (1), 126–39.

—(2007), "Conscientisation in Castalia: A Freirean teading of Hermann Hesse's *The Glass Bead Game.*" *Studies in Philosophy and Education* 26, (6), 509–23.

—(2009), "Education, death, and awakening: Hesse, Freire and the process of transformation." *International Journal of Lifelong Learning* 28, (1), 57–69.

—(2010), *Paulo Freire in the 21st Century: Education, Dialogue, and Transformation.* Boulder, CO: Paradigm Publishers.

Robinson, Phyllis (2005), "Whose oppression is this? The cultivation of compassionate action in dissolving the dualistic barrier," in C. A. Bowers and F. Apffel-Marglin (eds), *Rethinking Freire: Globalization and the Environmental Crisis.* Mahway, NJ: Lawrence Erlbaum, 99–112.

Rodrigues, S. T. (1984), "An investigation into the educational theories of Mohandas Gandhi and Paulo Freire for a framework for adult basic education in India." Doctoral dissertation, New York University.

Rogers, Carl (1969), *Freedom to Learn: A View of What Education Might Become.* Columbus: Charles Merrill.

—(1977), *On Personal Power.* New York: Delacorte.

Rojas, V. P. (1988), "An exploration of Habermas' theory of communicative competence and Freire's theory of literacy: Towards a critical ESL pedagogy for castelike Hispanics in higher education." Doctoral dissertations, Rutgers University.

Romao, Jose E. (2001), "Paulo Freire e o pacto populista," in *Freire, Paulo, Educaçao e Atualidade Brasileira.* São Paulo: Cortez.

—(2007), "Sociology of education or the education of sociology? Paulo Freire and the sociology of education" in C. A. Torres and A. Teodoro (eds), *Critique and Utopia: New Developments in the Sociology of Education in the Twenty-First Century.* Lanham, MD: Rowman and Littlefield, 131–38.

Rosas, Paulo (2001), "Reflexoes sobre a Pedagogia do Oprimido," in Ana M. Araujo Freire (ed.), *A pedagogia da libertação em Paulo Freire.* São Paulo: UNESP.

Rossatto, César (2005), *Engaging Paulo Freire's Pedagogy of Possibility. From Blind to Transformative Optimism.* Lanham, MD: Rowman and Littlefield.

Rule, Peter (2010), "Bakhtin and Freire: Dialogue, dialectic and boundary learning." *Educational Philosophy and Theory.* no. doi: 10.1111/j.1469–5812.2009.00606.x.

Salm, Joao, and Jared Ordway (2010), "New perspectives in public administration: A political process of education and leadership through mediation." *Administrative Theory and Practice* 32, (3), 438–44.

Sanders, M. (2004), "Social issues and education: Commentary on the use of Freirian, Hortonian and Boalian pedagogies in a graduate college classroom." *Mid-Western Educational Researcher* 17, (4), 34–8.

Sarkar, Pabitra (2003), "India's literacy scenario: Achievements and failure," in Tandra Mitra, Asoke Bhattacharya and Jayanti Alam (eds), *Education and Development*. Kolkata: Jadavpur University.

Sartre, Jean Paul (1947), *Situations 1*, Paris: Gallimard.

Saviani, Demerval (1983), *Escola e Democracia*. São Paulo: Cortez.

Sawyers, L. L. (1994), "Liberating the adult learner: A critical and comparative analysis of the philosophies of Malcolm S. Knowles and Paulo Freire." Doctoral dissertation, Columbia University.

Scapp, R. (1997), "The subject of education: Paulo Freire, postmoderism, and multiculturalism," in P. Freire, J. W. Fraser, D. Macedo, T. McKinnon, and W. T. Stokes (eds), *Mentoring the Mentor: A Critical Dialogue with Paulo Freire*. New York: Peter Lang, 283–91.

Scatamburlo, Valerie, Juha Suoranta, Nathalia Jaramillo, and Peter McLaren (2006), "Farewell to the 'bewildered herd': Paulo Freire's Revolutionary dialogical communication in the age of corporate globalization." *Journal for Critical Education Policy Studies* 4, (2), URL: www.jceps.com/?pageID=article&articleID=65

Schachtner, Christina (1999), "A Recepção do Enfoque Teórico de Paulo Freire na Europa," in Danilo Streck (ed.), *Paulo Freire: Ética, Utopia e Educação*. Petrópolis: Vozes.

Schapiro, Steven (1999), "Toward a pedagogy of the 'Oppressor'," in Steven Schapiro (ed.), *Higher Education for Democracy: Experiments in Progressive Pedagogy*. New York: Peter Lang Publishers.

Schipani, Daniel (1984), *Conscientization and Creativity: Paulo Freire and Christian Education*. Lanham, MD: University Press of America.

Schroeder, Christopher (1996), "From conscientization to connected knowing: The liberatory epistemologies of Paulo Freire and women's ways of knowing." Paper presented at the 47th Annual Meeting of the Conference on College Composition and Communication. Milwaukee, Wisconsin, March 27–30.

Schroeder, Joachim (2001), "A pedagogia do oprimido na alemania," in Ana M. Araujo Freire (ed.), *A pedagogia da libertação em Paulo Freire*. São Paulo: UNESP.

Schugurensky, Daniel (1997), "Paulo Freire: 'A man who lived, loved and tried to know'." *Taboo* 1, (2), Fall, 104–7.

—(1998), "The legacy of Paulo Freire: A critical review of his contributions." *Convergence—International Journal of Adult Education* 31, (1–2), 17–29.

—(2000), "Adult education and social transformation: On Gramsci, Freire and the challenge of comparing comparisons." *Comparative Education Review* 44, (4), 515–22.

—(2002), "La contribución de Freire a la educación. Una perspectiva histórica." *Uni-Pluri/versidad* 2, (1), 78–9.

—(2006), "'This is our school of citizenship.' Informal learning in local democracy," in Z. Bekerman, N. Burbules, and D. Silberman (eds), *Learning in Hidden Places: The Informal Education Reader*. New York: Peter Lang.

Schugurensky, Daniel and Kathy Madjidi (2008), "Reinventing Freire: Exceptional cases of citizenship education in Brazil," in James Arthur, Ian Davies, and Carole Hahn (eds), *The SAGE Handbook of Education for Citizenship and Democracy*. London: SAGE Publications.

Scocuglia, Alfonso (2006), "A pedagogia social de Paulo Freire como contraponto da pedagogia globalizada." Proceedings of the First International Congress of Social Pedagogy. São Paulo: Universidade de São Paulo, available at www.proceedings.scielo.br/scielo.php?script=sci_arttext&pid=MSC 00000000092006000100002&lng=en&nrm=iso.

Selander, Staffan (1990), "The case of Freire: Intellectuals and the transformation of ideas: Notes on ideology and context." *Journal of Curriculum Studies* 22, (6), 557–64.

Shaull, Richard (1970/1997), "Foreword," in P. Freire (ed.), *Pedagogy of the Oppressed*. New York: Continuum, 29–33.

Shim, S. H. (2008), "A philosophical investigation of the role of teachers: A synthesis of Plato, Confucius, Buber, and Freire." *Teaching and Teacher Education: An International Journal of Research and Studies* 24, (3), 515–35.

Shin, Hyunjung, and Graham Crookes (2005), "Exploring the possibilities for EFL critical pedagogy in Korea: A two-part case study." *Critical Inquiry in Language Studies* 2, (2), 113–36.

Shor, Ira (ed.) (1987), *Freire for the Classroom: A Sourcebook for Liberatory Teaching*. New Hampshire: Boynton/Cook.

Shor, Ira and Paulo Freire (1987), *A Pedagogy for Liberation: Dialogues on Transforming Education*. Massachusetts: Bergin & Garvey.

Siddhartha (1999), *Education as a Liberalizing Tool*. India: Gentlemen. Reproduced by UNESCO, available at www.unesco.org/most/freirearticle.htm (accessed May 10, 2010).

—(2005), "From conscientization to interbeing: A personal journey," in C. A. Bowers and F. Apffel-Marglin (eds), *Rethinking Freire: Globalization and the Environmental Crisis*. Mahway, NJ: Lawrence Erlbaum Associates, 82–98.

Sieber, T. (1997), "Pedagogy, power, and the city: Paulo Freire as urban school super-intendent," in P. Freire, J. W. Fraser, D. Macedo, T. McKinnon, and W. T. Stokes (eds), *Mentoring the Mentor: A Critical Dialogue with Paulo Freire*. New York: Peter Lang.

Singhal, Arvind, Lynn Harter, Ketan Chitnis, and Devendra Sharma (2007), "Participatory photography as theory, method, and praxis: Analyzing an entertainment-education project in India." *Critical Arts* 21, (1), 212–27.

Slaner, S. E. (2004), "Teacher perspectives on the use of film in higher education to promote conscientization." Doctoral thesis, Harvard University.

Slater, Judith, Stephen Fain, and Rossatto, C. (2002), *The Freirean Legacy: Educating for Social Justice*. New York: Peter Lang.

Sloop, Joyce (1992), "Education and critical consciousness: Freire, Freud and Hegel." *The Owl of Minerva* 23, (2), 227–8.

Smith, Betty (1999), "Freire, Boal, You and Me." *Transformations* 10, (2), 10–11.

Smith, L. F. (1995), "A spirituality-centered model of conscientization in transformative Christian education." Doctoral thesis, Southern Baptist Theological Seminary.

Smith, Vivienne (1999), "Everyone's a criminal? Reflections on critical reading in the primary classroom." Paper presented at the Biennial Conference of the International Federation for the Teaching of English. Warwick, England, July 7–10.

Smith, William (1976), *The Meaning of Conscientização: The Goal of Paulo Freire's Pedagogy*. Amherst: University of Massachusetts.

Solberg, R. L. (1999), "'A permanent act of discovery': Montaigne, Freire, and the socially constructed essayist." Ph.D. thesis, Indiana University of Pennsylvania.

Souto-Manning, Mariana (2010), *Freire, Teaching, and Learning: Culture Circles across Contexts*. New York: Peter Lang.

Spicer, Chris (2000), "Carrying on despite the violent twentieth century: A tenacious history of people's education," in Ron Miller (ed.), *Creating Learning Communities*. Vermont: Foundation for Educational Renewal.

Spielman, J. (1999), "'The Family Photography Project': Families articulate what they teach their children." Ph.D. thesis, The Union Institute.

Spigolon, Nima (2009), "Pedagogia da Convivência: Elza Freire, uma vida que faz educação." Masters' thesis, Universidade Estadual de Campinas.

Stanley, Manfred (1972), "Literacy," in Stanley Grabowski (ed.), *Paulo Freire: A Revolutionary Dilemma for the Adult Educator*. Syracuse, NY: Syracuse University Publications in Continuing Education.

Steinberg, Shirley (ed.) (2010), *Nineteen Urban Questions: Teaching in the City*. New York: Peter Lang.

Steiner, David, and Susan Rozen (2004), "Preparing tomorrow's teachers: An analysis of syllabi from a sample of America's schools of education," in Frederick Hess, Andrew Rotherham, and Kate Walsh (eds), *A Qualified Teacher in Every Classroom? Appraising Old Answers and New Ideas*. Boston, MA: Harvard Education Press.

Steiner, Stanley, Mark Krank, Peter McLaren, and Robert Baruth (eds) (2000), *Freirean Pedagogy, Praxis and Possibilities*. New York: Falmer Press.

Stern, S. P. (1994), "Social science from below: Grassroots knowledge for science and emancipation." Ph.D. thesis, City University of New York.

Stern, Sol (2009), "Pedagogy of the oppressor. Another reason why U.S. education schools are so awful: The ongoing influence of Brazilian Marxist Paulo Freire." *City Journal* 19, (2), available at www.city-journal. org/2009/19_2_freirian-pedagogy.html

Stevens, David (2010), "A Freirean critique of the competence model of teacher education, focusing on the standards for qualified teacher status in England." *Journal of Education for Teaching* 36, (2), 187–96.

Stotsky, Sandra (1990), "On literacy anthologies and adult education: A critical perspective." *College English* 52, (8), 916–23.

Strasburg, Jeffrey (2001), "'The only way to teach these people is to kill them': Pedagogy as communicative action in the major plays of David Mamet." Ph.D. thesis, University of Nevada.

—(2005), "Performing pedagogy: Teaching and confidence games in David Mamet's *House of Games* and *The Spanish Prisoner*." *Journal of the Midwest Modern Language* 38, (1), 31–43.

Streck, Danilo (2008), "The Utopian Legacy: Rousseau and Freire," in C. A. Torres and P. Noguera (eds), *Social Justice Education for Teachers. Paulo Freire and the Possible Dream*. Rotterdam: Sense Publishers, 69–80.

—(2010), *A New Social Contract in a Latin American Education Context*. New York: Palgrave-Macmillan.

Streck, Danilo, Euclides Redin, and Jaime José Zitkoski (eds) (2008), *Dicionário Paulo Freire*. Belo Horizonte: Auténtica.

Stromquist, Nelly (1997), *Literacy for Citizenship: Gender and Grassroots Dynamics in Brazil*. Albany, NY: State University of New York Press.

Suzuki, Marika (2003), "Empowering minority youth in Japan: The challenge of the AmerAsian School in Okinawa." Master's thesis, Stanford University.

Taber, Nancy, Aine Humble, and Deborah Norris (2006), "A Freirean approach to family life education: Teaching a graduate institute in Jamaica." *Convergence* XXXIX, (1), 45–60.

Taylor, Paul (1991), "Retexturing the word and the world." Unpublished doctoral dissertation, University of Warwick.

—(1993), *The Texts of Paulo Freire*. Buckingham: Open University Press.

Teodoro, Antonio (2007), "Educational policies and the sense of possibility: A contribution to democratic education in a progressive age," in C. A. Torres and A. Teodoro (eds), *Critique and Utopia: New Developments in the Sociology of Education in the Twenty-first Century*. Lanham, MD: Rowman and Littlefield, 87–96.

Thomas, David (2009), "Revisiting *Pedagogy of the Oppressed*: Paulo Freire and contemporary African studies." *Review of African Political Economy* 36, (120), 253–69.

Tilley, S. A. B. (1998), "Becoming familiar: Exploring stories of schooling with women in prison." Ph.D. thesis, Simon Fraser University.

Toh, Swee Hin (2004), "Education for international understanding toward a culture of peace: A conceptual framework," in Virginia Cawagas (ed.) *Education for International Understanding toward a Culture of Peace: Teachers Resource Book*. Seoul: Asia-Pacific Center of Education for International Understanding.

Tornhill, Chistopher (2002), *Karl Jaspers. Politics and Metaphysics*. New York: Routledge.

Torres, Carlos (1976), "A dialéctica Hegeliana e o pensamiento lógico-estructural do Paulo Freire. Notas para uma analise e confrontação dos pressupostos filosóficos vigente na dialética da pedagogía dos oprimidos e do pensamento freireano." *Revista Sintese* 3, (7), 61–78.

—(1990), *Paulo Freire: Twenty Years Later: Similar Problems, Different Solutions*. Athabasca: Aurora.

—(1993), "From the Pedagogy of the Oppressed to the Luta Continua: The political pedagogy of Paulo Freire," in P. McLaren and P. Leonard (eds), *Paulo Freire: A Critical Encounter*. London: Routledge.

—(1994), "Paulo Freire as secretary of education in the municipality of São Paulo." *Comparative Education Review* 38, (2), 181–214.

—(1998a), *Education, Power and Personal Biography. Dialogues with Critical Educators*. New York: Routledge.

—(1998b), Introduction to *Paulo Freire: Politics and Education*. Los Angeles, CA: Latin American Center, University of California-Los Angeles.

—(2001), *Paulo Freire e a agenda da educação latinoamerica do século XXI*. Buenos Aires: CLACSO.

—(2002), "The state, privatisation and educational policy: A critique of neoliberalism in Latin America and some ethical and political implications." *Comparative Education* 38, (4), 365–85.

—(2007), "Paulo Freire, education, and transformative social justice learning," in C. A. Torres and A. Teodoro (eds), *Critique and Utopia: New Developments in the Sociology of Education in the Twenty-first Century*. Lanham, MD: Rowman and Littlefield, 155–60.

—(2008), "Paulo Freire and social justice education: An introduction," in C. A. Torres and P. Noguera (eds), *Social Justice Education for Teachers. Paulo Freire and the Possible Dream*. Rotterdam: Sense Publishers, 1–11.

Torres, Carlos and Pedro Noguera (eds) (2008), *Social Justice Education for Teachers. Paulo Freire and the Possible Dream*. Rotterdam and Taipei: Sense Publishers.

Torres, Myriam, and Louis Reyes (2008), "Resurrecting democracy in public education through Freire's pedagogy of indignation and hope," in M. Shaughnessy, Elizabeth Galligan, and Romelia Hurtado de Vivas (eds), *Pioneers in Education: Essays in Honor of Paulo Freire*. New York: Nova.

Torres, Rosa Maria (1987), *Alfabetización popular. Diálogo entre 10 experiencias de Centroamérica y el Caribe*. Quito: CRIES.

—(1988), *Educación popular: un encuentro con Paulo Freire*. Buenos Aires: Centro Editor de América Latina.

—(1999), "The million Paulo Freires." *Adult Education and Development* 53, 239–50.

—(2010), "Paulo Freire, los sexshops y la comida tailandesa," available at www.fronesis.org.

Trilla, Jaime, ed. (2001), *El legado pedagógico del siglo XX para la escuela del siglo XX*. Barcelona: Graó.

UNESCO (1992), "Paulo Freire and Bogdan Suchodolski." UIE Report 6. Hamburg: Unesco Institute for Education.

Urban, Wayne (1972), "Comments on Paulo Freire." Paper presented at a meeting of the American Educational Studies Association in Chicago. February 23.

Van Heertum, Richard (2008), "Freire, apathy and the decline of the American left: The future of utopia in the age of cynicism," in C. A. Torres and P. Noguera (eds), *Social Justice Education for Teachers. Paulo Freire and the Possible Dream*. Rotterdam: Sense Publishers, 129–46.

Vazquez, G. (2005), "Nurturance in the Andes," in C. A. Bowers and F. Apffel-Marglin (eds), *Rethinking Freire: Globalization and the Environmental Crisis*. Mahway, NJ: Lawrence Erlbaum, 31–47.

Vieira Pinto, Alvaro (1982), *Sete lições sobre educação de adultos*. São Paulo: Cortez.

Vittoria, Paolo, and Ana Maria Araujo Freire (2007), "Dialogue on Paulo Freire." *International Journal of Education for Democracy* 1, (1), available at www.ried-ijed.org.

Wagner, Daniel (1989), "Literacy campaigns." *Comparative Education Review* 33, (2), 256–60.

Waldow, V. R. (1992), "The conscientization of oppression in Brazilian nursing through feminist pedagogy: A case study." Ed.D. thesis, Columbia University Teachers College.

Walker, Jim (1980), "The end of dialogue. Paulo Freire on politics of education," in R. Mackie (ed.), *Literacy and Revolution: The Pedagogy of Paulo Freire*. New York: Continuum, 120–50.

Wallace, Belle (2008), "A vision of Paulo Freire's philosophy: understanding his essential dynamism of learning and teaching," in M. Shaughnessy, E. Galligan, and R. H. de Vivas (eds), *Pioneers in Education: Essays in Honor of Paulo Freire*. New York: Nova.

Wallerstein, N. B. (1988), "Empowerment education: Freire's theories applied to health: A case study of alcohol prevention for Indian and Hispanic youth." Doctoral thesis, University of California, Berkeley.

Walsh, J. (2008), "The critical role of discourse in education for democracy." *Journal for Critical Education Policy Studies* 6, (2), 54–76.

Walters, Shirley, and Linzi Manicom (1996), *Gender in Popular Education: Methods for Empowerment.* London: Zed Books.

Wang, Caroline, Mary Ann Burris, and Xiang Yue Ping (1996), "Chinese village women as visual anthropologists: A participatory approach to reaching policymakers." *Social Science & Medicine* 42, (10), 1391–400.

Wang, Caroline, Susan Morrel-Samuels, Peter M. Hutchison, Lee Bell, and Robert Pestronk (2004), "Flint photovoice: Community building among youths, adults, and policymakers." *American Journal of Public Health* 94, (6), 911–13.

Wang, Ruotao (2000), "Critical health literacy: A case study from China in schistosomiasis control." *Health Promotion International* 15, (3), 269–74.

Watling, Rob, and Helen Clarke (1995), "'Our village': Freire, Freinet, and practical media work in the early years." *Early Years: An International Journal of Research and Development* 15, (2), 6–12.

Wattsa, Roderick, and Jaleel Abdul-Adilb (1998), "Promoting critical consciousness in young, African-American men." *Journal of Prevention & Intervention in the Community* 16, (1–2), 63–86.

Weiler, K. (1996), "Myths of Paulo Freire." *Educational Theory* 46, (3), 353–71.

—(1993), "Freire and a feminist pedagogy of difference," in K. Geismar and G. Nicoleau (eds), *Teaching for Change: Addressing Issues of Difference in the College Classroom.* Cambridge, MA: Harvard Educational Review.

Weiner, Eric (2003), "Secretary Paulo Freire and the democratization of power: Toward a theory of transformative leadership." *Educational Philosophy and Theory* 35, (1), 89–105.

West, Cornel (1993), "Preface," in P. McLaren and P. Leonard (eds), *Paulo Freire: A Critical Encounter.* London: Routledge, xiii–iv.

Westheimer, Joel, and Kahne, Joseph (2004), "What kind of citizen? The politics of educating for democracy." *American Educational Research Journal* 41, (2), 237–69.

Wilson, Tom, Peter Park, and Anaida Colón-Muñiz (eds) (2010), *Memories of Paulo.* Rotterdam: Sense Publishers.

Woock, Roger (1972), "Paulo Freire." Paper presented at a meeting of the American Educational Studies Association in Chicago. February 23.

Yagelski, R. P. (2006), "'Radical to many in the educational establishment': The writing process movement after the hurricanes." *College English* 68 (5), 531–44.

Youngman, Frank (2000), *The Political Economy of Adult Education and Development.* London: Zed Publishers.

Zacharakis-Jutz, Jeff (1986), "Review of Issues for an Evaluation of Freire-Inspired Programs in the United States and Puerto Rico." *Adult Literacy and Basic Education* 10, (3).

Zachariah, M. (1986), *Revolution through Reform: A Comparison of Sarvodaya and Conscientization*. New York: Praeger.

Zapata, Vladimir (2002), "Actualidad de Paulo Freire." *Uni-pluri/versidad* 2, (1), 72–8.

Zheng, Tongtao (2005), "Designing online Chinese language courses: New roles for educators." *Journal of Information Technology Education* 4, 275–86.

Index